Country Analysis

For the next generation

Jaden, Leo, Kessiah, Benjamin, Oliver, Jonah
Andrej, Marša, Mietta, Damian, Maria Elena

Country Analysis

Understanding Economic and Political Performance

DAVID M. CURRIE

GOWER

Gower Applied Business Research
Our programme provides leaders, practitioners, scholars and researchers with thought provoking, cutting edge books that combine conceptual insights, interdisciplinary rigour and practical relevance in key areas of business and management.

Published by
Gower Publishing Limited
Wey Court East
Union Road
Farnham
Surrey, GU9 7PT
England

Gower Publishing Company
Suite 420
101 Cherry Street
Burlington,
VT 05401-4405
USA

www.gowerpublishing.com

British Library Cataloguing in Publication Data
Currie, David M., 1946-
   Country analysis : understanding economic and political
   performance.
   1. Economic indicators. 2. Investments, Foreign--Decision
   making. 3. Macroeconomics.
   I. Title
   330.9-dc22

Library of Congress Cataloging-in-Publication Data
Currie, David M., 1946-
   Country analysis : understanding economic and political performance / David M. Currie.
      p. cm.
   Includes bibliographical references and index.
   ISBN 978-0-566-09237-4 (alk. paper) -- ISBN 978-0-566-09238-1 (ebk.) 1. Country risk. 2. Economic indicators. 3. Political indicators. I. Title.
   HG4538.C87 2011
   339.3--dc22

                                                                                                2010046980

ISBN   978-0-566-09237-4 (hbk)
ISBN   978-0-566-09238-1 (ebk)

Printed and bound in Great Britain by the
MPG Books Group, UK

Contents

List of Figures and Tables

Figures

Tables

Foreword

Why I Wrote this Book

After teaching finance and international economics for several years, I noticed two things. First, many students who had been trained in economics were well-versed in theory. They generally understood how a country was supposed to perform, at least under the idealizing assumptions of economic theory. However, if these same students were asked to analyze a country's performance, they were not as successful. They were not always able to apply the theory to actual circumstances.

The second observation was that executives, the readers of country reports from publications such as *The Economist* or *Financial Times*, frequently did not understand the reasoning behind the analysis. They would encounter terms such as GDP growth, inflation, and Current Account deficit, but either did not know what the term meant or didn't understand why the term was important. They saw the effects of all these variables on their business operations but didn't always understand the principles that caused what they observed.

There apparently was a disconnection between academic training in economic theory and the practice of evaluating the performance of a country. This book is an attempt to make that connection. It shows how to apply economic principles to evaluate the performance of a country. It thus extends the traditional economic curriculum into the realm of reality. At the same time, the book explains the principles underlying the analysis so that users of country analysis understand why the principles are important.

You won't find much theory in this book. There are plenty of economics texts that explain theory at various levels: to novice undergraduates, to advanced graduates, and to the general public. This isn't to imply that economic theory is unimportant. Just as you'll do better in finance if you have more exposure to accounting, you'll do better at applying economic principles if you're trained in the theory behind the principles. Who knows, perhaps reading this book will spur you to study economics if you haven't already, or bring back pleasant memories of your study of economics.

Two hundred years ago, economics was known as political economy because it was recognized that economic decisions were made in a political context. This book follows the same path. In fact, the book opens with politics not only because it is recognized as the major factor in country analysis, but also because governments adopt the economic policies that are the subjects of the remaining chapters. If you don't include government in risk analysis, you're omitting the major agent in macroeconomics.

Who Should Read this Book?

This book is oriented toward executives making investment decisions. In today's world, it is possible to invest beyond the borders of one country. But if that's the case, how do you decide where to direct your investment? What makes some countries more attractive and others less attractive? The investing decision is a tradeoff of risk relative to return, but how do you evaluate risk? This book is a step in that direction; it is about one of the major risks of investing globally: country risk.

A principle of investing is to diversify risk, which is the financial way of saying not to put all your eggs into one basket. Risk can be diversified in many ways, such as buying a variety of stocks rather than only one or buying bonds as well as stocks. In the modern world, diversifying increasingly means investing in other countries, something that has become possible only within the past few years. But investing globally creates other risks that aren't always apparent to investors accustomed to investing only in one country. This book is my attempt to identify and help you understand many of these risks.

In this book, you'll find four approaches that are not typical of most economic or investment books:

1. *Country Analysis* focuses on the analysis of economic and political information rather than on the derivation of theoretical principles. Most economics texts are filled with theory, so this is a departure from the norm.
2. *Country Analysis* has a global perspective throughout. Many people who study economic principles don't realize that the principles apply to other countries, not only in the United States or the United Kingdom or Japan. Because this book is intended for a US audience and I teach in a US business school, many of the background explanations relate to the US. However, the examples that illustrate the principles are drawn from around the world.
3. *Country Analysis* includes political and cultural aspects of economic decisions. Because governments create the environment in which investment decisions are made, investors should understand politics as well as economics. And because governments are part of the culture of a country, it is equally important to understand culture.
4. *Country Analysis* provides a frame of reference – the Washington Consensus – that allows us to determine whether a country's performance is good or bad. Economists traditionally don't like to make value judgments, but we won't shy away from the task. After all, it's your money, so you'd better have an idea about what is a good or a bad risk.

There have been other books titled Country Analysis. This one differs from almost all of them in at least two aspects. Some country analysis books are attempts by practitioners to write down some of the principles they used when making decisions about investing. In most cases, these attempts do not do a thorough job of explaining why the principles were used. It's one thing to say that a country with a government budget deficit equal to 15 percent of GDP is a risky investment, but it is more helpful to explain why a budget deficit is important when analyzing risk and what creates the deficit.

The other type of book about country analysis frequently relies on mathematics. Many of the principles of economics and finance can be expressed through mathematics. Although doing so is efficient, it limits the audience because many of us do not think in mathematical terms. This book uses mathematics in a few places where necessary, but it doesn't use mathematics as a shortcut to explain principles.

Attributions

Numerous people have helped improve the final product. At the Crummer Graduate School of Business, Dean Craig McAllaster provided financial support as well as encouragement. Special thanks go to Prof. Serge Matulich and Prof. Frank Dasse for suggesting ideas for several topics and reviewing chapters. I am grateful to colleagues at Jurai Dobrila University of Pula, Croatia, for their discussions about many of the topics. Prof. Denisa Krbec let me share her office, leading to innumerable opportunities for discussion. Finally, the Fulbright Program encouraged me to enhance relationships with colleagues from other countries, which I have done enthusiastically.

1 *Global Investing*

When you have a spare moment to think about globalization, what comes to mind? Do you think of the flood of imports from China, explaining why you see "Made in China" on everything from clothing to toys to housewares? Do you think of outsourcing jobs to Mexico or India, where labor rates are lower than in the US? Or do you think of the money you save as a consumer by purchasing less-expensive imports, or the fact that your company can survive a little longer by lowering labor costs?

These are all aspects of globalization, both the good and the bad. But there is another aspect of globalization that many people overlook: the ability to invest in almost any country around the world. Globalization is breaking down many of the barriers that previously prevented investing, or at least limited it to a few major companies with a global reach. Now even common folks like you and me can invest in another country, sometimes directly, sometimes through a financial intermediary that specializes in the process.

Look at firms catering to average traders, such as eTrade® or Charles Schwab® to see how they make it possible to invest globally. If you prefer to rely on others to do the research and trading, you can still invest globally through mutual funds such as Franklin Templeton Investments® or exchange-traded funds such as Wisdom Tree®, just to pick two whose ads have appeared in periodicals recently. At any of these locations, you will find the ability to either purchase assets (shares, bonds, real estate) in another country directly or invest in a fund that will do it for you. Globalization has made it easier to invest abroad. In fact, many investment advisors encourage investing abroad, as you will read in Box 1.1. Even after the global financial crisis of 2008, financial advisors suggested keeping a portion of an investor's portfolio in international assets.

The ability to invest abroad doesn't mean you know what you're doing. Ability doesn't equal knowledge. Just because the day is approaching when you can invest anywhere around the world, it doesn't mean that you know where the right places are to invest. There are myriad issues to consider. Which countries have a climate favorable for foreign investors? Which countries create growing, thriving markets that will enable firms within the country to prosper? Which countries experience economic fundamentals that enhance or at least don't diminish the return on your investment? Which countries have stable political regimes and policies that help ensure the safety of your investment? Which countries allow you to take your money out when you liquidate your position?

Notice that all the questions focus on a country's environment for investing. Financial advisers and books about investing usually have plenty of advice about which are the right firms or industries in which to invest. But in a global investing environment, understanding countries and their governments are equally important. Governments create the climate that attracts or repels investment from abroad. This book is about the interplay between economic and political forces and how they determine the climate for investing in a country. It is part of a process called *country analysis*: the process used by potential investors to analyze the political, economic, and cultural environment of a country.

Box 1.1   Invest globally

For years, investment advisers and securities managers have encouraged United States investors to look beyond United States borders. In the mid-2000s, when markets were booming domestically and abroad, fund managers recommended investing 10 to 20 percent of a portfolio overseas.

One argument was that overseas securities markets were performing better than United States markets. For example, one index of stocks in developed countries provided a 23.3 percent annual return to United States investors for the five years from 2002 to 2007. A similar index for developing countries returned 46.5 percent. During the same period, an index for the United States market returned 12.8 percent annually.

Another argument was that the United States dollar was depreciating steadily against many foreign currencies. Although it sounds counter-intuitive, a weakening dollar actually increases returns to United States investors. When you cash out your foreign investment, that currency is worth more United States dollars, so you get not only the market return but an additional return due to that currency's appreciation. Dollar depreciation is one reason why returns on the overseas indexes were so high during the five years.

Even after the financial crisis of 2007 and the recession of 2008 led to declining markets worldwide, market pros continued to recommend foreign securities as part of an investing portfolio. One bond analyst recommends 10 to 40 percent of a portfolio in overseas bonds, which is consistent with the pre-recession weights. Regardless of economic conditions, investing outside the home country is a reality.

Sources: Ian McDonald, "Forget Xenophobia: Go abroad for gains", *Wall Street Journal*, Mar 6, 2006, p. R1; Karen Hube, "Going global: How do you get there from here?", *Wall Street Journal*, Sep 8, 2008, p. R1; Jennifer Levitz, "Why foreign bonds make sense for income-oriented investors", *Wall Street Journal*, Dec 8, 2009, p. C9.

Types of Investing

Of course, this idea of investing globally is not new. Big corporations have been doing it for years and continue to do so. In fact, the principles of country analysis were developed decades ago by oil companies and commercial banks as part of their global expansions.

You're familiar with one type of investing because it frequently makes the news: investing done by large corporations. When Belgium's InBev purchased Annheuser-Busch, the US's largest brewery in 2008, it seemed like an American institution was passing. When China National Offshore Oil Company, a firm partially owned by the Chinese Government, wanted to purchase Unocal, one of the US's largest oil companies in 2005, it set off such a brouhaha that the US Government nixed the sale. The same reaction didn't occur seven years earlier when BP, a British-Dutch oil company, purchased Amoco, another of the US's largest oil companies; that sale was allowed. It's obvious that governments play a role in investing, even in the US.

A variation on this type of investing occurs when a foreign enterprise builds a new facility in a host country. In 2009, Toyota Motor built its eighth North American manufacturing facility, this one near Tupelo, Mississippi. A decade earlier, Mercedes built a manufacturing plant in Alabama. BMW built a plant in South Carolina a few years before that. Of course, US auto manufacturers such as General Motors and Ford have made similar investments in other countries. Now foreign manufacturers are returning the favor.

Economists have a term for these two investments: direct investment. *Direct investment* occurs when a foreign organization builds a facility in a host country or buys controlling interest in a host company. This is the style of investment that has been occurring for a century or more. Some countries welcome direct investment, while other countries discourage it.

Another kind of investing, *portfolio investment*, occurs when foreign investors purchase securities such as stocks or bonds. Portfolio investment is a more recent phenomenon that has blossomed in the past two or three decades. In the old days, many countries had what were termed closed capital markets: governments of those countries adopted policies that either limited investment to locals or discouraged foreign investment by limiting inflows or outflows of cash. Or else the countries were not sufficiently developed that they had stock or bond markets. In the past few decades, more countries have developed capital markets and even more countries have relaxed limitations on inflows and outflows of capital, so portfolio investing has increased globally.

At the same time, there were few mechanisms through which investors in one country could purchase securities in other countries. Virtually all of the investment was by large financial institutions rather than by individual investors. But over time, financial institutions developed mutual funds and exchange-traded funds that made it possible for smaller investors to invest abroad. It's also possible to bypass domestic financial intermediaries and go directly to an intermediary in another country to invest. We can invest directly in some other countries by opening an account at a brokerage firm in that country.

All of these changes – creation of capital markets, removal of restrictions on investing, and enabling small investors to invest in other countries – have created a global market for securities, as you will read in Box 1.2.

The upshot of all this is that smaller investors like you and me are gaining the ability to invest globally, either directly or through financial institutions. And the investments are not simply in securities such as stocks and bonds. We can purchase currencies, real estate, corporate stocks and bonds, government bonds, and even exotic investments such as derivatives.

Thomas Friedman calls this trend the "democratization of finance." Power is moving toward the individual and away from large institutions. A financial cold anywhere in the world (but particularly in the US) causes sniffles throughout the world. If you doubt that, look at the effect of the US mortgage meltdown in 2007, the subsequent financial crisis in 2008, and the global recession in 2009. As you read Box 1.3, look for evidence that investing has become easier for individuals and that the variety of investments has expanded.

Box 1.2   Global investing involves risk

Although investing globally makes sense, it is not without risks, and the risks are of a different type from investing domestically. *Business Week* began an article with this sentence: "Seek profit from strong economies in emerging markets, where demographics and government policies are driving impressive growth." That sounds simple enough, but how do you identify a strong economy? What demographics drive growth? What government policies promote economic growth and make your investment safer or riskier? Those issues are the topic of this book.

As developed countries become more closely integrated, their markets tend to move together. To increase returns, investors begin to move to less developed countries – known as frontier markets – where markets present both the potential for higher returns but also increased risk.

Here are some of the risks that we will discuss in this book:

- Credit risk: lending to a foreign government exposes you to risk that it won't pay you back. How do you determine when a government is a good or bad credit risk, or when it has policies that protect your investment? We'll cover these in Chapters 4, 5, and 7.
- Inflation: high inflation in the foreign country potentially reduces your return because it devalues that currency. How do you tell whether a central bank is credible? We cover this in Chapter 6.
- Currency exposure: the return you earn from investing abroad magnifies when the foreign currency appreciates. What indicators help you forecast whether a currency will appreciate or depreciate, and how do you protect against the currency moving the wrong way? We cover these in Chapters 7, 8, and 9.

Other risks tend to focus more on markets than on the environment for investing, so we don't go into detail about these risks:

- Volatility: markets in frontier countries are generally more volatile than are markets in developed countries. The investment's value goes up or down quickly, and sometimes the changes are drastic.
- Liquidity: frontier markets aren't as liquid as in developed countries, so it's not as easy to bail out if you need to exit quickly.
- Correlation: returns in frontier markets are not as closely correlated to returns in developed markets, so there is greater advantage in diversification.

Sources: Ben Steverman, "The action stays offshore", *Business Week*, Dec 28, 2009, p. 60; Ben Levisohn, Tara Kalwarski, "Cashing in on foreign debt", *Business Week*, Jun 29, 2009, p. 56; Jeff D. Opdyke, "The Street's rush into far frontiers offers big game and bigger risks", *Wall Street Journal*, Jun 16, 2008, p. C1.

Box 1.3   Investing possibilities are endless

If you want to invest overseas, there is no end of ways to do it. Thanks to globalization, you can buy securities directly in many countries. If securities aren't your bag, you can purchase real estate in a foreign country. To do this kind of investing, you need to have a certain amount of expertise, so this book helps.

If you don't know anything about the bond market in Moscow, Russia or the stock market in Zagreb, Croatia and choose not to make the decisions yourself, you can invest in Wall Street funds that achieve the same purpose. Mutual funds and exchange-traded funds offer portfolios oriented toward overseas bonds, overseas stocks, securities from developed countries or from developing countries, or combinations of any of the above. If you don't know anything about real estate abroad, find a Real Estate Investment Trust that does.

Of course, executives in multinational corporations regularly make decisions about expanding into foreign countries. Their access to information is different from what you have, but the process they follow and the factors they consider are similar to the factors discussed in this book. They also contend with the same risks that we discuss. For example, Wal-Mart spent more than $5 billion in 2009 as part of its international diversification strategy. It operates more than 3,700 stores in 14 countries, and it faces the same risks that were covered in Box 1.2. You have more in common with Wal-Mart than you think.

Sources: Jane J. Kim, Aaron Lucchetti, "Jumpy investors gain reasons to look ahead", *Wall Street Journal*, Mar 27, 2007, p. D1; Eleanor Laise, "Why venturing abroad still makes sense for fund investors", *Wall Street Journal*, Feb 2, 2009, p. R1; Jeff D. Opdyke, "Real-estate investors head overseas", *Wall Street Journal*, Jun 21, 2007, p. D1; Miguel Bustillo, "After early errors, Wal-Mart thinks locally to act globally", *Wall Street Journal*, Aug 14, 2009, p. A1.

Country Analysis

When large institutions did the investing, they developed contacts to help them collect economic and political information about the target country and processes for analyzing information once it was collected. Collecting timely, reliable information has always been a formidable task. Big institutions had the resources necessary to obtain information about economic growth, inflation, incomes, trade flows, government policies, and underlying social currents. Once they had the information, institutions had the staff to analyze the risk of investing in the target country. Even so, analyzing risks of investing was "more an art than a science," according to Ronald Solberg. There was no standardized methodology for evaluating risk.

The world changed with the development of the Internet. Information became available at low cost to anyone with the wherewithal to find it. Governments, who collect and disseminate the information, learned that it was to their advantage to provide information in a timely manner. Suddenly, you and I can find a country's rate of economic growth or inflation, or get wind of changes in government policy by typing a few keys as part of an Internet search.

One thing that individuals didn't have was a process for analyzing the information once we had it. Most of us don't possess the expertise to interpret detailed economic information, and we don't have a framework to tell us what differentiates good performance from poor performance. That's where another link in the chain helps.

During the 1980s, at about the same time the Internet was developing, an analyst at a Washington think tank summarized the criteria that institutions such as the International Monetary Fund (IMF), the World Bank, the US Treasury, and several other major lenders used to help them identify good credit risks. John Williamson called these criteria the Washington Consensus. Among the criteria were: whether the government or the free market determined what went on in a nation's economy, the extent of government control over interest rates, capital flows and exchange rates, the level of corruption in the government, and whether the government adopts sound economic policies.

Over the next decades, investors around the world adopted elements of the Washington Consensus – knowingly or unknowingly – because it provided a framework to use in evaluating the economic and political performance of a country. Maybe everyone didn't agree on all of the elements of the Washington Consensus, but investors used many if not most of the criteria because they made sound economic and financial sense.

So we have almost the perfect storm that affords everyone the ability to collect and analyze information to help them invest anywhere around the globe. Governments produce information on a more-timely basis, the Internet allows us to collect the information at relatively low cost, and the Washington Consensus provides a framework through which we can analyze the information we obtain. The stage is set for global investing to flower.

The trick is to know what the information means. Statistics become meaningful only when there are guidelines to help us interpret what they mean. The Washington Consensus provides the standard by which to evaluate the statistics, but even then we must understand how the statistics influence the decision to invest. This book will help us understand the information so that we can discriminate between country environments that promote investment success and those that impede success.

Both direct and portfolio investors use the criteria of the Washington Consensus when making the decision to invest. Some of the criteria may carry more weight for one type of investment than for the other, but all of the criteria are important. Thus, this book matters for investors in real assets such as buildings and factories as well as for investors in financial assets such as stocks and bonds.

Principles of Investing

Finance theory incorporates several principles that help guide the investment decision. We will discuss several principles, emphasizing the ones that relate to country analysis. For a more comprehensive introduction to investment principles, you may wish to refer to a finance textbook or tradebook.

RETURN ON INVESTMENT

What is a return on an investment? Suppose you have an opportunity to purchase a security for $100. You anticipate that in one year the security will be worth $110. If you make that investment, you will receive a $10 profit on an investment of $100, so you get a return of $10/$100 = 10 percent. The *return on investment* consists of the increase or decrease in value compared to the original investment; the return on investment usually is expressed in percentage terms.

Notice that the return could consist of a decrease in value. Reality may not turn out according to what you anticipate. If the security instead is worth $90 in one year, your return on investment will be $-10/$100 = -10 percent. You lost money on that investment, so your return was negative.

Obviously, it matters what kind of security you invest in. If the security is a corporate stock, there is a real possibility that the value in one year may be different from what you anticipate. Stocks don't have any guarantees about what the future price will be, so they entail more risk. Stocks are called equities because you own a share of the equity of the corporation. You gain or lose according to the market's perception of the value of your share in the profits or losses of the corporation.

Or the security may have been one-year debt obligation issued by the same corporation. Debts are different from equities because you don't own a share in the profits or losses of the corporation. Instead, you get an assurance that the corporation promises to repay you $110 in one year. Now you're breathing easier because you have a promise that you will receive a 10 percent return on your investment.

Unfortunately, the promise is only as strong as the organization that issues the promise. Corporations occasionally experience financial difficulty and are unable to repay the debts they have incurred, as investors learn during a recession. Even governments sometimes have difficulty repaying debts, so a government that shows an ability to repay its debts is safer than a government that is in danger of not repaying its debts. Discriminating between the two is where analysis comes in.

RISK VS. RETURN

The most basic principle is that investors measure at least two dimensions: the return they expect to earn from the investment and the risk associated with the investment. Comparing investments based solely on their expected returns gives a misleading view of the spectrum of investments because it ignores risk.

Think of investing in securities in the US. Securities include bonds issued by the US Treasury, bonds issued by the governments of 50 states and thousands of political subdivisions such as cities, counties, airport authorities, and other municipal agencies, bonds issued by corporations, and common and preferred stocks issued by corporations, just to name the obvious types of securities.

Now think for a moment about the risk of each of those securities: Is there a market where the securities are traded, so you can buy and sell the securities whenever you wish? Is there a chance that the issuer of the security will not be able to pay interest or principal on bonds or dividends on stocks? Is the issuer in a growing or a dying industry or market? Has the issuer borrowed too much in the past so that it might not be able to repay new borrowing? It should be obvious that securities differ in each of these, and perhaps other, aspects of risk. Ignoring the risks would mark you as a naïve investor indeed!

The basic principle is that, if the risk between two investments is the same, an investor will choose the one with the higher return. The principle applies in the other direction, too. If the return is the same between two investments, investors will choose the one with the lower risk. Modern finance theory is based on this principle.

The difficulty lies in measuring and evaluating risk, which has many dimensions. Here are several important risks. There may be other risks involved with investing in certain assets, so this is not a complete list. But the list will give you an idea of what's in store for a global investor.

- *Country risk* is the risk that the political or economic situation in a country will affect the value of an investment in that country. Country risk is affected by the degree of development of a country, the attention that a country's politicians pay to international investors, and the degree of confidence that global investors have in a country and its administrators. Iceland provides an example of country risk. Iceland's financial collapse in 2008 caused investors to take money out of the country, leading to collapse of the Government and the nation's banking system.
- *Exchange rate risk* is the risk that a country's currency will appreciate or depreciate on the global currency market so that it affects the return you receive on the investment. Investors from the eurozone have experienced a significant decline in the euro value of investments in the US over the past few years due to depreciation of the US dollar, for example.
- *Credit risk* is the risk that whoever you lend money to will not repay it. Credit risk is the most basic risk associated with lending, because there always is the chance that the person, company, or government to whom you lent money will not pay you back. A synonym for credit risk is default risk. Owners of mortgage-backed securities around the world encountered credit risk when homeowners in the US, Spain, and several other countries were unable to make mortgage payments in 2008.
- *Business risk* is related to the performance of the industry in which the firm operates. Economic conditions may change so that the industry performs better than previously, or they may change so that the industry deteriorates. A good example of business risk is what happened to the world auto industry in 2008 and 2009, when even industry leaders experienced sales declines and several firms faced bankruptcy.
- *Financial risk* reflects how a firm is financed. Firms that are financed through borrowing rather than owner's investment have a higher degree of financial risk. Financial risk relates to a firm's *leverage*, which is debt relative to equity. Leverage is great during good times because it magnifies returns to the owners, but it is deadly during bad times because it also magnifies losses. The financial crisis of 2008 showed that many firms had incurred too much financial risk because they borrowed when times were good. When the downturn came, the firms were unable to repay the interest and principal on borrowing.
- *Liquidity risk* measures how easy or difficult it is to sell an asset in exchange for cash. A characteristic of financial markets in many developed countries is that they are liquid: it is relatively easy to sell a stock or bond when you want to cash out. Of course, during panics you may not receive as high a price, but at least you can liquidate the investment. Many homeowners in the US in 2008 were unable to sell their houses because prices were declining, people were not willing to buy houses, and willing buyers found it difficult to obtain financing. The housing market was not liquid.

Most finance or investment books focus on business, financial, and liquidity risks because they help discriminate between companies and industries. As a nod toward global investing, the books usually mention country risk and may even devote a chapter to discussing exchange rate risk. This is to be expected, because most investment books are aimed at an audience investing in stocks and bonds.

Our focus in this book is on country and exchange rate risks. The title of this book, *Country Analysis*, gives you a hint about its country risk orientation. And because exchange rates are so important in international finance, they will be a theme throughout this book. We won't spend much time analyzing business, financial, and liquidity risks. It's not because they aren't important; they are. Rather, it's because we are focusing on how countries behave rather than how companies or industries behave. You can find numerous investment books focusing on company and industry risks, but this is one of the few focusing on country risk.

COMPENSATING FOR RISK

Another principle relates to the riskiness of different investments. One way that investors compensate for investment risk is by adjusting the return they require for the degree of risk. The reasoning is along this line: I will be willing to accept a greater degree of risk if there also is a chance that I will earn a higher return. Sometimes it is called the *risk-return tradeoff* because you are willing to trade more risk in exchange for a higher expected return.

The risk-return tradeoff has several dimensions. One dimension relates to the risks mentioned above. If a firm or a country has a higher degree of risk, you will demand a higher return on your investment. That's why investing in the US or Germany is not equivalent to investing in Bulgaria or Vietnam. Investors in Bulgaria or Vietnam will expect a higher return due to the risks associated with those countries.

For US investors, the least risky investment they can make is to purchase securities issued by the US Treasury. The US Treasury has never defaulted on its borrowings, so credit risk is low. Although it may seem like the Federal Government borrows excessively, the borrowing isn't out of line when compared to other developed countries; financial risk isn't high. The political and economic systems in the US are among the world's most stable, so there is little country risk. Securities representing the Treasury's debt are traded on markets, so liquidity is not an issue. In short, US investors in US Treasury securities don't face much risk. We could call them the lowest-risk securities in the US.

A second dimension relates to time. An investor in Treasury securities might encounter one risk that we haven't mentioned already: the risk of inflation. Inflation decreases purchasing power, so a dollar in the future won't be as valuable as a dollar right now. Investors are subject to inflation because they give up the opportunity to purchase now when they invest. Investors hope to make up for the loss of purchasing power by earning a return that exceeds the rate of inflation.

The Treasury issues securities that repay the borrowed amount, called the principal, at different times. Short-term securities repay the principal in three months; these are called Treasury Bills. Long-term securities repay the principal in two to 20 years; these are either Treasury Notes or Treasury Bonds. Investors can avoid most of the negative effect of inflation by purchasing Treasury Bills.

We see that there are at least two dimensions to adjusting for risk: an adjustment for the riskiness of the borrower, and an adjustment for the length of time that the funds will be invested. The way to compensate for these risks is to invest in a short-term Treasury security, called a Treasury Bill. In fact, an investment in three-month Treasury Bills frequently is called a risk-free investment and the return on that security is called the risk-free return.

No other investment in the US compensates for risks as well as three-month Treasury Bills do, so the return on this investment frequently serves as a benchmark on which other interest rates are based. Investors then compensate for risks by adjusting upward the return they expect to receive, so it is known as the *risk-adjusted return*. The percentage added to the risk-free return is known as the *risk premium*.

Thus, investors will add a risk premium to the return on Treasury Bills when evaluating an investment in Treasury Bonds. The risk premium compensates investors for the additional time that their money is invested. Investors also will add a risk premium to the return on Treasury Bills when evaluating an investment in short-term borrowing by corporations. The risk premium compensates investors for assuming credit risk because there is a possibility that a corporation might default.

The investment world is filled with risk premiums that are functions of the riskiness of different investments. For example, rates on 30-year mortgages are a function of the rate on a 30-year Treasury Bond. Expected returns on corporate stocks are higher than expected returns on corporate bonds because stocks are riskier than bonds. The Government of Mexico has to pay a higher interest rate to borrow dollars than the Government of the US does because Mexico entails greater risk. There's no escaping the risk-return tradeoff.

The trick is in knowing how much the risk premium should be. It's easy to say, "Adjust the expected return to compensate for additional risk." It's more difficult to say, "Adjust the expected return by 4 percent to compensate for the additional risk." Is 4 percent sufficient to compensate you for the additional risk you assume? Or if you insist on an additional 4 percent, will you price yourself out of the market because other investors are willing to settle for 3 percent? (As an example, in 2010, the Government of Greece paid a risk premium of 3.8 percent over the rate the Government of Germany paid to borrow because Greece was perceived as a greater risk than Germany.) Answers to those questions come from experience and knowledge. This book can't give you experience, but it can give you knowledge.

DIVERSIFICATION

Another principle of investment is that you can reduce risk through diversification. A *portfolio* is the mix of assets that you invest in. A portfolio can include cash, stocks, bonds, real estate, mutual funds, art, gold, or any asset in which you can invest. A portfolio can consist of one asset or hundreds of assets.

In the 1950s, finance professors began to use mathematics to examine the nature of risks and returns of portfolios. Harry Markowitz showed that an investor can reduce the riskiness of a portfolio by adding assets to the portfolio, as long as the assets are not highly correlated with each other. This means that a portfolio composed of two stocks will be less risky than a portfolio of one stock, as long as the stocks do not move in tandem. Markowitz' idea was so innovative and important to the fields of economics and finance that he was awarded the Nobel Prize for economics.

Investors have followed Markowitz' advice for decades. Portfolio diversification implies that investors should have a variety of assets in their portfolios. It also implies that investors should diversify beyond the US. Think about it. Even if you invest in a variety of assets, if the assets are all in the US, you are still subject to risk of business and political events in the US. Your portfolio will rise or fall according to the success of the US.

To overcome the US-specific risk, you have to invest in assets outside the US. That's one of the big reasons why you should invest globally, and one of the big reasons you should know how to analyze the investing climate in countries. If you're going to invest globally, you need to know what you're doing.

STRATEGY OF INVESTING

Investing is a strategic decision. Businesses invest to expand market share, exploit profit opportunities, reduce costs, or achieve another of the organization's goals. Most businesses use a process called capital budgeting to evaluate the potential return on an investment. *Capital budgeting* is a method for investing the firm's financial resources so they help achieve the organization's objectives. Capital budgeting focuses on the cash inflows and outflows that result from the investment; the amount of cash flows is important, as is their timing.

We won't cover the techniques of capital budgeting because they are not the focus of this book. You can find descriptions and examples of capital budgeting techniques in corporate finance textbooks. Instead, we focus on the factors that determine the potential return from and the risks associated with making the investment, particularly when those risks arise from investments in other countries.

Fifty years ago, when national borders determined the extent of many markets, global investing was done by only a few firms such as banks, oil companies, and a few manufacturers. As the decades passed, it became easier to expand globally. New markets opened, new profit opportunities were created, and global investing increased.

Similar strategic reasoning applies to investing by individuals. Individuals invest to earn returns on their savings, to speculate, to accumulate funds for retirement, or a variety of other reasons. The nature of the assets in which people invest is influenced by the age of the investor, and the riskiness of the assets is influenced by the individual's attitude toward risk. *Financial planning* is the process used by individuals to decide which assets to invest in to achieve personal investment objectives. Like capital budgeting, financial planning focuses on the amounts and timing of cash flows.

In the twenty-first century, it has become not only possible, but almost desirable to invest globally. The US now accounts for less than half of the value of worldwide equities and about one-third of the world's debt, so investing only in the US means you're passing up a majority of the world's available investment opportunities. Not only that, but markets in other countries frequently provide higher returns than markets in the US, so you're also passing up profits.

So whether you're a business executive interested in improving the performance of your firm or an individual interested in improving the performance of your portfolio, expanding beyond the domestic market is a key strategic move. Doing so may improve the return you expect to earn, but it also exposes you to more risks. It pays to understand the risks if you are to be an intelligent investor.

Our Approach

Country Analysis takes an approach that has been used in corporate finance – financial analysis – and applies the approach to economic analysis of a country. The book thus takes an analytical perspective rather than a theoretical perspective. My experience is that students studying economics have been exposed to theory *ad nauseum*, but when given a set of economic indicators for a country, may not be able to interpret the performance of the country.

From another perspective, many readers of economic and financial periodicals encounter the results of some author's analysis in the form of country summaries such as those from *The Economist, Financial Times,* or *Euromoney*. However, the readers may not understand why the indicators presented in the summary are important, how the indicators are derived, or how one indicator relates to another. The readers are missing the background behind the numbers.

This book tries to link the two perspectives by explaining the derivation of the most frequently used indicators, showing how they relate to an investor's evaluation of risk, then applying the indicators in a variety of situations to give practice in analyzing results. The book includes a chapter on analyzing government performance, and discusses political aspects of economic decisions in other chapters. Including government with economics puts modern economics into its historical framework of political economy: economics as part of the legal, political, and social environment of a country. Throughout the book, we relate the indicators and the analysis to the criteria of the Washington Consensus so that we have a guide to what constitutes good or bad performance.

TEXT BOXES

Perhaps you've already noticed one of the prominent features of this book: the use of text boxes. These are an integral part of the book, not simply an author's trick. Text boxes serve multiple purposes. First, they illustrate a point made in the text. When there is a section discussing economic growth, for example, there will be a text box containing an illustration of economic growth and its importance in country analysis. In this way, text boxes reinforce what you read.

Second, the readings in text boxes come from business periodicals, so they represent information that you can obtain for only the price of a subscription. It's amazing what you can learn about the world via regular reading and paying attention to other media. Text boxes thus provide guides to obtaining additional information relating to what's in the text.

Third, the text boxes represent a lesson in how to filter information. Articles like these appear regularly in business publications such as *The Wall Street Journal, Business Week,* and *The Economist,* but many people skim over them so they can read about hot stocks or growing industries. Even people who pay attention to information about countries may not approach the process systematically. The text boxes help you organize the process by identifying information relevant to appropriate topics, so that you learn to spot information that you then can analyze using the framework of country analysis.

As you're reading this book, don't skip the text boxes because you think they're fluff. They aren't. They're intended to reinforce and extend the material in the text. I've done lots of background work by selecting readings from a variety of sources. I would have copied the articles directly so you could read real world applications of the principles, but I would have gone broke paying for copyright permissions. Instead, I've summarized several articles relating to the point under discussion. Unfortunately, by the time you read them, these readings are months or years old. You'll have to learn to spot current ones during your study and future reading.

INVESTMENT ADVICE

One thing that you won't find in this book is investment advice. The purpose of this book is to help you become conversant in the terms, concepts, and relationships underlying country analysis, not to sell investment advice. If you want investment advice, there are several commercial sources where you can purchase it. Their explanations will discuss the same topics that are covered in this book, so now you will have a better understanding of what they are saying. In fact, after reading this book, you may know more about world events and how they influence investing than the average financial advisor knows.

Events change so rapidly in the world that up-to-date information is a valuable commodity. You can start the process by paying attention to political, economic, and social news from around the world. The more you learn about these issues, the more you will appreciate how they influence the climate for investing in a country. Gaining this understanding will help you evaluate the quality of information you receive from other sources.

EFFECT OF THE ECONOMIC CRISIS OF 2008

Another feature of the book is that I've tried to update everything to include the effects of the economic recession that began in 2008 and the financial crisis that began in 2007. Many of the issues raised by the recession and financial crisis have not been resolved by the time this book went to press, so there isn't always a conclusion to the story. But you should have a better understanding of what transpired as a result of reading this book.

Further Reading

Easterly, W. (2001) *The Elusive Quest for Growth*, Cambridge: MIT Press.

Friedman, T. (2000) *The Lexus and the Olive Tree*, New York: Anchor Books.

Markowitz, H.M. (1959) *Portfolio Selection: Efficient diversification of investments*, New Haven: Yale University Press.

Porter, M.E. (1990) *The Competitive Advantage of Nations*, New York: The Free Press.

Reilly, F.K. and K.C. Brown (2006) *Investment Analysis and Portfolio Management*, 8th ed., Thomson South-western.

Solberg, R.L. (1992) *Country-risk Analysis*, London: Routledge.

Stiglitz, J.E. (2003) *Globalization and its Discontents*, New York: W.W. Norton.

Williamson, J. (1990) What Washington means by policy reform, http://www.petersoninstitute. org/publications/papers/paper.cfm?ResearchID=486, accessed 4/18/07.

2 *Economic Indicators*

In some ways, managing a country is similar to managing a business. Just like business executives, managers of a country must have an idea of what they want to accomplish, they must develop indicators to help measure progress toward the goal, and they must be able to adjust performance in response to the indicators. The major difference, of course, is that in most cases, managing a country does not involve a board of directors or chief executive officer to develop and implement strategy. Furthermore, governments have powers beyond those of corporations or individuals.

Because the majority of this book concerns economic analysis, we begin by introducing several important indicators through which the health of a nation's economy can be evaluated. Because they measure the economy as a whole, they frequently are referred to as indicators of a country's macroeconomic performance. You encounter them in the news on a regular basis, so let's begin by making sure we understand what they mean.

Learning Objectives

After studying this chapter, you should be able to:

1. explain a variety of economic indicators such as GDP, inflation, per capita income, unemployment, and interest rates;
2. explain the difference between real and nominal indicators;
3. explain why per capita figures do not reflect income distribution;
4. evaluate two different approaches to translating figures from a variety of currencies into a common currency.

Gross Domestic Product

Gross domestic product (GDP) is the most comprehensive measure of the performance of a nation's economy: the market value of all final goods and services produced in a nation during a period of time. There are many nuances associated with measuring a country's GDP, which you will find in any economics textbook or in the article *Measuring the Economy* listed at the end of this chapter. For our purposes, think of GDP as an indicator of the economic health of a nation because it measures the output of goods and services that are the basis of an economy. When an economy is growing, its GDP is increasing, businesses are selling more goods and services, and more people are earning higher incomes.

The government isn't looking over your shoulder to observe every transaction you make during a day, of course. Instead, the government conducts surveys and collects data from a variety of sources, then uses the results to estimate the number and value of other transactions. Surprisingly, measuring a nation's economy is a relatively recent concept; for example, the US didn't begin the process until the 1930s. In the US, the Bureau of Economic Analysis (BEA) of the Department of Commerce estimates GDP. The BEA's quarterly estimates of GDP are one of the most eagerly anticipated statistics in the US because organizations from manufacturing to financial institutions use the information.

At the end of the month following the end of a quarter, the BEA releases an Advanced Estimate of GDP for the quarter just completed. As the weeks go by, more complete data and more reliable data become available, so the BEA publishes a Preliminary Estimate in the second month following the end of the quarter. A month later, it publishes a Revised Estimate for the quarter, before the cycle begins again for the next quarter. The point of all this is that GDP is a series of estimates that are only as good as the underlying information. Even in developed countries, there is a tradeoff between speed and accuracy: the information you obtain quickly may not be as reliable as the information obtained later. Box 2.1 discusses how the GDP figures for the US ultimately revealed the depth of the recession that began in 2008.

Box 2.1   Gross domestic product

Gross domestic product (GDP) is the most famous measure of a country's economic performance, so investors, policy makers, and the general public are anxious for its release each quarter. In late 2008, the United States appeared to be in recession even though the most recent statistics showed that the economy grew slightly.

When statistics for the fourth quarter of 2008 were released in January 2009, the Commerce Department reported a 3.8 percent decline in annualized GDP. The United States had indeed been in recession. The following month, more data was available, so the Commerce Department revised its estimate about fourth quarter GDP: the economy declined 6.2 percent on an annualized basis, not the 3.8 percent in the original estimate. This meant that the United States was in its worst recession since 1982.

The United States would not be able to count on its trading partners to help it out of the recession. Japan's economy declined at an annual rate of 12.7 percent in the fourth quarter of 2008. Europe declined 5.9 percent. Many of the world's major economies were in recession by the end of 2008.

Sources: Conor Dougherty, Kelly Evans, "Economy in worst fall since '82", *Wall Street Journal*, Feb 28, 2009, p. A1; Yuka Hayashi, "Export slide hits Japan's economy", *Wall Street Journal*, Feb 17, 2009, p. A6; "Odd numbers", *The Economist*, Feb 2, 2008, p. 86.

ACCOUNTING AND POLICY ASPECTS OF GROSS DOMESTIC PRODUCT

GDP is part of a system for organizing accounting information at the national level called National Income and Product Accounts (NIPA). The framework for NIPA can be found in the System of National Accounts, an effort by the United Nations and several other organizations to standardize the principles for collecting macroeconomic information throughout the world. Even so, each country is responsible for preparing its own statistics, and the reliability varies. Developed countries have more sophisticated methods for and transparency in collecting data, so their estimates of GDP tend to be more reliable.

Economists allocate GDP according to the entities who purchase the goods and services: Consumption (C) by individuals, Investment (I) by businesses, Government (G) purchases and investment, and net Exports (X), which are purchases of US-produced goods and services by other nations less US purchases of goods and services produced by other nations. This allocation creates the fundamental equation in the System of National Accounts:

$$GDP = C + I + G + X_{net}$$

Each of the components is broken down further into subcategories, as you see in Table 2.1:

- *Consumption* consists of purchases of durable goods, which last three years or longer, nondurable goods, which last less than three years, and services.
- *Investment* to an economist is not the same as what most people tend to think of as investment. To an economist, investment by businesses means building plant and equipment – the assets that will help the economy generate more GDP in the future. Investment also consists of residential housing and additions to inventories. The average person thinks of investment in its financial connotation, such as purchasing shares of stock. To an economist, these financial exchanges involve trading one asset (money) for another asset (shares), so they have no impact on economic growth. It is possible to get rich (at least on paper) when share prices increase, but the nation's productive capacity is unchanged. This is a hint that there is a difference between financial aspects of the economy and real aspects of the economy.
- *Government* consumption consists of federal, state, and local purchases of goods and services as well as investment by all levels of government.
- *Net exports* are composed of exports minus imports. An export means some of the goods and services produced in the US were sold to other countries, so we need to count them in US production. An import means that some of the goods and services produced in other countries were sold in the US, so we need to subtract them to avoid a misleading picture of US production. As you see in Table 2.1, the number is negative, indicating that the US imported more goods and services than it exported.

Although an increase in any of the components will cause GDP to increase, policymakers frequently focus on certain aspects of the economy. For example, reducing corporate taxes will encourage businesses to invest more, leading to an increase in GDP now and potentially increasing future GDP. Providing a tax rebate to households may lead them to purchase more goods and services, so consumption will increase. Higher incomes in other nations will cause them to purchase more US-produced goods and services, so US exports will increase.

The private sector consists of households, businesses, and foreign purchasers. The public sector is government at all levels. A famous economist of the 1930s, John Maynard Keynes, argued that it was the duty of government to increase spending when the private sector wasn't generating economic activity sufficient to lead to full employment. The theory behind this argument is the basis for most macroeconomics courses at universities. The philosophical debate about the proper role of government in society has gone on for years.

Table 2.1   United States gross domestic product, 2006 and 2007 (billions of dollars)

Line		2006	2007
1	**Gross domestic product**	**13,194.7**	**13,841.3**
2	**Personal consumption expenditures**	**9,224.5**	**9,734.2**
3	Durable goods	1,048.9	1,078.2
4	Nondurable goods	2,688.0	2,833.2
5	Services	5,487.6	5,822.8
6	**Gross private domestic investment**	**2,209.2**	**2,125.4**
7	Fixed investment	2,162.5	2,122.4
8	Nonresidential	1,397.7	1,481.8
9	Structures	405.1	472.1
10	Equipment and software	992.6	1,009.7
11	Residential	764.8	640.7
12	Change in private inventories	46.7	2.9
13	**Net exports of goods and services**	**-762.0**	**-708.0**
14	Exports	1,467.6	1,643.0
15	Goods	1,030.5	1,152.9
16	Services	437.1	490.1
17	Imports	2,229.6	2,351.0
18	Goods	1,880.4	1,979.4
19	Services	349.2	371.6
20	**Government consumption expenditures and gross investment**	**2,523.0**	**2,689.8**
21	Federal	932.5	976.0
22	National defense	624.3	660.1
23	Nondefense	308.2	315.9
24	State and local	1,590.5	1,713.8

Source: Bureau of Economic Analysis, Table 1.1.5.

COMPARING GROSS DOMESTIC PRODUCT YEAR-TO-YEAR

The GDP figures in Table 2.1 are called *nominal GDP* or *GDP at current prices* because they are the GDP figures measured in the prices that occur in the year GDP is measured. In 2006, the US produced $13.2 trillion of goods and services measured in 2006 prices. In 2007, the US produced $13.8 trillion of goods and services measured in 2007 prices. It is tempting to conclude that the US economy grew by $0.6 trillion (that's $600 billion) during the year, an increase of 4.9 percent. But you may be incorrect. The problem is that 2006 GDP is measured in 2006 prices, while 2007 GDP is measured in 2007 prices, and prices may have changed over the year. We need to separate the 4.9 percent increase into its two components. How much of the change was due to an increase in prices, and how much was due to an increase in output of goods and services?

  If prices increased during the year, the actual amount of goods and services changed by less than $600 billion. If prices decreased during the year, the actual amount of goods and services changed by more than $600 billion. The point is that we don't know exactly how many more goods and services were produced over the year because the numbers include two effects: a change in the number of goods and services and a change in prices. If we are to measure the change in goods and services, first we need to develop a measure of prices.

Inflation

Prices frequently go up, and occasionally come down, for a variety of reasons. For example, more people wishing to purchase an item (such as corn produced for ethanol) may cause its price to increase. On the other hand, improvements in technology may cause prices to decrease. Pocket calculators were very expensive when they were introduced 40 years ago, but you can purchase them for less than $1 now. These changes in relative prices (some prices go up or down relative to prices of other products) are important in determining income distribution (who gets how much) in an economy.

  To measure the general level of prices in a country, statisticians compute a *price index* – an indicator that goes up or down depending on the prices of a variety of goods and services, much like a thermometer goes up or down depending on the temperature. The Dow Jones Industrial Average is a price index based on a selection of 30 industrial stocks trading on the New York Stock Exchange. Just expand the concept to the entire economy and you have a feel for an index designed to measure prices of goods and services. There is much economic and statistical theory involved in constructing a reliable price index, featuring concepts such as Laspeyres or Paasche processes. As difficult as it is to believe, some people enjoy that sort of work.

  There are several famous price indices. Perhaps the most newsworthy is the *consumer price index (CPI)*, which measures the value of a basket of goods and services that are purchased by consumers. Each month, representatives of the Labor Department's Bureau of Labor Statistics (BLS) survey establishments about the prices of about 80,000 goods (such as computers) and services (such as hospital stays). The BLS folks try to find goods or services that are identical to be sure they are comparing the same product from one month to the next. However, this sometimes is difficult to accomplish. To make sure that the basket of goods and services reflects actual goods and services purchased by consumers, the BLS surveys 30,000 consumers about once each decade about the goods and services they purchase. The BLS then changes the components and weights of the components according to results of the survey.

To illustrate the problems facing the BLS, consider computers. Personal computers didn't exist until the late 1970s, so they weren't included in the price survey. In the intervening years, computers have become so common that they make up a portion of most households' purchases. The basket of goods and services had to be revised to include computers. Another issue is that computing power has increased dramatically since computers were introduced in the 1970s (have you ever heard of the 286, 386, or 486 chips?), while computer prices have generally fallen. To compensate for the increase in computing power, the price index has had to be adjusted to reflect that each dollar purchases more computing power. These are not easy decisions, but they are typical of the judgments that must be made when measuring price changes.

A more comprehensive index that measures prices for all the goods and services is the *GDP deflator*. Although this price index is not as glamorous as the CPI, it has the advantage of including a broader range of goods and services. The GDP deflator, rather than the CPI, is the index that economists use when measuring the general price level for the economy.

An increase in prices as measured by the price index is called *inflation*; a decrease is *deflation*. Prices increase in most countries, which means that some inflation is typical. A few countries, such as Japan, face the opposite problem of declining prices, so Japanese policy makers are concerned about deflation. Table 2.2 shows rates of inflation for selected countries from 2005 to 2006. Notice the relatively modest rates of inflation in developed countries such as Canada, the US, and the eurozone, the deflation in Japan, and the dramatic rate of inflation in Zimbabwe.

Table 2.2   Rates of inflation for selected countries, 2006

Country	Inflation
Canada	2.3%
China	3.6%
Eurozone	2.3%
Japan	-0.9%
United States	3.2%
Zimbabwe (2005)	237.9%

Source: World Bank, World Development Indicators.

Of course, inflation is more than a measurement problem. Inflation, particularly unexpected inflation, distorts decisions by consumers and business executives. For example, inflation leads to more borrowing because debtors repay debt with money that has reduced buying power. Inflation introduces uncertainty into decisions about investing or consuming because prices are distorted, and prices convey a multitude of information in a market economy. Inflation also changes horizons; the long run becomes a few weeks or months rather than several years because prices are changing so rapidly. A good example is a country experiencing *hyperinflation* – a rate of yearly inflation in high double digits, triple digits, or sometimes, quadruple digits. In these countries, it may be impossible to borrow money for more than a month, and even then the interest rate will be very high.

Inflation also promotes social unrest. People begin to point fingers at others they believe are taking advantage by raising prices. Workers blame corporations, executives blame suppliers or laborers or bankers, in an endless chain of accusation. Inflation sometimes leads to revolt, such as in 2008 when people rioted or protested in several countries about dramatic increases in prices of food. In fact, the protests forced the Prime Minister of Haiti to resign.

Because of this potential for social unrest, governments are hardly disinterested observers when it comes to measuring inflation. Even in the US, political careers are made or lost because of inflation (look up Jimmy Carter and the misery index for proof), and each time the Commerce Department proposes revising the statistics, there is a political dogfight. In other countries, it is even worse. Governments have been known to prepare "official" figures that are distant from the actual level of inflation. Sometimes governments even enact laws forbidding price increases (look up Richard Nixon and price controls, for example), but these efforts almost always fail. Box 2.2 explains how inflation sometimes leads to social unrest.

NOMINAL VS. REAL GROSS DOMESTIC PRODUCT

Now that we have developed a price index, we can determine how much of the change in nominal GDP in 2007 was due to a price change. The GDP deflator at the end of 2006 was 116.568; the deflator at the end of 2007 was 119.668 (BEA, Table 1.1.4 Price Indexes for Gross Domestic Product). This means that prices increased 2.7 percent during the year 2007 (119.668/116.568 – 1 = 2.7 percent). If the total change in nominal GDP was 4.9 percent and 2.7 percent of that was due to increased prices, then the increase in production of goods and services must have been 2.2 percent. (In reality, the relationship is multiplicative rather than additive, but this is a good approximation.)

Another way to address the same issue is to divide each year's nominal GDP by the price index for that year to obtain a price-adjusted figure. *Real GDP* is nominal GDP adjusted for the price level. Table 2.3 shows nominal and real GDPs for 2006 and 2007. If we measure the change in real GDP from 2006 to 2007, we obtain the same 2.2 percent increase we just calculated. The figure for real GDP frequently is multiplied by 100 so that it is in same scale as nominal GDP. Alternatively, real GDP sometimes is presented as an index to facilitate year-to-year comparisons.

Once we have calculated real GDP, we have a measure of the output of goods and services. When real GDP increases, it means that more goods and services were produced. *Economic growth* is the increase in goods and services from one period to the next, and it is measured by the increase in real GDP. We have solved the problem of separating observed GDP figures into the two components of inflation and output of goods and services.

What happens when the output of goods and services declines? Obviously, it's not a good thing because it means that the economy is contracting. We frequently call these declines *recessions*, although the organization that declares a recession in the US does not focus solely on the output of goods and services. Table 2.4 shows rates of inflation and economic growth for the same sample of countries.

Box 2.2   Inflation's subtle influence

Inflation has a subtle effect on society because it promotes mistrust and blame. Executives blame workers for demanding higher wages. Workers blame businesses for raising prices. John Maynard Keynes, a famous economist, agreed with Vladimir Lenin, a famous revolutionary, when he said that there was no surer way to tear the fabric of society than to create inflation. The big winner in the process is the government, which is able to repay its debts with money that is less valuable.

Among the countries experiencing protests against inflation in 2008 were:

- Spain and Portugal: Fishermen conduct nationwide strikes protesting increases in fuel costs.
- Iceland: The economy collapsed amid a financial crisis. Protests occur regularly against government officials responsible for the crisis and against inflation of 19 percent.
- Egypt: Inflation of 23 percent leads to factory strikes and urban riots.
- South Africa: Mines, shops, and factories closed when 25,000 protestors marched in Johannesburg, complaining of 11 percent inflation, particularly a 28 percent increase in electricity rates.
- South Korea: Protests against inflation and a slowing economy forced the president to make a public apology.

Because of the threat of social unrest, governments frequently take steps to disguise the true rate of inflation. In 2009, Venezuela used price controls, setting prices on many commodities (particularly food), on interest rates, and on pay for workers in some industries. Argentina goes further by dictating to the statistics office the figures that it will release for inflation. In both countries, the true rate of inflation is higher than the official rate released by the government.

Sources: J.M. Keynes, *The Economic Consequences of the Peace*, p. 235; Ciaran Giles, "Iberian fishermen strike over fuel costs", *Orlando Sentinel*, May 31, 2008, p. A7; "After the thaw", *The Banker*, Mar 2009; "Will the dam burst?", *The Economist*, Sep 13, 2008; Tom Burgis, "South Africa hit by strikes over rising living costs", *Financial Times*, Jul 24, 2008, p. 2; Anna Fifield, "Inflation and protests create economic storm", *FT.com*, Jun 21, 2008; "Venezuela", *Caribbean Update*, Sep 2009, p. 20; "Marital bliss", *The Economist*, Dec 15, 2007, p. 43.

In the US, the National Bureau of Economic Research (NBER) is responsible for deciding whether the nation is in recession. The NBER defines a recession as "a significant decline in activity spread across the economy, lasting more than a few months, visible in industrial production, employment, real income, and wholesale-retail trade." A committee of economists – the Business Cycle Dating Committee (BCDC) – declares a recession by interpreting a variety of statistics measuring the phenomena described in the explanation, and they do so after waiting several months so that the information is reliable. The task is more difficult than one might think because not all statistics move in the same direction at the same time. Some indicators may actually improve even though the economy is in recession. The NBER emphasizes that it does not focus strictly on changes in real GDP.

Table 2.3   US nominal and real GDP, 2006 and 2007

	2006	2007
Nominal GDP (billions of dollars)	13,194.7	13,841.3
Price deflator (2000 = 100)	116.568	119.668
Real GDP	113.193	115.664
Real GDP (billions of dollars)	11,319.3	11,566.4

Source: Bureau of Economic Analysis.

Table 2.4   Rates of inflation and economic growth for selected countries, 2006

Country	Inflation	Economic growth
Canada	2.3%	2.8%
China	3.6%	10.7%
Eurozone	2.3%	2.7%
Japan	-0.9%	2.2%
United States	3.2%	2.9%
Zimbabwe (2005)	237.9%	-5.3%

Source: World Bank, World Development Indicators.

Per Capita Figures

GDP is a measure of how a country's economy is performing over time, but it is not a measure of how individuals within the country are doing. For that, we need to calculate *GDP per capita (GDPpc)*, which means GDP per person. It is possible to calculate nominal GDPpc or real GDPpc, depending on what the analyst wishes to measure. We calculate real GDP per capita because it is possible for real GDP to increase (which means that the nation is producing more goods and services) but real GDPpc to decrease (which means that production of goods and services per person is declining). This could happen if population was growing faster than real GDP.

China encountered this problem in the 1950s and 1960s. Mao Zedong, who was leader at the time, encouraged families to have plenty of children so that China could catch up to western countries. Unfortunately, the economy did not grow as rapidly as did the population, so GDP per person declined. The next leader, Deng Xiaoping, instituted a one-child policy in an effort to slow population growth. In the 1980s and 90s, economic growth outpaced population growth, so GDPpc increased. The one-child policy apparently worked, at least from an economic standpoint.

Table 2.5 shows real GDPpc for each of the countries in the sample, except that Germany replaces the eurozone because the IMF doesn't publish GDPpc for the eurozone. As you look at the table, focus on each country by comparing 2006 to 2000. If 2006 real

Table 2.5   GDP per capita, domestic currency in constant prices, 2000 and 2006

Country	2000	2006
Canada (Canadian dollar)	35,905	39,327
China (Yuan)	3,944	6,676
Germany (Euro)	25,073	26,513
Japan (Yen)	3,966,842	4,303,631
United States (US dollar)	34,773	37,848
Zimbabwe (Zimbabwean dollar)	30	23

Source: International Monetary Fund, World Economic Outlook Database.

GDPpc is higher than in 2000, it means that the average person is better off because the average person is producing more goods and services. Can you identify the country in which the average person was worse off in 2006 than in 2000? (Don't be confused by the monetary units, because each statistic is in the currency of that country. At this point, you can't compare the numbers for Canada to the numbers for Japan because they are measured in different currencies.)

Income Distribution

Although it is a widely accepted indicator of development, GDPpc still is not the ideal indicator. Measuring something on a per capita basis means that we are taking an average per person. The trouble is that incomes may be distributed unequally in a country. A few families, an educated elite, owners of valuable resources, or some other special group may earn high incomes, while a large majority of the population earns low incomes.

Economists address the issue of income distribution by using any of several indicators. The most straightforward measure of income distribution is to compare the share of income held by the richest 10 percent or 20 percent of the population to the share of income held by the poorest 10 percent or 20 percent of the population. In a country with a more unequal income distribution, the ratio will be higher.

Another, more sophisticated measure of income distribution was developed by an Italian statistician. The *Gini Coefficient* measures income distribution by comparing how much income shares for each segment of the population deviate from what the shares would be if incomes were distributed equally. If incomes are distributed equally, the Gini Coefficient is 0 because there is no deviation. If incomes are distributed unequally, the Gini Coefficient has a maximum value of 1. If the Gini Coefficient is multiplied by 100, the result is the Gini Index, which can range from 0 to 100.

Table 2.6 shows these two indicators for the countries in the sample. You'll see that according to the Gini Index, incomes are distributed most unevenly in Zimbabwe, followed by China and the US. According to the ratio of incomes, China is the most uneven, followed by Zimbabwe and the US. Compared to other developed countries such as Canada, Germany, or Japan, incomes are much less evenly distributed in the US.

Table 2.6   Indicators of income distribution

Country	Gini Index*	Ratio of richest 20% to poorest 20%
Canada	32.6	5.5
China	46.9	12.2
Germany	28.3	4.3
Japan	24.9	3.4
United States	40.8	8.4
Zimbabwe	50.1	12

Notes: * The Gini Index is the Gini Coefficient multiplied by 100. A number closer to zero represents more equal distribution of income.

Source: United Nations Development Programme, Human Development Indicators.

A word of caution: measuring income distribution is not equivalent to measuring poverty. Income distribution is a relative measure: what share of incomes does a certain segment of the population earn? Poverty is an absolute measure: is the income sufficiently high to enable the household to eat, for example? When it comes to poverty, most of the world's population exists on less than the equivalent of $2 per day. Try getting by on that sometime.

Another interesting approach is to compare income distribution within a country over time. According to the US Census Bureau, income inequality in the US increased from 1968 through 1998, the year of the most recent study. The trend continued into 2002, according to the study by Smeeding. Incomes were distributed more unequally in the US than in all of the high-income countries in the Organization for Economic Cooperation and Development (OECD), which includes countries such as Germany, France, Italy, Norway, Canada, and Switzerland.

Globalization has helped alleviate poverty around the world, but it has been accompanied by increased disparity of incomes. Average incomes have increased, but distribution of incomes has become more unequal. Economists are still investigating why the two results have occurred. In Box 2.3, you will read about income redistribution and how it may lead to undesirable consequences.

US Dollar Equivalents

We need to address one other topic before leaving GDP. Countries measure their GDPs in their own currencies, which is fine if you're only worried about one country. But when you try to make international comparisons, you'd like to have GDPs for all the countries in a common currency, such as the US dollar.

There are two approaches to converting statistics from one country's currency to a different currency. The most direct method is to use market exchange rates, which reflect the values of the currencies on the currency market. Although this method is easy, it is potentially more volatile because exchange rates fluctuate. The picture of two economies may vary drastically from one year to the next simply because of changes in the exchange rate.

Box 2.3   Globalization and income distribution

Globalization has increased living standards around the world, but a closer examination of the evidence indicates that the distribution of incomes is becoming more unequal. Income distribution in Latin America is more unequal than anywhere outside of Africa because a wealthy elite skews tax laws and government programs toward them. In Mexico, for example, workers in the top 10th percentile earned 4.7 times what workers in the bottom 10th percentile earned in 2004; in 1987, the number was 4.0. The Chinese Communist Party worries about increasingly unequal income distribution because its legitimacy depends on widespread participation in the country's growth. A study by the Asian Development Bank revealed that inequality had increased in 15 of the 21 countries it studied.

Income disparity also has widened in the United States. Real (adjusted for inflation) after tax incomes declined in the United States during the 2000s. The gap between the highest and lowest income percentiles narrowed during the 1950s and 1960s, but widened since the 1980s. In 2004, the top 1 percent of Americans received 15 percent of the country's incomes, compared to 8 percent in the 1960s. One difference is that Americans don't seem to care about income inequality as much as people in other countries do. According to *The Economist*, "Americans want to join the rich, not soak them."

Still, there are potential consequences to growing income inequality. Studies have shown that income inequality stifles economic growth, so it is to a country's advantage to distribute incomes more equally. Even some wealthy Americans warn against the country becoming an aristocracy in which a wealthy ruling class governs the country. The biggest danger is that income inequality can lead to social unrest and class warfare.

Sources: Bob Davis, John Lyons, Andrew Batson, "Globalization's gains come with a price", *Wall Street Journal*, May 24, 2007, p. A1; "Improving the Latin rate of growth", *The Economist*, May 20, 2006, p. 40; "For whosoever hath, to him shall be given, and he shall have more", *The Economist*, Aug 11, 2007, p. 36; "Dividing the pie", *The Economist*, Feb 4, 2006, p. 70; "The rich, the poor and the growing gap between them", *The Economist*, Jun 17, 2006, p. 28; David Cay Johnston, "Richest are leaving even the rich far behind", *New York Times*, Jun 5, 2005, p. 1.

The method favored by economists is to adjust GDP statistics for differences in purchasing power between countries before translating into a common currency. The adjustment is necessary because $1 in the US will purchase a certain amount of goods or services, but the equivalent of $1 in another country may purchase many more goods or services. Because relative prices vary less than exchange rates, *purchasing power parity (PPP)* provides a more reliable, less volatile measure of countries' economies.

Table 2.7 shows GDPpc for each of the countries in the original currency, then in US dollars using either market exchange rates or PPP. Notice that adjusting for purchasing power changes the amount of each country's GDPpc, but the adjustment is greater for less developed countries, where the change in purchasing power is likely to be greatest. The adjustment for developed countries is 10 percent or less, but the adjustment for developing countries is more than 100 percent for China and 50 percent for Zimbabwe.

Table 2.7   GDP per capita in USD using exchange rates and PPP, 2006

Country	GDPpc Domestic currency	GDPpc USD	GDPpc USD (PPP)
Canada (Canadian dollar)	44,360	39,114	36,837
China (Yuan)	16,042	2,012	4,650
Germany (Euro)	28,218	35,432	32,432
Japan (Yen)	3,983,875	34,263	32,031
United States (US dollar)	44,118	44,118	44,118
Zimbabwe (Zimbabwean dollar)	69,958	123	195

Source: International Monetary Fund, World Economic Outlook Database, April 2008.

Using PPP also can change the way the world's economies rank. China, which was slightly smaller than Germany in 2007 using exchange rates to compare economies, becomes the world's second largest economy (and twice the size of Germany) when the comparison is based on PPP. The other seven economies in Table 2.8 are the world's seven largest industrialized economies, and are known as the G-7. Obviously, China has become one of the seven largest economies! There is much discussion about when China's economy will overtake the US's economy. If both economies continue to grow at their current rates, it will happen sometime around the middle of this century. Of course, there was similar discussion in the 1980s about when Japan would overtake the US economy because Japan was growing so rapidly, but as you see in the table, it hasn't happened yet.

Table 2.8   World's largest economies in USD ranked by exchange rates and PPP, 2007

Country	GDP USD	Country	GDP USD (PPP)
United States	13,808	United States	13,808
Japan	4,382	China	7,035
Germany	3,321	Japan	4,292
China	3,280	Germany	2,812
United Kingdom	2,804	United Kingdom	2,168
France	2,594	France	2,068
Italy	2,105	Italy	1,788
Canada	1,436	Canada	1,270

Source: International Monetary Fund, World Economic Outlook Database, October 2008.

Is Gross Domestic Product the Best Measure of a Nation's Health?

Almost from the time GDP was invented, it has been subject to criticism. The criticisms range from the accounting principles used to develop GDP to its shortcomings as a measure of social welfare in a country. Although some of the criticisms are valid, GDP continues to be the most widely used measure of a nation's performance. You can read a detailed evaluation of GDP in the article by Van den Bergh in the references at the end of this chapter. The article by Ritter explains several of the issues arising from preparing the national accounts.

Alternatives to GDP have been developed, but they are not yet widely accepted. A typical alternative is the *Human Development Index (HDI)* that was developed by the United Nations Human Development Programme. The HDI measures development using three dimensions: GDPpc, adult literacy rates, and life expectancy at birth. Table 2.9 shows the countries ranking in the top ten and bottom ten according to the HDI.

Until a more appropriate measure is developed and used more widely, GDP will continue to be the measure of a nation's performance.

Table 2.9   Top ten and bottom ten countries in Human Development Index, 2007

Top 10		Bottom 10	
1.	Iceland	168.	Congo, Democratic Republic
2.	Norway	169.	Ethiopia
3.	Australia	170.	Chad
4.	Canada	171.	Central African Republic
5.	Ireland	172.	Mozambique
6.	Sweden	173.	Mali
7.	Switzerland	174.	Niger
8.	Japan	175.	Guinea-Bissau
9.	Netherlands	176.	Burkina Faso
10.	France	177.	Sierra Leone

Source: United Nations Human Development Programme http://hdr.undp.org/en/statistics/.

Unemployment

Although it sounds straightforward, unemployment actually is difficult to measure because people have different motives for working and it is a challenge to evaluate their willingness to work. Attitudes toward work and unemployment also are closely tied to a country's culture, so that actual unemployment sometimes is disguised through techniques such as keeping surplus workers on the payroll.

Unlike the System of National Accounts, there is no standardized method for measuring unemployment internationally. This means it is up to each country to define and measure unemployment, so comparing results between countries is potentially misleading. Nevertheless, the OECD prepares standardized statistics for the 41 countries that are members. These figures come with a lag of about one month because of the time

Table 2.10   Standardized unemployment rates, March 2008

Country	Standardized unemployment rate
Canada	6.0%
China	(not an OECD member)
Germany	7.3%
Japan	3.8%
United States	5.1%
Zimbabwe	(not an OECD member)

Source: OECD.Stat, Standardized unemployment rates http://stats.oecd.org/WBOS/Index.aspx?QueryName =251&QueryType=View.

it takes to standardize the figures from each country. Table 2.10 shows the standardized unemployment rates for the countries in our sample that are members of the OECD.

One also can learn about a country's performance by looking at changes in job creation or employment over time. In the US, the Department of Labor conducts two surveys each month to measure the labor market. The most famous is the Current Population Survey (household survey) of approximately 60,000 households, providing an indicator known as the unemployment rate. The focus of the survey is to measure the percentage of the work force that is actively looking for work but is unable to find it.

The second survey is the Current Employment Statistics survey (establishment survey) of approximately 400,000 businesses. The establishment survey measures hours worked, hourly earnings, and job gains or losses to help evaluate whether the economy is generating jobs. Analysts tend to pay more attention to the establishment survey than to the household survey because the establishment survey is more comprehensive (it measures more indicators) and covers a larger sample.

Table 2.11 shows results of each survey for two months in 2008. You'll see that the unemployment rate declined slightly even though the economy lost 20,000 jobs during the month. These seemingly conflicting results occurred at the time several notable executives and politicians were stating that they thought the US was in recession. Remember the previous point about how difficult it is to identify a recession? In this case, one employment indicator is up (an improved unemployment rate) while another is down (job losses).

Table 2.11   Results of US establishment and household surveys, March and April 2008

Indicator (Survey)	April	March
Nonfarm payrolls (Establishment survey)	-20,000	-81,000
Civilian unemployment rate (Household survey)	5.0%	5.1%

Source: Briefing.com http://www.briefing.com/Investor/Public/Calendars/EconomicReleases/employ.htm.

Interest Rates

Interest is a price, but it is a special price. Just like a loaf of bread costs $1.49 at the supermarket, money costs $5.50 per $100 at the bank. You can buy the use of $100 for one year by paying the bank $5.50 in interest, or an interest rate of 5.5 percent. *Interest* is the price you pay for money, while the interest rate is the price per $100, which is why the rate is called a percent. If you borrow $100 from the bank for one year at 5.5 percent, you repay the bank $105.50 at the end of the year. The $105.50 is made up of the amount you borrowed ($100), which is called the *principal*, and the interest.

The math gets slightly more complicated when you borrow for longer periods, but the process remains the same. If you borrow the same $100 for two years rather than one, you pay $5.50 interest for the first year, then repay the bank $105.50 in principal and interest at the end of the second year.

An interest rate reflects all the factors that go into the decision to borrow or lend, but economists typically separate the factors into three categories:

- The basic lending rate as if you were lending at zero risk; this is usually referred to as the *risk-free* rate.
- An extra amount to compensate for all the risks of lending to a borrower who does not have zero risk, such as the length of time of the loan, the chance that the borrower won't repay the loan, the risk of lending in another currency, or any other dimensions of risk.
- An extra amount to compensate for any inflation that could occur during the time of the loan; sometimes inflation is included as one of the risks above, but we shall separate it for this discussion.

Let's explore the dimensions of interest rates by starting with the safest loan we can think of: a loan to the US Treasury. The reason we chose the Treasury is that the US Government is the least risky borrower in the US. There is little or no chance that it will default on its borrowing (at least it hasn't so far!), and every other loan in the US (such as to a corporation, an individual, or a different level of government) involves some greater degree of risk. Let's call the interest rate on the loan to the Treasury the risk-free rate of interest because the borrower is risk-free.

If you decide to lend to any other borrower, that borrower is more risky than the risk-free borrower, so you will require a higher return on your loan to compensate for lending to a higher-risk borrower. You charge a higher interest rate. That's why, when you look at any interest rates that are for the same time period (such as three months or 30 years), the lowest interest rate is the US Treasury rate. All other rates are built upon the Treasury rate. Sometimes this additional interest rate to compensate for additional risk is called the *risk premium*.

Another dimension of interest rates is time. Over longer periods of time, there are more opportunities for things to go wrong with a loan. Besides, you're giving up your money, which means you can't do anything else with it during the period of the loan. For these reasons, you expect a higher return when you lend money for a longer period of time, so you require a higher interest rate on the loan. That's why, when you look at interest rates for any borrower (where the risk is the same), short-term interest rates usually are lower than long-term interest rates. When you plot a graph of the market interest rates for securities of the same risk but for different time periods, you obtain a *yield curve*, which sometimes is called the term structure of interest rates. Figure 2.1 shows the yield curve for US Treasury securities.

The problem is that the principle in the previous paragraph isn't always true. There are occasions when short-term interest rates are higher, not lower, than long-term rates. This seemingly counter-intuitive result has intrigued economists for decades. The discrepancy revolves around the concept of expectations about the future of the economy, particularly inflation. You can see an animated view of the Treasury yield curve over time at yieldcurve.com (http://www.yieldcurve.com/marketyieldcurves.asp).

Still another dimension of interest rates is how to incorporate inflation. If inflation is zero, interest rates will behave according to the other dimensions: a risk premium and a time premium. But inflation usually is positive, which means that each time you lend money, you face the threat of losing purchasing power. If something costs $100 today and you expect inflation to be 3 percent over the coming year, the same item will cost $103 next year. If you lend money, you'll need to charge at least 3 percent interest to compensate for the loss of purchasing power. If you don't, you won't be able to purchase as much when you get the money back (plus interest). Because of this principle, interest rates react to expectations about inflation: higher rates of inflation create higher interest rates.

However, the opportunities for inflation differ according to how long a loan is outstanding. If you lend money for one night, there's little chance of getting hurt from inflation, at least under normal circumstances. (If your country experiences hyperinflation – inflation of 1,000 percent or even 150 percent – then one day matters, but those aren't normal circumstances in the US.) But if you lend for 30 years, there is a good chance that inflation will occur, so you'll build the expected rate of inflation into the interest rate that you charge.

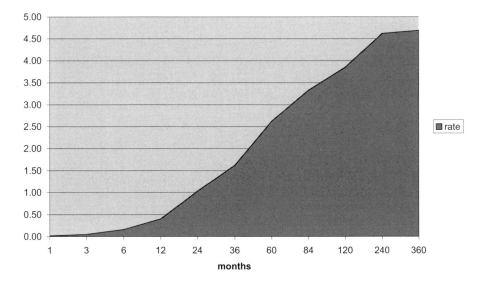

Figure 2.1   Treasury yield curve, 1/7/10

Source: US Department of the Treasury.

Here's the situation so far. The market interest rate has to include the risk-free rate, an adjustment for risk, and an adjustment for inflation. We could write this as a formula:

Market interest rate = risk-free rate + risk premium + inflation premium

That's a pretty useful way to think about interest rates, and you'll encounter the principles every time you borrow or lend money.

Let's explore one more topic. The discussion above describes what interest rate you should charge before you lend money; we're looking forward. What happens if we look backward and see what happens to your actual return if some of the factors change? In particular, what happens to the actual return because of inflation? Suppose you lent out money at 5 percent, but inflation turns out to be 3 percent. You actually received a real return on your loan of only 2 percent. There is a difference between the market interest rate (the *nominal interest rate*) and the *real interest rate* (the nominal rate adjusted for inflation). Just as we adjusted nominal GDP for inflation to obtain real GDP, we adjust nominal interest rates for inflation to obtain real interest rates.

Of course, if you're a smart lender and 2 percent isn't sufficient to compensate you for the risk-free rate and the risk premium, then next time you lend, you'll adjust your lending rate upward to compensate for a new level of inflation. But if you don't do a good job of forecasting, it's possible for the real interest rate to be negative. Do you see how?

Conclusion

Indicators help us determine whether a country and its citizens are better off or worse off. Indicators used frequently to measure a country's welfare include gross domestic product, inflation, unemployment, and interest rates. Indicators measuring individual welfare include GDP per capita and income distribution.

Further Reading

Bureau of Economic Analysis (2007) Introduction to the NIPA accounts, http://www.bea.gov/scb/pdf/national/nipa/methpap/mpi1_0907.pdf, accessed 5/22/08.

Bureau of Economic Analysis (2006) Measuring the economy, http://www.bea.gov/national/pdf/nipa_primer.pdf, accessed 5/22/08.

Bureau of Labor Statistics (2007) BLS *Handbook of Methods*, Chapter 17, The Consumer Price Index http://stats.bls.gov/opub/hom/pdf/homch17.pdf, accessed 5/19/08.

Bureau of Labor Statistics (2007) Monthly employment situation report: Quick guide to methods and measurement issues http://www.bls.gov/bls/empsitquickguide.htm#payroll, accessed 5/28/08.

Cage, R.J. Greenlees and P. Jackman (2003) Introducing the chained Consumer Price Index, International Working Group on Price Indices http://stats.bls.gov/cpi/super_paris.pdf, accessed 5/19/08.

Callen, T. (2007) PPP versus the market: Which weight matters? International Monetary Fund, Finance and Development http://www.imf.org/external/pubs/ft/fandd/2007/03/basics.htm, accessed 5/20/08.

Jones, A.F. and D.H. Weinberg (2000) The changing shape of the nation's income distribution, US Bureau of the Census http://www.census.gov/prod/2000pubs/p60-204.pdf, accessed 5/22/08.

National Bureau of Economic Research, The NBER's recession dating procedure http://www.nber.org/cycles/jan08bcdc_memo.html, accessed 5/24/08.

OECD Observer, Is GDP a satisfactory measure of growth? http://www.oecdobserver.org/news/fullstory.php/aid/1518/, accessed 5/25/08.

Ritter, J.A. (2000) Feeding the national accounts, *Federal Reserve Bank of St Louis Review* http://research.stlouisfed.org/publications/review/00/03/0003jr.pdf, accessed 5/27/08.

Smeeding, T.M. (2005) Public policy, income inequality, and poverty: The United States in comparative perspective, *Social Science Quarterly* (86) p. 955.

Stewart, K.J. and S.B. Reed (1999) Consumer Price Index research series using current methods, 1978–98, Bureau of Labor Statistics, *Monthly Labor Review* http://stats.bls.gov/opub/mlr/1999/06/art4full.pdf, accessed 5/29/08.

United Nations Human Development Programme (2008) http://hdr.undp.org/en/statistics/, accessed 5/23/08.

United Nations, System of National Accounts (1993) http://unstats.un.org/unsd/sna1993/introduction.asp, accessed 5/23/08.

Van den Bergh, J.C.J.M (2007) Abolishing GDP, Tinbergen Institute http://www.tinbergen.nl/discussionpapers/07019.pdf, accessed 5/25/08.

World Bank (2007) 2005 International Comparison Program preliminary results http://siteresources.worldbank.org/ICPINT/Resources/ICPreportprelim.pdf, accessed 5/22/08.

World Bank, Measuring inequality http://web.worldbank.org/WBSITE/EXTERNAL/TOPICS/EXTPOVERTY/EXTPA/0,contentMDK:20238991~menuPK:492138~pagePK:148956~piPK:216618~theSitePK:430367,00.html, accessed 5/26/08.

3 *A Frame of Reference: The Washington Consensus*

So I'm reading *The Wall Street Journal* one day over my morning glass of fresh Florida orange juice, and find an article about problems in the stock market in India. The article says that until recently, India's stock market has been able to withstand the financial and economic problems in the US. However, there is evidence that the Sensex (India's stock market index) is beginning to fall, and a big initial public offering has been withdrawn due to lack of investor interest. Two days later, an article in the *Journal* says that investors are flocking to foreign bonds. In the past year, US investors have parked an additional $19 billion in foreign-bond funds, bringing the total to $84 billion. The article says that there are different types of foreign government bonds, from ultrasafe bonds in Germany paying 4 percent yields, to riskier bonds in Brazil paying 13 percent or more.

What goes on here? I thought this was the *Wall Street Journal*, but it contains articles about investing in India, Germany, and Brazil. What this tells me is that investors can put money almost anywhere around the globe these days, thanks to globalization of financial markets. The *Journal* is forced to take a global perspective because US investors have alternatives beyond Wall Street. Another thing this tells me is that if you're going to invest globally, you'd better be aware of the risks of doing so. Why is Germany considered ultrasafe while Brazil has to pay three times as much interest in order to attract investors? And if the risk of each country is different, how can I as an investor evaluate the risk and incorporate it into my investing decision?

Back in the 1960s when I studied economics, a course called "Comparative Economic Systems" was common in most economics programs in US colleges and universities. The course attempted a typology of economic systems around the world. At one extreme were the capitalist countries, in particular the US. At the other extreme were the communist countries, in particular the Soviet Union. It was easy to tell the good from the bad because we were taught early on that capitalism was good and communism was bad. I assumed that every country that professed capitalism was good, like the US, and every country that professed any form of communism was bad.

It wasn't until several years later that I visited some of these countries and interacted with their people. In the process, I learned that there were many shades between market-controlled and government-controlled economies. For example, in France, which most Americans consider a capitalist country, the government owns or owned some of the firms that I took for granted were owned by private investors. In Australia, another capitalist country, there is a high degree of government influence over business behavior, and it has a reputation as one of the world's highly regulated economies. In Canada and the United

Kingdom, government provides many services that are provided by the private sector in the US. Even in the US, government owned some sources of production and protected certain sectors of the economy. It turned out that all of the world's economies were mixed – a combination of capitalism and government control. If that was the case, how could you tell the good from the bad?

Evaluating risk involves two aspects: assessing and analyzing. Assessing risk means to measure the likelihood of some event affecting the value of an investment, such as when a socialist government threatens to nationalize an industry. Experience, knowledge, and access to information lead to better risk assessment. Analyzing risk means to develop an underlying theory about which factors to consider, how to measure them, and how to develop a system of rating the factors. The theory and practice of analyzing risk have been developed over the past few decades and are still evolving.

In this chapter, we focus on analyzing risk. We discuss a frame of reference that emerged during the 1990s: the Washington Consensus. Countries that meet the criteria of the Washington Consensus are considered safer places to invest than are countries that do not meet the criteria. The Washington Consensus represents a method that investors could use to evaluate the risk of investing globally.

Learning Objectives

After studying this chapter, you should be able to:

1. explain modern investing principles in their historical context;
2. discuss the criteria investors consider when investing in another country;
3. explain the risk-return tradeoff that faces every investor.

A Brief Historical Background

To put today into its historical context, it is necessary to go back to the Great Depression. The US in the 1930s was gripped by a prolonged economic collapse; millions of workers couldn't find jobs, factories shut down, and the mechanisms of traditional economics seemed not to function. The unemployment rate reached 25 percent in 1937: one in four workers couldn't find a job. The economic problems were leading to social unrest; socialism was gaining adherents as a replacement to the capitalist system. It was obvious to some economists and policy makers that the market system no longer worked; people couldn't rely on a collection of independent decisions by people and businesses to achieve employment, happiness, or social stability. Some alternative way out of the problem had to be found.

A solution that appealed to many was a greater role for government. If the individual actors in the economy – people and businesses – couldn't generate a level of economic activity sufficient to generate employment, then the government had an obligation to intervene to help stimulate economic activity. In fact, one of the twentieth century's prominent economists, John Maynard Keynes, developed a theory of when and how a government could intervene and how the economy would behave when it did.

The interpretation of the government as the solution to society's problems wasn't shared universally among economists or policy makers, of course. When the government gets involved, the process becomes centralized and people lose a degree of freedom. Decisions previously made by workers or business executives instead are made by government officials. Some economists at the time, such as Friedrich von Hayek, argued that government intervention was worse than leaving the economy to solve its own problems, and that individuals should not be required to cede to the government their freedom about making decisions. In addition, several analysts have examined the period in retrospect and discovered that bad government policy accounted for at least some of the economic ills of the Great Depression, so government was the problem rather than the cure. But none of this was apparent to the majority of policy makers in the 1930s.

Anyway, in 1944, toward the end of the Second World War, representatives of the Allied nations met at a resort in Bretton Woods, New Hampshire, in the US to discuss what the world economic environment would be once the war concluded. The conference featured some of the prominent economic and financial experts of the era, such as John Maynard Keynes of England and Harry Dexter White of the US. Participants remembered the economic collapse that occurred following the First World War and a decade of misery during the Great Depression, and they feared that the world would return to those conditions after the Second World War. To them, government intervention appeared to be the solution.

Attendees at Bretton Woods created two major global institutions to help countries cope with potential economic problems:

1. International Bank for Reconstruction and Development (IBRD). The IBRD's purpose was to lend to governments to repair a country's infrastructure – rail systems, roads, port facilities, airports, electricity generation, and distribution systems – damaged during the war. Repairing the infrastructure would enable a nation's economy to grow, generating revenues for the government to repay the loans. The IBRD still exists as part of the World Bank (WB) group of financial institutions.
2. International Monetary Fund (IMF). The IMF's mission was to help a government weather the economic crisis that results when a country loses foreign exchange due to temporary trade imbalances. A nation without foreign exchange would not be able to purchase goods and services from other countries, so the IMF would lend reserves to the country experiencing the crisis. These imbalances sometimes result from bad economic policies on the part of the government, so the loans typically come with conditions designed to rectify the bad economic policies. Once the situation was stabilized, the country would follow the IMF's guidance and the underlying economic problems would be solved. The improved trade position would generate the funds necessary to repay the IMF.

Notice that both of the organizations resulting from Bretton Woods personified centralization, as if the WB or the IMF could determine what projects or policies were best for an individual country. But the organizations represented economic and political thinking of the time. The people who make public policy do so with the mindset in which they were educated, experienced, or came to power, and the 1930s and 1940s were tumultuous decades. These large, centralized global institutions were the culmination of the idea of government intervention. Not only did the government of a particular nation have the responsibility to intervene, but now the world economic system was structured around intervention by global institutions.

Things continued along this vein for the next 30 years until economic and political thought migrated toward a contradictory view – that government and centralization were not the solutions to national or world problems. During the 1980s, revolutions in economic thought and policy occurred in the United Kingdom when Margaret Thatcher was elected Prime Minister, then in the US when Ronald Reagan was elected President. Both leaders espoused free-market rather than government-intervention approaches to solving economic problems, and the WB and IMF began to follow that guidance. The free-market approach gained credence when the Soviet Union collapsed in 1989, which appeared to prove that a government-directed approach was not a viable solution to economic problems.

The outcome was a group of Washington, DC-based global institutions (the IMF and WB headquarters are in Washington, as are several others) that advocated free-market solutions to the world's economic problems. Furthermore, the institutions applied the principles to every country under all circumstances. It was centralized control promoting market-based principles.

The Washington Consensus

In 1990, an economist at one of the Washington think tanks summarized the general feeling about desirable economic policies as viewed by official Washington – the US Treasury and Federal Reserve, the WB, the IMF, and other organizations. He called this view the Washington Consensus because it was a summary of the thoughts of the majority of the organizations in Washington DC. In the original article, the principles of the Washington Consensus represented desirable reforms only for Latin American countries, which were undergoing one of their periodic financial crises. However, before long the principles began to be considered the official view of Washington and the global institutions toward all countries.

The principles of the Washington Consensus represent desirable economic policies that a country should follow to attract global investment:

1. *Fiscal discipline.* Governments should practice fiscal discipline, which means that the government should spend no more than it generates through tax revenues.
2. *Public spending priorities.* Governments should spend most on purposes that will improve public welfare, such as education, health, and the nation's infrastructure.
3. *Tax reform.* Governments should broaden the tax base and adopt moderate tax rates.
4. *Interest rates.* Interest rates should be determined by the market rather than by government edict. Governments should keep inflation low enough that market interest rates exceed the rate of inflation and investors earn a positive return on investment after inflation.
5. *Exchange rate.* Exchange rates should be determined by the market rather than by government edict. The exchange rate should be sufficiently competitive that the country's flow of funds with the rest of the world can be improved through export growth.
6. *Trade policy.* Governments should gradually reduce import restrictions such as tariffs and quotas.

7. *Foreign direct investment.* Governments should place no restrictions on investment by foreigners for purposes such as building physical facilities or ownership of businesses.
8. *Privatization.* Whenever possible, governments should sell off state-owned enterprises so that they are subject to market competition.
9. *Deregulation.* Governments should promote competition by removing regulations and reducing protection of industries from market forces.
10. *Property rights.* Governments should create a legal environment that encourages and enforces private property rights.

One thing you'll notice is that the focus in each of these principles is on what the government should (or should not) do. As the ultimate decision maker and enforcer in any nation, government determines the country's economic environment. It has the power to intervene as it wishes, but the Washington Consensus mentions several places where the government should not intervene. Another thing you'll notice is the emphasis on free-market principles. The point of the Washington Consensus is that governments have a choice: They can move toward letting the market determine the competitive environment in a country, or they can move toward greater government control over the competitive environment. The Washington Consensus favors less government intervention. If it is a choice between the market or the government determining economic behavior, the Consensus comes down squarely on the side of the market.

One value of the Washington Consensus is that it provides a way to interpret people and events in the world. Here are some examples:

- Citizens in many European countries have a tradition that the government should play a more active role in society. Nevertheless, many of the governments are moving toward the principles of the Consensus and in the process creating dissatisfaction in some sectors of society. For example, in many European countries, the communication system, the railroad network, and even banks are or have been owned by the government. Because government ownership is contrary to the privatization principle of the Consensus, many governments are privatizing these sectors, endangering the job security and pensions of employees. It's not surprising that there are public demonstrations such as those that led to the resignation of one French prime minister and greeted a newly-elected president of France.
- After collapse of the Soviet Union, representatives from the IMF and the US assisted Russia in setting up economic and political systems that were closer to the Washington Consensus. In other words, they tried to establish free-market principles in a country that had never (even in pre-Soviet times) been free of centralized control. Russian citizens had difficulty becoming accustomed to a different institutional environment, so the transition toward capitalism has not been easy. Of course, there are other reasons for Russia's hesitancy to move toward the free market, but there is no question that the Russian economy is becoming more open even if its political system is not.
- Hugo Chávez, the President of Venezuela, advocates many principles of government that are contrary to the Washington Consensus, and he tries to enlist other Latin American governments to his point of view. One source of conflict between Chávez and officials in Washington is that he flaunts principles such as government ownership of or control over business and opposition to many principles of globalization. When you have an opportunity, research some of the Chávez ideas and compare them to the principles of the Consensus.

We see that the Washington Consensus is a useful way to view political and social changes in the modern world. But it is more than that. As an investor, you have a choice to put your money almost anywhere around the world these days. In fact, if you want to diversify your portfolio, you'll invest in several different countries so you're not at the mercy of what happens in only one country. How do you decide where to invest? Wouldn't you prefer to invest in a country in which the government sets a climate that is most favorable for foreign investors? That's where the Consensus comes in. It provides a set of criteria that we can use to evaluate whether a country has an economic and political environment favorable for investors.

Major corporations and large financial institutions have been doing this for years. In fact, the concepts of country analysis originated with corporations like the big oil companies. But now even smaller investors have an opportunity to invest in securities around the world, and we don't want to do it blindly. The Consensus helps us understand whether countries are adopting good or bad policies that establish the environment in which securities markets operate. It's all part of what Thomas Friedman calls the *democratization of finance*: the spreading of risks and rewards away from large financial institutions and toward individual investors and borrowers.

As financial markets have grown, as exchange rates have been freed from control, and as countries have liberalized rules about investing, more small players have been able to invest globally. But small investors don't always understand the way international financial markets operate, so they need to get educated. (It's like the old adage about a man with experience meeting a man with money. When they parted, the man with experience left with the money and the man with the money left with the experience.) We don't want to be losers because we choose lousy places to invest. We want to put our money in the places it's most likely to be safe, and that's where country analysis helps us. That's the purpose of this book.

More Detail about the Criteria

Because we will use criteria along the lines of the Washington Consensus throughout the book, let's spend a little time investigating the criteria in more detail so we understand why they are important and how they influence the investing environment.

FISCAL DISCIPLINE

Any time you see the word fiscal, think of a budget. A company has a fiscal year that relates to its annual budget. Governments are the same. Governments determine the amount they plan to collect in tax revenue and the amount they plan to spend. Some governments have a habit of spending more than is generated through revenues. In large part, the blame can be placed on politicians, who face more favorable chances for election if they promise to reduce taxes and provide more services. It takes a pretty responsible government to live within its means by spending only what it receives as revenues.

Spending more than revenues means that a government must borrow to finance the difference, and more borrowing increases the national debt. Countries in which the government persistently spends more than its revenues have high deficits and high national debts compared to the size of the country's economy.

As a global investor, where would you prefer to invest: in a country where the government acts responsibly by balancing its budget, or in a country where the government habitually runs a budgetary deficit because it spends more than its revenues? The Consensus answer is that governments that balance their budgets are more responsible, more courageous, and ultimately, more successful. It's called fiscal discipline because running a balanced budget requires self-control on the part of government policy makers.

PUBLIC SPENDING PRIORITIES

How governments allocate their spending is a function of the priorities of the people making the decisions. Sometimes those priorities are directed toward what is good for the general population, but other times the priorities are directed toward special constituencies. The special constituency may be a privileged elite that influences or controls the people in the government who make spending decisions. It may be a ministry or a government agency that holds power during the budget process. In these situations, government spending priorities may reflect the priorities of the ruling elite or the powerful ministry rather than what is good for the population in general.

One particular constituency frequently is a government-owned enterprise. Governments throughout the world (even in the US) own some sectors of the economy. In directed economies such as Russia or China, the proportion may be much higher, but even there the trend is toward less government ownership.

The problem arises when the government-owned enterprise doesn't make a profit, so it becomes a drain on the government's budget. The government has to subsidize the operation. These kinds of subsidies can have a real impact on government spending, and they force the people who pay the taxes to subsidize the owners and employees of the unprofitable enterprise. And guess who gets stuck with paying taxes in most countries? Working stiffs like you and me, not the wealthy, who frequently are able to avoid taxes.

The Consensus view about public spending priorities is that the government ought to spend on things that are good for the nation as a whole: education, health, roads, and bridges. Having the working class subsidize certain sectors of the economy, particularly unprofitable, state-owned enterprises, doesn't make sense. And too many countries do just that.

The sole exception to the Consensus view of spending priorities is the military. Defense budgets are virtually untouchable in any country. You and I might argue that they are too high or too low given the possibility of conflict, but military spending is a separate issue that the Consensus doesn't address.

So the question is, as a global investor, where would you rather invest: in a country that seems to be spending on purposes that are beneficial for the population as a whole, or in a country that is spending to support special interests, particularly state enterprises? The Consensus answer is that you prefer countries in which the government spends to help the nation as a whole, not just a particular class or sector of the population.

TAX REFORM

One of the lessons of the Thatcher and Reagan eras is the importance of taxes as incentives to behavior on the part of the people or businesses that pay them. Economists had known for ages that taxes and subsidies affect the behavior of those who pay or receive them, but during the years following the Second World War, the incentive effect had become buried relative to the other thing taxes do: raise money for the government.

In the 1970s, several economists gained credibility in political circles by pointing out that tax rates were too high. A *tax rate* is the proportion of someone's income, for example, that the government confiscates as tax. When applied to the taxes you pay on additional earnings, the rate is called the *marginal tax rate*. In the US during the 1950s, the marginal tax rate was as high as 91 percent on incomes above $400,000; in other words, the individual kept only 9 percent of the income he or she earned above $400,000. (The marginal rate was 94 percent during the Second World War.) Imagine the incentive effect of that tax!

Some economists and politicians pointed out that these high tax rates were hurting the economy by discouraging people from doing things that were good for the economy, such as investing, saving, and working. They reasoned that it might be possible for the government to obtain the same amount of revenue by lowering tax rates, provided that doing so had the effect of stimulating people to work more so that taxable incomes went up. The same principle applies to other taxes, of course; the principle isn't limited to only income taxes.

Another principle of taxation is that a tax system shouldn't play favorites by allowing some people to avoid taxes while others have to pay them. The figure on which the government collects taxes is called the *tax base* (for the personal income tax, the tax base is taxable income, after all adjustments, deductions, and exemptions have been made). The Consensus argues that the tax base should be broadened so that everyone shares in the tax burden. Governments in every country have a tendency to allow some people to avoid paying taxes on specific activities. For example, in the US, we are allowed to deduct from income contributions to charitable causes, interest paid on a primary mortgage, and some educational expenses, to name a few. Whether these deductions are legitimate depends on your point of view. They may be beneficial for society, but they allow some people to escape paying taxes while shifting the burden to others. As you read Box 3.1, see whether you can identify the tradeoff between tax rates and the tax base, and the incentive effects of taxes.

Examples of avoiding taxes may be more egregious in other countries. The point of the Washington Consensus is that the government shouldn't put the entire tax burden on the working people while wealthy families with government connections are exempt from paying their fair share. That sounds like a reasonable idea, doesn't it?

These two principles – lowering tax rates while broadening the tax base – became pillars of the Washington Consensus. The neat thing is that they appeared to work. When the principles were applied in developed countries such as the UK or the US, the result was a higher rate of growth of the economy. When applied to less developed countries where governments were starving for tax revenues, the result was that people didn't resist paying taxes as much, and tax revenues increased. The principles were the basis of the monumental US tax reforms that occurred in 1986, which were described in a book about the episode, *Showdown at Gucci Gulch*. It's a great lesson on the interplay between economics and politics and I encourage you to read the book.

The interesting aspect is that manipulating tax rates and the tax base doesn't imply that taxes themselves are inherently bad, or even that government tax revenues should decline. Tax reform means that the burden of taxes should be distributed fairly across society. The appropriate level of tax revenues ultimately is a function of what role individuals expect government to play in society. It therefore depends on how the revenues will be spent, which is the issue discussed in the previous section on public spending priorities. Believe it or not, people in some countries expect a significant level of services from government and are willing to pay for them through taxes. It's hard for us to believe that in the US, where we traditionally distrust the government, but it's true.

As a global investor, wouldn't you prefer to invest in a country where the tax system isn't used as a political tool and where the burden of paying for government is shared by everyone? That's the view of the Consensus, anyway.

Box 3.1   Corporate tax rates

Countries use corporate tax rates as a tool to attract corporations to invest in the country. Here is a snapshot of the discussion about corporate tax rates around the world in 2007. The discussion also shows the difference between the tax rate and the tax base.

In India, the Government considered a budget that reduced the corporate tax rate to 25 percent from 34 percent. At the same time, the Finance Minister proposed eliminating several exemptions that allowed corporations to escape paying the tax.

In Germany, the Finance Minister proposed a budget that cut corporate tax rates below 30 percent from about 39 percent, the highest in the European Union. He also proposed reducing the amount of interest expenses that could be deducted from tax liability. Business executives in Germany were strongly in favor of the reduction in the tax rate, but strongly opposed limiting tax deductibility of interest expense.

The Government in China enacted a tax law that equalized treatment of foreign and domestic companies. The previous law favored foreign companies by giving them tax breaks and exemptions that allowed them to avoid many taxes. Although foreign and domestic firms were taxed at the same 33 percent rate, the loopholes allowed foreign firms to pay an effective 15 percent tax rate compared to 25 percent for domestic firms. The favorable treatment for foreign investors began when China opened its economy in the 1980s.

The Chancellor of the Exchequer in the UK lowered the corporate tax rate to 28 percent from 30 percent, but reduced capital allowances, a deduction from tax liability for certain investments.

Corporate tax rates at the time in the United States were 40 percent, although most corporations paid a lower effective rate due to tax breaks.

Sources: Amit Mukherjee, "What's in Chidambaram's bag?", *Business Today*, Mar 11, 2007, p. 96; "German tax changes could damage investment", *International Tax Review*, Mar 2007, p. 1; "Levelling the playing field", *Business Asia*, Mar 19, 2007, p. 5; "UK corporate tax", *Financial Times*, Mar 22, 2007, p. 28; Marcus Walker, "Europe competes for investment with lower corporate tax rates", *Wall Street Journal*, Apr 17, 2007, p. A12.

INTEREST RATES

There was a time only a few decades ago when interest rates were controlled to a great extent by government edict. In some countries, they still are. The US got out of the interest rate control business in the 1980s and left responsibility for determining interest rates to the market: the people borrowing and lending money. If interest rates get too high, borrowers won't borrow as much. If rates get too low, investors aren't willing to invest. The interplay between these two forces determines the level of interest rates throughout the US economy, from daily rates such as federal funds to long-term rates such as 30-year home mortgages. In fact, perhaps the only rate that is set is the discount rate, the rate at which the central bank lends money to commercial banks that are members of the Federal Reserve System.

The advantage of letting markets determine rates is that the money is allocated according to priorities of borrowers or lenders, which means their need for profit. It gets government out of the business of subsidizing some borrowers by lending to them at lower rates. *Interest is the price of money.* Economists have long recognized that prices perform important functions in an economy. Prices: 1) transmit information about tastes and resource availability, 2) provide incentives for efficiency in production, and 3) distribute incomes by determining who gets what. Interest rates perform those functions in the money market. Markets are a much more efficient way to make these decisions than governments are, and keeping the government out removes the possibility of favoritism.

A market is a wondrous mechanism, and it is very good at allocating resources according to the priorities of the people trying to buy and sell in the market. Any economist will tell you that when things interfere with the operation of a market, a number of undesirable results can occur. That's why, when there's a choice between the market or the government deciding something, the Consensus prefers the market.

When governments control interest rates, they have an incentive to keep rates low because low rates stimulate borrowing and consumption, or because the government wishes to lend to certain sectors of the economy. The trouble is that the government might control rates so they are below the rate of inflation, which means that lenders lose purchasing power when they lend. Pretty soon, lenders decide not to lend under those circumstances, and capital starts to leave the country so it can be invested in more favorable places. Sometimes it's a hard pill to swallow, but the best solution regarding interest rates is to let the market decide the appropriate level.

As a global investor, you'll tend to steer clear of countries where interest rates are set by the government rather than by the market. In those countries, governments are apt to use interest rates to achieve purposes other than keeping investors happy. This is the situation in Venezuela, as you'll read in Box 3.2.

EXCHANGE RATES

The same choice about how interest rates should be determined – by the government or by the market – applies to the price of a country's currency. Prior to 1972, currency prices were fixed by government agreements. The only way the price of a country's currency could change was for governments from several countries to agree on the new price. However, that system of fixed exchange rates broke down in 1972, and since then currency prices have been free to fluctuate according to market forces, although some countries continue to try to set the exchange rate for their currency.

Box 3.2   Venezuela's banking system

Venezuela's President Hugo Chávez nationalized several banks in 2008 and began passing legislation and issuing directives dictating operating practices to private banks. Some of the rules required banks to lend 100 percent of the purchase price on home mortgages, a practice that haunted the United States financial system during the financial crisis.

Directives also require banks to lend at lower rates to sectors favored by the government, such as farming and housing, and to increase microlending, the practice of making small loans to poor borrowers. The government sets a cap on rates banks can charge for loans and controls the difference between the bank's borrowing and lending rates. The government requires banks to increase lending, including purchasing securities issued by the government.

When Venezuela began to experience a financial crisis in 2009, Chávez said he would take over more banks if necessary, and the government closed several small banks. The financial positions of banks have deteriorated to the point that they receive lower ratings from agencies such as Moody's Investors Services or Standard and Poor's Corporation.

Sources: "The autocrat of Caracas", *The Economist*, Aug 9, 2008, p. 36; Dan Molinski, Darcy Crowe, "Venezuelan leader warns of crackdown", *Wall Street Journal*, Dec 8, 2009, p. A12; Brian Caplen, "Venezuela's banks survive in the face of adversity", *The Banker*, Sep 2009.

A number of factors influence the value of a currency, including the country's trade with other countries, the level of interest rates in each country, and the level of inflation in each country. These forces change so rapidly that only markets unconstrained by government interference have the ability to react by adjusting the price of a country's currency.

In many cases, government attempts to interfere with the market's power to determine exchange rates lead to financial crisis in a country. Financial crises in Mexico, Russia, and Southeast Asia in the 1990s were largely the result of economic conditions that were made worse by government exchange rate policies, illustrating the futility of governments trying to dictate an exchange rate. Just as the Consensus favors market-determined interest rates, it also favors market-determined exchange rates. Box 3.3 describes attempts by several governments to fix the value of their currencies.

TRADE POLICY

Governments sometimes try to improve the position of their country relative to trading partners. They do this for a number of reasons, particularly to protect domestic manufacturers from foreign competition. You're probably familiar with terms such as tariff and quota, two of the common techniques for establishing barriers to trade. There may be justification for trade barriers in a few circumstances, such as when a country is emerging into world competition or when the industry is in its early stages of development. In these situations, it is possible to build a reasonable case for protecting the country or the industry from the nightmare of global competition. The trouble is that once a trade barrier is erected, it is difficult to remove.

Box 3.3   Currency pegs

When the government of a country tries to maintain the value of its currency against another currency, it is called a currency peg. Currency pegs can be successful, but generally a government finds it difficult go continue the policies necessary to maintain the peg, so it abandons the peg. Here are some examples of recent experiences with currency pegs.

Vietnam began pegging its currency, the dong, against the United States dollar around 1997. Initially, the peg was beneficial at encouraging investment in Vietnam. Over the years, the United States dollar began to depreciate against other currencies, making imports into Vietnam more expensive and driving up Vietnam's rate of inflation. The Government began to abandon the currency peg in 2008 and allowed the dong to appreciate against the United States dollar.

Bulgaria fixed its currency, the lev, against the euro because it planned to enter the European Monetary Union (EMU). When Bulgaria's economy slowed in 2008 and 2009, currency markets began to speculate that Bulgaria would allow the lev to depreciate against the euro. The Government had few options if it wanted to maintain the peg: raise interest rates to encourage investors to own leva, or use its foreign currency reserves to purchase leva on the currency market. Both alternatives would further slow the economy, so were not attractive.

Like Bulgaria, the Baltic countries – Estonia, Lithuania, Latvia – pegged their currencies against the euro because they planned to enter the EMU. The Baltic economies were hit especially hard by the economic downturn; their economies were expected to shrink by 10 percent in 2009. The economic situation caused riots in the capitals and led to the downfall of Latvia's government. The Baltic governments had the same choice that faced Bulgaria: take steps to protect the peg, but fall into further economic decline, or abandon the peg and make it more difficult for the many individuals and companies that had borrowed euros.

Sources: James Hookway, "Vietnam tries to cut loose from falling dollar", *Wall Street Journal*, Mar 19, 2008, p. A8; Jens Bastian, "No time to dither over policy options", *Financial Times*, Jun 19, 2009, p. 23; Robert Anderson, "Pressure on Lithuania as economy shrinks", *Financial Times*, Apr 29, 2009, p. 3; Gideon Rachman, "Latvia's appalling currency choice", *Financial Times*, Oct 9, 2009, p. 12.

A *tariff* is a tax on an import, so imposing a tariff makes imported goods more expensive relative to domestic goods. This enables the domestic manufacturer to charge higher prices and potentially earn a profit. A *quota* is a numerical limit on the number of foreign goods that can enter a market. By limiting the number of foreign goods, the quota enables domestic manufacturers to sell more.

These results sound attractive, but they frequently have undesirable consequences. Domestic manufacturers may charge higher prices than warranted. The quality of domestically-produced goods may fall. Employment and wages in protected industries may be higher than they should be. Consumers may not have a choice of products at various prices or of various qualities. We see that restricting trade benefits one sector of the economy at the expense of other sectors, so now we're back in the political arena. Governments, rather than markets, choose who wins or loses. Such is the case with several tariffs in the US and China, as you see in Box 3.4.

Box 3.4   Tariffs and China–United States trade disputes

The World Trade Organization (WTO) is the arbiter that decides whether countries can impose trade restrictions such as tariffs and quotas. The WTO issues its rulings after a country brings an official complaint about trade restrictions. In 2009, the WTO heard 27 percent more cases concerning tariffs imposed to counteract dumping (selling at artificially low prices) compared to 2008. The major target of the complaints was China.

The United States has imposed tariffs on several products from China, including steel pipe and tires. In 2009, the United States imposed tariffs ranging from 10 to 16 percent on steel pipe used in drilling for oil and natural gas. Also in 2009, the United States imposed a 35 percent duty on tires manufactured in China. China's Government called the tariffs "abusive protectionism" and threatened to investigate imports of United States automobiles.

China also has tariffs, of course. Research in Motion (RIM), a Canadian manufacturer of BlackBerry smartphones, faced tariffs trying to sell in China. Even though RIM's products were more technologically advanced, the tariffs prevented it from competing successfully against China Mobile, the largest mobile phone operator. In 2009, RIM signed arrangements with Digital China and with China Mobile to distribute BlackBerry in China.

China also imposed an unusual tariff on exports in 2007. When the world economy was growing in 2006 and 2007, the prices of industrial minerals in China increased drastically. Because China needed the raw materials for its domestic economy, the Government imposed tariffs of up to 95 percent on exports of raw materials from China. The effect of the export tax was to make it more attractive to Chinese raw materials producers to sell to the domestic market. The United States and the EU filed complaints with the WTO against China in 2009 to stop the export tariff.

Sources: Aaron Back, Patricia Jiayi Ho, "Beijing slams US tariffs in growing clash", *Wall Street Journal*, Nov 7, 2009, p. A6; James Haggerty, "New tariff on China-produced tires expected to put prices into overdrive", *McClatchy-Tribune Business News*, Sep 18, 2009; Kathrin Hille, "BlackBerry maker seals China distribution deals", *Financial Times*, Dec 8, 2009, p. 19; John W. Miller, "US and EU file case over China's tariffs", *Wall Street Journal*, Nov 5, 2009, p. A14.

The Consensus opposes most barriers to trade because they interfere with operation of the market. In many cases where trade barriers exist, they have the effect of allowing inefficient enterprises to remain in operation. If they were faced with competition on the open market from more efficient firms, the firms would not be successful, so they seek protection from the government.

FOREIGN DIRECT INVESTMENT

Besides trading with one another, countries have been investing in one another for hundreds of years. Remember, the US started as colonies of a variety of countries, particularly Britain. Those countries invested in their colonies by establishing manufacturing facilities or trade and distribution channels. More recently, companies have invested in other countries as a means of coping with globalization. Sometimes it is advantageous to manufacture in another country because wages are more favorable or because the company can gain access to resources that aren't available elsewhere. Other times, it may be advantageous to invest in distribution systems so the company can gain access to a market at lower cost.

When a company invests in physical facilities in another country, it is called *foreign direct investment*. Guess what position the Consensus takes regarding foreign direct investment? There shouldn't be any restrictions. That answer shouldn't be surprising, given that the Consensus favors an environment favorable for global investors. Box 3.5 describes what happened in France when one of its largest banks was the target of takeover offers from other European banks.

Countries have developed a variety of mechanisms for limiting foreign investment. Sometimes a country will put a specific sector off limits to foreign investors, as when the US prohibits foreign ownership of defense companies or Mexico prohibits foreign investment in its oil industry. Other times a country will limit foreign ownership to a minority percentage so domestic investors (or the government) maintain a majority

---

Box 3.5   Foreign direct investment and Société Générale

In 2007, at the same time United States banks were failing because of the mortgage meltdown, a financial crisis of a different sort was taking place in France. Executives at Société Générale (SocGen) discovered that a trader in the derivatives division had taken positions that cost the bank more than its capital. The bank was insolvent.

Jérôme Kerviel had not only executed unauthorized trades that lost money, he also had hacked into the bank's computer system in an effort to hide his losses. When the losses were discovered in January 2008, M. Kerviel had cost SocGen almost €5 billion. When combined with a loss of €2 billion from mortgage losses, SocGen did not have capital sufficient to meet regulatory standards.

The issue became where would SocGen obtain additional capital. Several foreign banks, including others from the European Union (EU), were potential candidates to take over SocGen's operations. But the Government of France opposed ownership outside of France, so made public statements that it would not allow SocGen to be sold to foreign investors. "The state will not remain just a bystander and leave Société Générale at the mercy of any predator," said an advisor to French President Sarkozy.

The Government's position was contrary to the position of the EU. One EU official stated "The rules on free movement of capital mean that potential bidders must be treated in a nondiscriminatory way in the situation of cross-border takeovers." The EU favored the impartial treatment of potential acquirers, regardless of whether they were foreign or domestic. In addition to French banks, banks from Spain, Italy, and the United Kingdom were thought to be interested in acquiring SocGen.

Sources: David Gauthier-Villars, Carrick Mollenkamp, Alistair MacDonald, "French bank rocked by rogue trader", *Wall Street Journal*, Jan 25, 2008, p. A1; Helen Dunne, "SocGen's independence still hangs in the balance", *The Business*, Feb 2, 2008, p. 1; Nicola Clark, James Kanter, "Regulators warn France against protecting bank", *New York Times*, Feb 1, 2008, p. C3.

share. Countries also frequently adopt rules about what can be done with the proceeds from an investment by foreigners, such as limiting the amount of profits that can be taken out of the country.

As a global investor, you'd like to put your funds in a country that doesn't restrict what you can do with the investment or its earnings. That's the view of the Washington Consensus.

PRIVATIZATION

One fact of the modern world is that governments own some enterprises. The countries range from the US, where the government owns Amtrak, the Pension Benefit Guaranty Corporation, and the Tennessee Valley Authority, to China, where government-owned entities constitute a significant portion of the economy. In between are countries such as Mexico, where the government owns the oil industry, and France, where the government owns or has owned the national railway system, the telecommunications system, several major banks, and numerous other sectors.

Beginning with the Thatcher/Reagan revolutions, many of these firms have been privatized, which means that the government is selling some portion of the ownership to private investors. Government ownership doesn't necessarily lead to bad management, but politicians and economists have found that many times, governments manage firms for purposes other than improving returns to investors. A government might own a firm as a means of providing employment, for example, or to protect a firm from the forces of market competition. These firms frequently became unprofitable, and therefore a drain on the government's budget. Turning these firms over to the private sector is a way to relieve bloated employment and improve efficiency, while it saves the government treasury the expense of supporting an unprofitable firm.

The trend around the world over the past 20 years has been toward increased privatization. The airline industry presents an interesting example. In the 1950s and 1960s, almost every country had a national airline: Iberia in Spain, Sabena in Belgium, BOAC in the United Kingdom, and many others. In most cases, the national airlines were government-owned. It was a matter of national pride to fly the country's colors in a growing, glamorous industry. As the airline industry matured, countries found that their airlines couldn't compete. A national carrier became a drain on the country's budget and labor issues made it difficult for the airlines to improve efficiency. The national carriers merged with other airlines, were privatized, or left the industry completely. Now there are fewer national carriers than there were 50 years ago.

The Consensus believes that governments ought to get out of the business of ownership. Firms should respond to forces in the market rather than being kept alive through government largesse. In Box 3.6, you'll read about nationalizations and privatizations in Latin America. Even though the government did not privatize the firm, it has decided to deal with the problems. You also can return to Box 3.2 to see the extent of nationalization in Venezuela. Nationalization is the opposite of privatization: the government, rather than the private sector, owns the firm.

Box 3.6   Privatization and nationalization in Latin America

Latin America has gone through waves of privatization (ownership by the private sector) and nationalization (ownership by the Government), depending on the economic philosophy of the party in power. Since the 1990s, Mexico has generally adopted the Washington Consensus of privatizing state-owned enterprises. In 2005, the Government privatized two airlines – Mexicana and AeroMéxico – that accounted for 80 percent of the passenger traffic in Mexico. The airlines had been owned by a Government holding company for more than a decade.

In late 2009, Mexico's President Calderón sent federal police to take control of the Government-owned power monopoly, Luz y Fuerza del Centro (LyFC). Before the takeover, LyFC employed more than 44,000 workers. Expenses were twice as high as revenues, forcing the Government to subsidize LyFC's operations by $3.5 billion annually. Following the takeover, the company employs about 8,000, and it has improved the quality of service. Although the monopoly was not privatized, ownership was transferred to a more efficient government-owned utility.

Venezuela has gone in the opposite direction, nationalizing several sectors that previously were in private ownership. President Chávez nationalized part of the oil industry, several commercial banks, and other segments of the economy that he considers of strategic value to the country: cement, telecommunications, dairy, and iron and steel.

Sources: David Field, "Mexican airlines head for private ownership", *Flight International*, Jul 12, 2005, p. 8; "Power to the people", *The Economist*, Oct 17, 2009, p. 50; José de Córdoba, "Mexico power takeover creates sparks", *Wall Street Journal*, Oct 12, 2009, p. A12; Richard Lapper, "Chávez shifts up a gear in his drive for 21st-century socialism", *Financial Times*, Jan 10, 2007, p. 15; "The autocrat of Caracas", *The Economist*, Aug 9, 2008, p. 36.

DEREGULATION

Since the days of Adam Smith, the father of economics in the late 1700s, economists have realized that unconstrained markets do not always produce outcomes that are good for society. There are times when the government needs to intervene by providing direction about market outcomes. The intervention frequently takes the form of government regulation. When used properly, regulation can promote outcomes that are more beneficial to society.

Unfortunately, some governments carry the idea of regulation too far. When used to excess, regulations penalize people and businesses by interfering with their ability to transact exchanges. Regulations frequently provide a shield that protects a firm from competition. Regulations also create an environment ripe for corruption. It becomes too tempting to try to circumvent a regulation by offering someone a payment for expediting the process or granting a favor. When this happens, resources are diverted away from the efficient performance of the market.

The US began to realize the inefficiency of regulation during the Carter administration of the 1970s. Several federal agencies responsible for regulating industries were either phased out or had their responsibilities curtailed. Other countries are beginning to realize that regulations sometimes interfere with commerce. For example, India was long known as the "Licensing Raj" due to its complex set of regulations, but through the years the regulations are being reduced.

The Consensus favors reducing regulations that exist primarily to protect firms or industries. The protected firms frequently are unprofitable, poorly managed, or use resources unwisely, creating a drain on society. As an investor, you look for countries where regulations are not as prominent or where the quality of regulation is higher.

PROPERTY RIGHTS

A *property right* gives the owners of a resource the ability to do with it as they please, including allowing someone else to use the resource and require payment for its use. Property rights are one of the fundamental tenets of a market economy. The concept of property rights is so ingrained in most European and American countries that we take the concept for granted. However, the concept is not shared by all nations around the world. When people or firms accustomed to enforceable property rights interact with people or firms accustomed to little or no enforcement of property rights, conflict can result.

An illustration of this point is US or European firms doing business in Asia, where property rights are not always enforced. A US firm introducing a product in many Asian countries may find the product copied and distributed without reimbursement to the owner. In Asia, the tradition has been that a resource was owned by the government, by a collective, or by society as a whole. This cultural tradition of public ownership conflicts with the idea of private ownership, so many western firms encounter unexpected difficulties when dealing with a country such as China, as you see in Box 3.7.

As you might expect, the Consensus, coming from a western-culture line of thought, favors private property rights. You would too, as an investor. Property rights enable you to capture the returns from your investment without having to share them with someone else.

Box 3.7   Property rights in China

For years, business executives from western countries have complained about the lack of protection of intellectual property in China. Property rights have long been characteristic of Western business practices, but they conflict with Confucian tradition and the Chinese Communist Party's concept of ownership by the state rather than the individual.

In 2009, a court in China sentenced executives of Chengdu Gongruan Network Technology Co. to prison and fined them $1.6 million for copyright infringement. The court ruled that Gongruan had illegally distributed software, including the Windows operating system. The size of the judgment against the executives was the largest in Chinese history, and led outsiders to think that the Government is getting serious about attacking the problem.

In 2007, 82 percent of the software installed on computers in China was counterfeit, so pirating software is not an unusual practice. Although China has laws protecting intellectual property rights, the laws are rarely enforced and fines are usually small. The Gongruan ruling reversed the pattern.

Beginning in 2006, China's Government declared that protecting intellectual property rights was a "strategic policy." The Government required all Government offices to use legal copies of software, and ran ads on television explaining the benefits of intellectual property rights.

Perhaps the event precipitating the change in attitudes about property rights occurred in 2005 when Lenovo Group, Ltd. purchased the computer division of IBM Corp., a major United States computer manufacturer. Lenovo has the largest share of the computer market in China and the Government is the largest single shareholder in Lenovo. Only a cynic would argue that there was an unbroken chain between the Government's announcement of a strategic policy, Lenovo's purchase of IBM, and the largest judgment in Chinese history.

Sources: "China's next revolution", *The Economist,* Mar 10, 2007, p. 11; Loretta Chao, "China court issues rare piracy penalty to Windows copycats", *Wall Street Journal,* Aug 22, 2009, p. A9; Andrew Batson, "As China reins in piracy, some see faster results", *Wall Street Journal,* Nov 27, 2006, p. A3; Jay Greene, "A big Windows cleanup", *Business Week,* Jun 4, 2007 p. 80.

The Principles in Action

Those are the basic principles of the Washington Consensus. So that you don't think of the Consensus as an arbitrary set of criteria, let's look at some examples of how it works in action.

CalPERS

The California Public Employees' Retirement System (CalPERS) is the largest investment fund in the US. For several years it has been investing in other countries, so has developed a set of criteria to guide where it should invest. Compare these criteria to the ten principles of the Consensus:

A.   Political Stability – Progress toward the development of basic democratic institutions and principles, including such things as: (1) a strong and impartial legal system; and (2) respect and enforcement of property and shareowner rights. Political stability encompasses:
   1. Political risk: internal and external conflict; corruption; the military and religion in politics; law and order; ethnic tensions; democratic accountability; bureaucratic quality.
   2. Civil liberties: freedom of expression, association, and organization rights; rule of law and human rights; free trade unions and effective collective bargaining; personal autonomy and economic rights.
   3. Independent judiciary and legal protection: an absence of irregular payments made to the judiciary; the extent to which there is a trusted legal framework that honors contracts, clearly delineates ownership, and protects financial assets.

B.   Transparency – Financial transparency, including elements of a free press necessary for investors to have truthful, accurate, and relevant information. Transparency encompasses:

1. Freedom of the press: structure of the news delivery system in a country; laws and their promulgation with respect to the influence of the news; the degree of political influence and control; economic influences on the news; the degree to which there are violations against the media with respect to physical violations and censorship.
2. Monetary and fiscal transparency: the extent to which governmental monetary and fiscal policies and implementation are publicly available in a clear and timely manner, in accordance with international standards.
3. Stock exchange listing requirements: stringency of stock exchange listing requirements with respect to frequency of financial reporting, the requirement of annual independent audits, and minimal financial viability.
4. Accounting standards: the extent to which US GAAP or IAS is used in financial reporting; whether the country is a member of the International Accounting Standards Council.

C. Productive Labor Practices – No harmful labor practices or use of child labor. In compliance, or moving toward compliance, with the International Labor Organization (ILO) Declaration on the Fundamental Principles and Rights at Work. Productive Labor Practices encompasses:
1. ILO ratification: whether the convention is ratified, not ratified, pending ratification, or denounced.
2. Quality of enabling legislation: the extent to which the rights described in the ILO convention are protected by law.
3. Institutional capacity: the extent to which governmental administrative bodies with labor law enforcement responsibility exist at the national, regional, and local level.
4. Effectiveness of implementation: evidence that enforcement procedures exist and are working effectively; evidence of a clear grievance process that is utilized and provides penalties that have deterrence value.

D. Corporate Social Responsibility and Long-term Sustainability – Includes Environmental sustainability. In compliance, or moving toward compliance, with the Global Sullivan Principles of Corporate Social Responsibility.

E. Market Regulation and Liquidity – Little to no repatriation risk. Potential market and currency volatility are adequately rewarded. Market regulation and liquidity encompasses:
1. Market capitalization.
2. Change in market capitalization.
3. Average monthly trading volume.
4. Growth in listed companies.
5. Market volatility as measured by standard deviation.
6. Return/risk ratio.

F. Capital Market Openness – Free market policies, openness to foreign investors, and legal protection for foreign investors. Capital market openness encompasses:

1. Foreign investment: degree to which there are restrictions on foreign ownership of local assets, repatriation restrictions or un-equal treatment of foreigners and locals under the law.
2. Trade policy: degree to which there are deterrents to free trade such as trade barriers and punitive tariffs.
3. Banking and finance: degree of government ownership of banks and allocation of credit; freedom financial institutions have to offer all types of financial services; protectionist banking regulations against foreigners.

G. Settlement Proficiency/Transaction Costs – Reasonable trading and settlement proficiency and reasonable transaction costs. Settlement proficiency/transaction costs encompasses:
1. Trading and settlement proficiency: degree to which a country's trading and settlement is automated; success of the market in settling transactions in a timely, efficient manner.
2. Transaction costs: the costs associated with trading in a particular market, including stamp taxes and duties; amount of dividends and income taxes; capital gains taxes.

H. Appropriate Disclosure – On environmental, social, and corporate governance issues.

These criteria are lifted directly from the CalPERS web site at the URL in the Further Reading at the end of the chapter, and are Copyright © 2007 by CalPERS. You must look at the details of some of the CalPERS criteria, but even after you adjust for social objectives typical of California, you'll notice the similarities between the CalPERS and Washington Consensus criteria. They focus on whether the government of the country establishes an environment that is favorable for foreign investors.

RATING AGENCIES

Here is another illustration. Rating agencies evaluate countries on behalf of clients interested in purchasing currencies or securities issued by governments. In the US, the major rating agencies are Moody's, Standard and Poor's, and Fitch Ratings. Table 3.1 shows the criteria used by each of the rating agencies.

The criteria listed are only headings, and within each heading are more details. For example, Moody's lists 53 indicators that it uses to measure the four criteria in the table. The rating agencies developed their criteria and methodologies independently from the Washington Consensus, but it is interesting that the criteria turn out to be similar.

The point of all this is that the criteria used in the Washington Consensus are used in other forms to evaluate a country's performance. They are acceptable for use by an investor wishing to evaluate a country as a place to invest because a country that either meets or is moving toward meeting the criteria should be a safer place than a country that is not doing so.

Meeting the criteria of the Consensus doesn't guarantee investment success, of course. Just think of the risk faced by investors in the US when the real estate market collapsed in 2007, taking with it financial institutions around the globe, or the junior employee in Société Générale in France who was able to make unauthorized trades that cost the bank

Table 3.1   Summary of sovereign ratings criteria

Moody's	Standard and Poor's	Fitch Ratings
Economic structure and performance	Political risk	Macroeconomic performance and prospects
Government finance	Income and economic structure	Political risk and governance
External payments and debt	Economic growth prospects	Public finance, public debt, fiscal financing
Monetary, external vulnerability, and liquidity indicators	Fiscal flexibility	Financial sector and banking system
	General government debt burden	External finances, trade balance, capital flows, external debt
	Offshore and contingent liabilities	
	Monetary flexibility	
	External liquidity	
	External debt burden	

Sources: Moody's *Sovereign Credit Analysis*, Standard and Poor's *Sovereign Credit Ratings: A Primer*, Fitch Ratings: Foreign Rating Methodology.

a loss of €5 billion. Companies succeed or fail, and stock markets rise or fall according to diverse forces, but at least you know the game is fair in a country that conforms to the criteria of the Consensus.

Criticisms of the Washington Consensus

Just because the world's largest pension fund and three rating agencies use criteria similar to the Washington Consensus doesn't mean that everyone agrees with it. In fact, some people have raised objections almost since the day the criteria were introduced. One notable critic was Joseph Stiglitz, a Vice President at the WB, one of the institutions considered part of the Consensus. Stiglitz pointed out that the criteria of the Consensus also are conditions that lead to a country's economic development. When they are applied in this manner, the conditions of the Consensus can be imposed at the wrong time, on an ideological basis, or too rigidly.

For example, the Consensus views privatization as a means of improving a country's economy. But if privatization is imposed simply for ideological reasons, it may not be beneficial. In some situations, a government-owned firm may be performing quite well, and there may not be a need to transfer the firm to the private sector. In other situations, a country may not be at a stage of development that the private sector can assume ownership and responsibility for managing a firm. It could even be deleterious for the country if ownership was transferred to foreign investors, so that domestic people or firms do not participate in the firm's development.

Another notable economist, Paul Krugman, disagreed with the principles of the Consensus because they were not able to predict whether or when an economic crisis would occur in a country. Krugman says that countries suddenly got "free market religion" when they converted to the principles of the Consensus, and that the Consensus may turn out to be a speculative bubble. One of these countries was Mexico, which had made great strides in adopting free-market principles. Mexico encountered a currency crisis in late 1994, similar to currency crises that other countries had encountered previously. Krugman asked if adopting the principles of the Consensus didn't help a country avoid crisis, what good were they? Krugman also points out that a country can adopt one or some of the principles of the Consensus without adopting others, and still achieve desirable economic growth.

You're welcome to read the thoughtful comments by Stiglitz and Krugman in the articles listed at the end of the chapter. As you do, you'll notice that both criticisms relate to the principles of the Consensus when used as conditions for economic development rather than as criteria for evaluating investment risk. We're using the Consensus in a slightly different way.

Regardless of whether a country adopts all of the principles of the Consensus, they are being adopted around the world. The principles of the Washington Consensus have become a global trend.

Another set of criticisms of the Consensus come from heads of state that either disagree with the criteria or refuse to abide by them. Perhaps the most prominent of these critics in the early twenty-first century is Hugo Chávez, the President of Venezuela, who advocates a centralized, socialistic approach using government resources to address social inequalities. Chávez calls his approach *Bolívarian socialism*, named for Latin America's liberator, Simón Bolívar. Chávez has gained a few adherents from other Latin American countries, but when you read about him in the American press, you're more likely to see him characterized as a renegade. Box 3.8 explains how the populist movement has attracted some adherents in Latin America, although other countries continue to adopt principles of the Washington Consensus.

Even countries that you might consider bastions of centralized control, such as Russia and China, are adopting principles of the Washington Consensus. Russia has privatized many firms, reduced regulation, allowed the ruble to float, and encourages foreign investment. China has moved further by adopting more free-market economic policies while retaining strict central political control. China still lags in terms of political freedom, but you'll notice that political freedom is not one of the criteria of the Consensus. If you take a snapshot of either of these countries, you're likely to miss how much they have moved toward the Washington Consensus. But if you take a video comparing them to the way they were 20 years ago, you would be amazed at the difference.

Even countries that would be considered least likely to adopt the Consensus are in fact adopting some if not many of its principles. Therefore, the Washington Consensus will serve us as our guide for evaluating investment risk.

Box 3.8   Hugo Chávez and twenty-first century socialism

Since his election as President of Venezuela in 1998, Hugo Chávez has attempted to exert influence in Latin America that would offset that of the United States. Chávez established a television network to offer news with a South American perspective other than CNN's Latin America network. He also tried to set up a free trade area to compete against the United States-oriented Free Trade Area of the Americas.

In some ways, Chávez's policies have benefitted countries adopting them. For example, in Venezuela, Chávez adopted programs that benefit the poor, such as hiring teachers and medical personnel from Cuba to raise the levels of education and health. Programs such as these not only help the country, but they make him popular with a class of citizens that previously had been neglected.

Part of what makes Chávez's programs socialistic is that he advocates Government provision of many goods and services, and in recent years, Government ownership of a country's resources. In Venezuela, Chávez has nationalized sectors of the economy such as banking, petroleum, telecommunications, and electricity.

A few other countries in Latin America have adopted Chávez's policies. Bolivia, for example, has become a close ally and has patterned its style of economic development after that of Venezuela. The grease that allows Chávez to accomplish many of his goals is money from Venezuela's oil industry. Chávez sells oil to other countries at below-market prices.

Chávez is having difficulty managing the economy of Venezuela, however. Inflation is much higher than the level that the Government dictates. The practice of subsidizing some goods and services creates distortions. In 2010, the Government mandated two exchange rates – one rate to make imports more expensive and another to make exports less expensive.

Despite Chávez's anti-United States rhetoric, Venezuela is tied closely to the United States. The United States is the largest market for Venezuelan petroleum, and Venezuela owns Citgo, a gasoline retailer in the United States. The United States also imports about 13 percent of its petroleum from Venezuela.

Sources: Franklin Foer, "The talented Mr Chávez", *Atlantic Monthly*, May 2006, p. 94; Richard Lapper, "Chávez shifts up a gear in his drive for 21st-century socialism", *Financial Times*, Jan 10, 2007, p. 15; José de Córdoba, David Luhnow, "New president has Bolivia marching to Chávez's beat", *Wall Street Journal*, May 25, 2006, p. A1; Dan Molinski, "Chávez struggles to tame black-market dollar might", *Wall Street Journal*, Jan 22, 2010, p. C2.

How we use the Criteria

We see that there are ways to evaluate risk when investing in another country. Each of the approaches mentioned in this chapter – Washington Consensus, CalPERS, or rating agencies – attempts to understand the risk of an investment. And that's the name of the game when investing: to understand the risk associated with the return you anticipate receiving. Investors adjust their expectations by adjusting for risk: they require a higher return to compensate for more risk. That's why bonds in Brazil pay 13 percent while bonds in Germany pay 4 percent; the risk of investing in each country is different.

The Washington Consensus is one way to evaluate the risk. As we saw, it is not the only way; the rating agencies and CalPERS incorporate other, but similar, criteria. But we use the Washington Consensus throughout the book as a guide to help us understand the various dimensions of risk in global investing.

The introduction to this chapter pointed out that analyzing risk requires an underlying theory about which factors affect risk. That's what the Washington Consensus gives us – a list of criteria that helps us analyze risk. When we're finished, we'll have a process and a set of standards for evaluating the risk of investing in different countries. That's why this book is called *Country Analysis*.

The Consensus and the World Financial Crisis

The world financial crisis and the subsequent economic recession that occurred in 2008 and 2009 led governments in many countries to adopt measures to protect their economies. In many cases, the measures violated principles of the Washington Consensus. The measures occurred in developed as well as developing countries, in countries that advocated the principles as well as those that opposed them.

Perhaps the most frequently-violated principle was the Consensus' preference for balanced government budgets. Keynesian economic theory says that when a government wishes to stimulate the economy, it should increase spending, decrease taxes, or both. The result would be a budget deficit, which is contrary to the first principle of the Washington Consensus. Because of the worldwide recession, governments adopted budget deficits amounting to significant percentages of GDP. In the US, for example, the 2009 budget deficit was $1.4 trillion, or about 10 percent of GDP. Even China, whose economy continued to grow despite the global recession, adopted a stimulus package equal to 7 percent of GDP.

Another frequently-violated principle was privatization. The Consensus argues that firms should be freed from government influence and instead face competition in the market. When the US Government faced the potential collapse of the banking system, the Government intervened massively. The process began with the Government taking control of two large financial institutions responsible for supporting the housing market – Fannie Mae and Freddie Mac. Then the Government provided financing to or took partial ownership of other financial institutions, including commercial banks, investment banks, and insurance companies. As a result, the US Government became the nation's largest insurer and lender. The US Government also provided financial support to automobile manufacturers such as General Motors and Chrysler, taking an ownership interest in those firms.

It is interesting that these efforts occurred under the presidential administrations of George Bush, a Republican, and Barack Obama, a Democrat. Political ideology appeared to have little to do with the effort to save the country's economy or with the willingness to abide by the principles of the Washington Consensus.

These violations of the Consensus occurred in other countries, too. In the United Kingdom, a Government minister suggested that the Government reconsider whether it should allow foreign ownership of UK firms. Previously, the Government had taken an approach more consistent with the Consensus, that countries should not adopt policies limiting foreign ownership.

South Korea, which had been liberalizing its financial sector since the Asian crisis of 1997, postponed further efforts. Part of the liberalization was to allow greater foreign ownership of domestic banks. The German Government debated adopting a policy to prevent foreign ownership of one of its automakers, Volkswagen. The Governments of India, China, Russia, and Canada adopted or considered new restrictions on foreign ownership. Because of the financial crisis, countries in the G20 (the world's major economies) debated new regulations on financial transactions.

In short, the crisis led countries to backtrack on their commitment to free-market principles. It's still too early to evaluate the extent to which governments went back on principles of the Washington Consensus, but many governments reconsidered the role the Consensus should play in their national economies.

Conclusion

The Washington Consensus was developed in the 1980s to summarize desirable characteristics leading to economic development. Since then, many countries have adopted several of the criteria. Investors use the criteria of the Consensus as a guide to determine in which countries they should invest. Rating agencies and pension funds use criteria comparable to those of the Washington Consensus.

Further Reading

Bhardwaj, A., J. Dietz and P.W. Beamish (2007) Host country cultural influences on foreign direct investment, *Management International Review*, 47(1) p. 29.

Birnbaum, J.H. and A.S. Murray (1987) *Showdown at Gucci Gulch*, New York: Random House.

Bolivarian Project, http://www.venezuelanalysis.com/analysis/project, accessed 8/22/08.

Brook, D. (2004) How Sweden tweaked the Washington Consensus, *Dissent*, Fall(4) p. 24.

Callick, R. (2007) The China model, *The American*, Nov/Dec, http://www.american.com/archive/2007/november-december-magazine-contents/the-china-model, accessed 8/22/08.

CalPERS (2007) Statement of investment policy, 2007 http://www.calpers.ca.gov/eip-docs/investments/policies/inv-asset-classes/equity/ext-equity/emerging-eqty-market-prinicples.pdf',604,550.

Caplen, B. (2006) Washington Consensus: A uniform policy that doesn't fit all, *The Banker*, 9/1/06.

Faux, J. (2001) The global alternative, *The American Prospect*, 7/2/01.

Finnegan, W. (2003) The economics of empire, *Harper's Magazine*, May.

Fitch Ratings (2007) *Sovereign Rating Methodology*.

Friedman, T. (2000) *The Lexus and the Olive Tree*, New York: Anchor Books.

Hetzel, R.L. (2007) The contributions of Milton Friedman to economics, Federal Reserve Bank of Richmond: *Economic Quarterly*, Winter.

Keynes, J.M. (1936) *General Theory of Employment, Interest and Money*, Cambridge: Macmillan Cambridge University Press.

Krugman, P. (1995) Dutch tulips and emerging markets, *Foreign Affairs*, July.

Moody's Investor Services (2006) *Moody's Sovereign Credit Analysis*.

Noman, A. (2005) Scoring the millennium goals: Economic growth versus the Washington Consensus, *Journal of International Affairs*, Spring 58(2) p. 233.

Ramo, J.C. (2004) *The Beijing Consensus*, London: The Foreign Policy Centre.

Rosenberg, T. (2007) The perils of petrocracy, *New York Times Magazine*, 11/4/07.

Soederberg, S (2001) The Emperor's new suit: The new international financial architecture as a reinvention of the Washington Consensus, *Global Governance*, Oct–Dec 7(4) p. 453.

Standard and Poor's (2006) *Sovereign Credit Ratings: A primer.*

Stiglitz, J. (2000) *Globalization and its Discontents*, New York: Norton.

Swiderski, K. (1992) ed., Financial Programming and Policy: The case of Hungary, Washington, DC: International Monetary Fund.

Vahtra, P., K. Liuhto and H. Lorentz, (2007) Privatization or renationalization in Russia?, *Journal for East European Management Studies*, 12(4) p. 273.

von Hayek F.A. (1944) *The Road to Serfdom*, Chicago: Univ. of Chicago Press.

Wall Street Journal (2008) India's IPO pillar shows fissures, 2/11/08.

Wall Street Journal (2008) Investors flock to foreign bonds, 2/13/08.

Williamson, J. (2000) What should the World Bank think about the Washington Consensus?, *World Bank Research Observer*, August.

Yergen, D. and J. Stanislaw (1998) *The Commanding Heights*, New York: Touchstone.

4 *Evaluating Governance and Culture*

The Washington Consensus is a good framework on which to base country risk analysis, but it may not be sufficient. If you look again at the criteria of the consensus, you see that most of them are economic in nature: government spending, inflation, international trade, and so forth. There may be noneconomic dimensions that we should consider when examining investment risk.

When economists conducted rigorous tests of the Washington Consensus, they found that the principles of the Consensus didn't do a particularly good job of predicting economic development. Some countries that adopted the principles didn't increase GDP per capita (a typical measure of economic development) any faster than average. Many Latin American countries fell into this category. Other countries that didn't adopt the principles showed better-than-average growth of GDP per capita. Many Asian countries fell into this category. Consequently, the Consensus was insufficient as a guide for a country's economic development.

Something else was needed to explain why some countries grew while others did not. Two explanations that emerged over the intervening two decades are governance and culture. Some countries had better governance – they were governed better or had in place institutions that enabled economic growth. Other countries had national cultures that created an environment for economic growth. These two dimensions – governance and culture – are the topic of this chapter. We'll have to add these explanations to our guide for our investing decisions.

Learning Objectives

After studying this chapter, you should be able to:

1. explain how quality of governance and institutions influence investing decisions;
2. interpret measures of quality of governance, such as transparency, corruption, and regulation;
3. interpret measures of culture, such as power distance, uncertainty avoidance, and assertiveness.

What do Governments do?

Governments create the environment in which individuals and businesses conduct their activities. In this chapter we examine the institutions and policies through which governments establish an environment that reduces risk to investors. These can be called a system of *governance*. They reflect the cultural traditions and heritage of a nation, and in part reflect the attitude that people have toward the role of government in society. According to the World Bank:

> Governance consists of the traditions and institutions by which authority in a country is exercised. This includes the process by which governments are selected, monitored and replaced; the capacity of the government to effectively formulate and implement sound policies; and the respect of citizens and the state for the institutions that govern economic and social interactions among them.[1]

We tend to think of *institutions* as tangible things or organizations created for a certain purpose. But institutions also are the ethos or moral compass of society – the set of practices that persist over time that influence behavior of the members of society. Institutions are the "rules of the game" and may be formal, such as laws and regulations, or informal, such as social norms or codes of conduct. In the US, institutions relating to economics and politics include the voting process, the legal system (especially the law of contracts), private property, and banking, among others. Institutions determine the social rules that determine individual actions. Whereas policies can change according to wishes of public officials, institutions tend to be more stable and persist through time.

When you read the term *policy* in this book, it refers to decisions made by a governmental authority that relate to general aims or goals for the authority. Public policy occurs within the context of the attitudes and institutions of a society. One example of the interplay between institutions and public policy is provided by fiscal policy, the set of decisions about the government's budget. Decisions about the government's budget are made yearly by politicians, but the decisions are made within the institutional framework of society, such as the public's attitude toward the level of service they expect from government and their willingness to pay for that level of service. These attitudes have evolved over generations. When taken collectively, the institutions and policies set the stage in which members of society make economic decisions.

Countries can grow if they adopt sound economic policies, but they may grow even faster if they also adopt sound governance policies. Noneconomic considerations such as corruption, the legal system, and regulations can enhance opportunities for growth or they can impede growth. These noneconomic factors are on the cusp between economics and politics and fall into the area that was traditionally known as political economy, as economics was called 200 years ago. Douglass C. North, who won the Nobel Prize for Economics in 1993, is probably the most famous researcher studying the role of institutions in economic behavior.

The first half of this chapter discusses several widely used indices of government performance. This list is by no means comprehensive. You'll notice that some of them overlap in that they consider similar factors when constructing the index. In fact, some of them use one or more of the other indices when computing their own index. You'll also notice the overlap between the criteria in some of the indices and the criteria of the Washington Consensus. This shouldn't be surprising because the ideas behind the Consensus and good government are similar, and the indices are promulgated by some

---

1   http://info.worldbank.org/governance/wgi/index.asp, accessed 1/10/10.

of the same organizations that developed the Consensus. However, the lack of alternative perspectives doesn't take away from the fact that the criteria are appropriate for measuring the quality of governance in an environment of globalization.

Why Institutions Matter

During their investigations into the importance of institutions, economists discovered some interesting results. For example, Rodrik, Sumbramanian and Trebbi found that institutions were more influential in determining growth of per capita incomes than two traditional causes: geography or international trade. In fact, they found that improving the quality of institutions by one standard deviation led to a six-fold increase in per capita incomes. A force of that importance is something we should include in our evaluation of investment risk. We would much rather place our funds in a country that has quality institutions than in a country without them.

The trick is to measure governance indicators such as institutional quality and the environment for foreign investment, and measuring is where great strides have occurred. Over the past two decades, several sources have attempted to identify principles of good governance and evaluate countries according to their performance relative to a standard. As with the Washington Consensus, the principles were identified and the evaluation performed by analysts from developed, capitalist countries, so many of the principles of good governance are similar to principles of the Washington Consensus. Keep that potential bias in mind as you read this chapter. Regardless, the techniques for evaluating countries have improved through the years as theory has focused on the sources of economic growth and analysts rely more on facts and hard data rather than impressions.

One potentially surprising finding is that there is no relation between a country's political regime – democratic or nondemocratic – and the performance of its economy. Many of us in capitalist countries are biased in favor of democratic governments that are elected by a majority of the voters. However, capitalism and democracy are not twin concepts. It is possible for a country to be capitalist but not democratic; Hong Kong is an example. And the relation between the type of government and economic growth is even less certain. Some nondemocratic nations, such as China, have shown phenomenal economic performance. Thus, the path to economic success does not necessarily go through the field of democracy.

Nevertheless, the pressure of globalization is forcing governments to adopt policies that are favorable to foreign investors. Globalization makes it easier for anything to move from one country to another: people, money, diseases, and ideas. Countries find that if they do not adopt principles of good governance, investors will find other places to park their money. Douglass North points out that institutions reduce uncertainty. Because investors try to avoid uncertainty, they try to find countries with quality institutions that are favorable for global investors.

WORLDWIDE GOVERNANCE INDICATORS[2]

The WB initiated a set of governance indicators in the mid-1990s. The Worldwide Governance Indicators (WGI) are compiled from a variety of data sources such as polls of experts and surveys across countries. Although many of the inputs are subjective (based on opinions) rather than objective (based on analysis of data), the authors believe that the indicators are reliable measures of governance.

The WGI measures governance according to six dimensions:

1. *Voice and accountability* measures the extent to which a country's citizens are able to participate in selecting their government, as well as freedom of expression, freedom of association, and a free media.
2. *Political stability and absence of violence* measures the perceptions of the likelihood that the government will be destabilized or overthrown by unconstitutional or violent means, including domestic violence and terrorism.
3. *Government effectiveness* measures the quality of public services, the quality of the civil service and the degree of its independence from political pressures, the quality of policy formulation and implementation, and the credibility of the government's commitment to such policies.
4. *Regulatory quality* measures the ability of the government to formulate and implement sound policies and regulations that permit and promote private sector development.
5. *Rule of law* measures the extent to which agents have confidence in and abide by the rules of society, in particular the quality of contract enforcement, the police, and the courts, as well as the likelihood of crime and violence.
6. *Control of corruption* measures the extent to which public power is exercised for private gain, including petty and grand forms of corruption, as well as "capture" of the state by elites and private interests.

The first two dimensions, "Voice and accountability" and "Political stability and absence of violence," measure how those in authority are selected and replaced: do citizens participate in the process and is there a threat that the government will be overthrown? The next two dimensions, "Government effectiveness" and "Regulatory quality," measure the quality and soundness of government policies. The final two dimensions, "Rule of law" and "Control of corruption," measure how much citizens and the government itself respect the rules that govern the country. Thus, the dimensions measure how a government is selected, how well it governs, and whether it is respected.

Although the WGI does not rank countries, the process allows comparison of countries because of the use of percentiles. There is no overall index incorporating all six dimensions. Instead, the WB provides percentile rankings for each of the dimensions for individual countries, either as a chart or as a table. It also is possible to group countries according to geographic area (such as Latin America) or degree of development (such as OECD). The process also permits comparisons for the same country over time, so you can determine whether the country is improving or regressing according to each indicator.

The authors of the indicators then analyzed whether the governance indicators helped predict measures of economic development such as per capita income, adult literacy, and

---

2   http://info.worldbank.org/governance/wgi/index.asp.

infant mortality. They found that governance indeed was an important determinant of development. You can read more about the indicators and the statistical interpretation of their results in the article by Kaufmann in the references at the end of the chapter.

Figure 4.1 is the summary for the US over two years of data in chart format. You see that some of the indicators have improved for the US from 2003 to 2008, but others have gotten worse. "Political stability" has improved since the terrorist attacks of 2001, but "Voice and accountability" has not. In many of the indicators, the US ranks above the 90th percentile. Box 4.1 describes one of Thailand's institutions – the military – and its role in the governance process. Decide which dimensions would be affected by the military's role, then visualize a ranking for Thailand. Go to the WGI homepage to see how well you did.

As an investor you prefer a country that runs its affairs effectively, uses regulations for the benefit of society, has a legal system to protect your investment, and is not corrupt. Political stability probably is more important than the system of government, which influences "Voice and accountability."

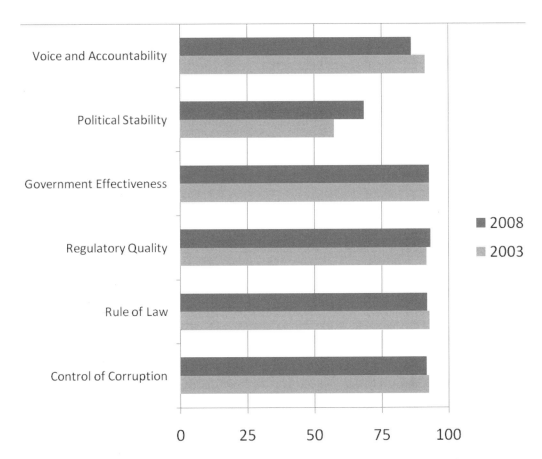

Figure 4.1   World Governance Indicators for United States, 2003 and 2008

Source: http://info.worldbank.org/governance/wgi/sc_chart.asp#.

Box 4.1   Thailand and the military

Like many countries, Thailand has a tradition of military influence in government. Prior to 1932, Thailand was a kingdom, but a military coup led to a constitutional monarchy that was to include elected governments. The military became one of the strongest institutions in the country.

From 1932 until 2009, the military conducted 18 coups to replace governments in power, an average of one every four years. The longest period between coups was 15 years. Occasionally, the coups pitted one faction within the military against another military faction in power. The military ruled the country for 48 of the 60 years from 1932 until 1992. In 1992, troops shot into crowds of pro-democracy protestors, killing at least 40 people and injuring hundreds more. The military had killed hundreds of students during similar protests in 1976.

The military plays a prominent role in Thailand's commerce. Thailand has almost as many generals as does the United States, whose military is more than four times the size. The military controls some legitimate businesses such as trading companies, but it also operates illegal activities such as drugs, guns, and gems. One of the reasons that the military opposes civilian controls on its activities is the fear that a civilian administration will reduce military spending, another major source of income for the generals.

In 2006, Thailand's Prime Minister left Bangkok to give a speech at the United Nations in New York City. While he was away, he was deposed in a military coup. The military administration created a panel of judges that annulled the results of the election and accused the Prime Minister of corruption and abuse of power. The judges also outlawed the Prime Minister's political party, leading to protests that were violently suppressed by the military in 2008. In an ironic twist in 2009, the deposed Prime Minister became an advisor to the President of Cambodia, a country that frequently has been an enemy of Thailand.

Military interference with the political process frequently leads to downgrades in the ratings of bonds issued by the Government of Thailand.

Sources: "Thailand marches in reverse", *New York Times*, Feb 26, 1991, p. A22; "Forward into the past", *The Economist*, May 23, 1992, p. 16; "Thailand, the generals and the King", *The Economist*, May 23, 1991, p. 35; "The party is over", *The Economist*, June 2, 2007, p. 41; "Where power lies", *The Economist*, Sep 19, 2009, p. 51; "A new way to annoy a neighbour", *The Economist*, Nov 14, 2009, p. 51.

CORRUPTION PERCEPTIONS INDEX[3]

Transparency International (TI) developed the *Corruption Perceptions Index* in 1995 to measure the extent of public sector corruption in a country. TI defines *corruption* as the misuse of public power for private benefit, such as bribing public officials, kickbacks in public procurement, or embezzlement of public funds. The index is based on the extent of corruption as perceived by business and government officials surveyed by TI, and that is why it is called the Corruption Perceptions Index. TI admits that it is difficult to obtain or compare hard data regarding the types of corruption it wishes to measure.

---

3   http://www.transparency.org/policy_research/surveys_indices/cpi.

Table 4.1 shows the top 10 and bottom 10 (plus ties) countries in the Corruption Perceptions Index. Countries are listed in the table from least to most corrupt, so New Zealand ranks as the least corrupt country in the world. The US, ranked 19 in 2009, does not make the top ten. Somalia ranks as the most corrupt. When you read the second article in Box 4.2, you'll get a better idea why China does not rank higher on the list.

Table 4.1   Corruption Perceptions Index, 2009

Rank	Country	CPI score	Confidence range
Top 10			
1	New Zealand	9.4	9.1–9.5
2	Denmark	9.3	9.1–9.5
3	Singapore	9.2	9.0–9.4
3	Sweden	9.2	9.0–9.3
5	Switzerland	9.0	8.9–9.1
6	Finland	8.9	8.4–9.4
6	Netherlands	8.9	8.7–9.0
8	Australia	8.7	8.3–9.0
8	Canada	8.7	8.5–9.0
8	Iceland	8.7	7.5–9.4
Bottom 10 (plus ties)			
168	Burundi	1.8	1.5–2.0
168	Equatorial Guinea	1.8	1.6–1.9
168	Guinea	1.8	1.7–1.8
168	Haiti	1.8	1.4–2.3
168	Iran	1.8	1.7–1.9
168	Turkmenistan	1.8	1.7–1.9
174	Uzbekistan	1.7	1.5–1.8
175	Chad	1.6	1.5–1.7
176	Iraq	1.5	1.2–1.8
176	Sudan	1.5	1.4–1.7
178	Myanmar	1.4	0.9–1.8
179	Afghanistan	1.3	1.0–1.5
180	Somalia	1.1	0.9–1.4

Source: http://www.transparency.org/policy_research/surveys_indices/cpi/2009.

Box 4.2   Corruption in China

Official and unofficial corruption are problems in modern China. Corruption has many causes, including personal greed, ties between government and business, lack of transparency, and a form of networking called guanxi.

Rapid economic growth creates opportunities for people in powerful positions to profit. A recent mammoth trial in Chongqing (a city of 31 million) involved 9,000 suspects, including 50 public officials. Allegations included graft by a public official who owned taxi and bus services, ties with the local mafia, and drug trafficking. Similar cases recently involved officials in Beijing, Shanghai, and Shenzhen.

The Communist Government controls the judicial system and police forces, and does not make decisions in a public forum, creating opportunities for corruption by party officials. A Government audit in 2009 discovered that 234.7 billion yuan ($34.3 billion) disappeared from public funds during the first 11 months of the year, leading to cases against 67 senior Government officials. China's President, Hu Jintao, frequently warns that corruption could destroy the Communist Party.

Guanxi, which has been part of Chinese culture for centuries, can be thought of as a system of social networking in which trust between individuals is important. One problem with guanxi is that it is difficult for an outsider to verify. In many developed countries, business relationships are based on contracts, laws, and transparency. Thus, there is an inherent conflict between the traditional Chinese way of doing business, based on relationships, and the western way based on laws. Some analysts think that the lack of a modern legal system could constrain China's growth.

In 2008 China's Government adopted the Regulations on Open Government Information with the intention of opening some Government information to public scrutiny. Activities such as administrative rulings, financial statements, and payments for land use must be made available on web sites or through news conferences. Previously, local bureaucrats guarded access to this information.

Source: Geoffrey A. Fowler and Juying Qin, "China moves to boost transparency, but much is kept hidden", *Wall Street Journal*, Apr 25, 2007, p. A6; Dominic Ziegler, "Tangled Web", *The Economist*, Apr 8, 2000, p. CS7; "Control freaks", *The Economist*, Dec 19, 2009, p. 16; Andrew Browne, "Beijing says billions in funds are missing", *Wall Street Journal*, Dec 30, 2009, p. A9; Andrew Jacobs, "Chinese trial reveals vast web of corruption and fuels a political career", *New York Times*, Nov 4, 2009, p. A6.

GLOBAL COMPETITIVENESS INDEX[4]

The World Economic Forum has become famous over recent years for its annual meetings in Davos, Switzerland, attended by some of the world's influential people. The meetings are frequently but not exclusively economic in nature, sometimes addressing diplomatic and social issues.

---

4   http://www.weforum.org/en/initiatives/gcp/Global%20Competitiveness%20Report/index.htm.

The Forum introduced a Global Competitiveness Index (GCI) in 2004. The GCI defines competitiveness as "the set of institutions, policies, and factors that determine the level of productivity of a country." Countries that are more competitive are able to generate higher per capita incomes because they are more productive. The GCI evaluates and ranks 180 countries according to what it calls 12 pillars:

1. *Institutions*, such as the legal system and property rights, regulation, transparency, and corruption.
2. *Infrastructure*, such as transport and communication systems.
3. *Macroeconomy*, particularly government deficits and inflation.
4. *Health and primary education* addresses the physical and mental abilities of the work population, particularly the work force.
5. *Higher education and training* measures the quality and extent of secondary and higher education, as well as worker training provided by businesses.
6. *Goods market efficiency*, such as the mix of goods and services and how well they reflect consumer needs, taxes, and rules on ownership.
7. *Labor market efficiency* measures how well the labor force matches needs of employers, as well as worker incentives for efficient production.
8. *Financial market sophistication* measures the efficiency of capital markets in providing funds to growing businesses.
9. *Technological readiness* measures how technology is incorporated into business needs, how knowledge is disseminated, and how information and communication technologies are used.
10. *Market size*, including the domestic market as well as the extent to which the country is globalized.
11. *Business sophistication* addresses the degree of development and the availability of support networks.
12. *Innovation*, such as designing and implementing technological improvements.

Table 4.2 shows the top ten and bottom ten countries ranked by the GCI. As you might expect, the top ten countries are developed economies which are likely to rank high according to the 12 pillars. The bottom ten countries are small, undeveloped, and frequently victims of political or social turmoil. The GCI adjusts for potential bias in favor of developed countries by adjusting the index according to the stage of a country's economic development. You should get a better understanding of many of the pillars after reading Box 4.3.

INDEX OF ECONOMIC FREEDOM[5]

The Heritage Foundation, a conservative think tank in the US, began the Index of Economic Freedom (IEF) in 1995. The IEF ranks 179 countries and classifies them as Free, Mostly Free, Moderately Free, Mostly Unfree, or Repressed. As you can guess from the index's title, it has a bias toward countries whose population is free to make economic decisions, even if they do not have equal political freedom. Economic freedom consists of personal choice, exchange coordinated by markets, freedom of the individual to enter and compete in markets, and protection of property rights against encroachment by other parties.

---

5   http://www.heritage.org/Index/.

Table 4.2   Global Competitiveness Index, 2009

| Country | GCI 2009–2010 | | GCI 2008–2009 |
	Rank	Score	Rank
Top 10			
Switzerland	1	5.60	2
United States	2	5.59	1
Singapore	3	5.55	5
Sweden	4	5.51	4
Denmark	5	5.46	3
Finland	6	5.43	6
Germany	7	5.37	7
Japan	8	5.37	9
Canada	9	5.33	10
Netherlands	10	5.32	8
Bottom 10			
Paraguay	124	3.35	124
Nepal	125	3.34	126
Timor-Leste	126	3.26	129
Mauritania	127	3.25	131
Burkina Faso	128	3.23	127
Mozambique	129	3.22	130
Mali	130	3.22	117
Chad	131	2.87	134
Zimbabwe	132	2.77	133
Burundi	133	2.58	132

Source: http://www.weforum.org/en/index.htm.

The IEF evaluates countries according to ten freedoms:

1. *Business freedom* includes the time, cost and regulatory delays in opening, operating and closing a business.
2. *Trade freedom* includes tariffs, quotas, and nontariff barriers to international trade.
3. *Fiscal freedom* includes total tax burden of the government as a percent of GDP, as well as marginal tax rates on businesses and individuals.
4. *Government size* includes government spending as a percent of GDP.

Box 4.3   India's competitiveness

In the 2009 Global Competitiveness Index, India ranks 49th, well behind China at 29. Whereas China has shown rapid economic growth for more than two decades, India's rapid growth began in the late 1990s when the Government gave up economic planning and replaced it with free-market principles.

Many people inside and outside of India are concerned about India's ability to maintain growth sufficient to raise the standard of living of its population of more than one billion. Here are some of the concerns:

Poor infrastructure. India has underinvested in infrastructure for half a century, both in building new facilities for a growing economy and maintaining existing facilities. The process of unloading ships and clearing cargo from the port requires 21 days in India compared to three in Singapore. Roads in India's cities are congested: The average speed in Delhi was 10 kilometers per hour in 2008 compared to 27 kph in 1997. Demand for power exceeds supply by about 15 percent, creating periods when power is off completely. Consumers steal about 35 percent of the power produced.

Poor health and education. Only about 13 percent of sewage is treated, creating conditions for water-borne diseases and malnourished children. Only 65 percent of the population was literate in 2001; the figure is 90 percent in China.

Inefficient goods markets. The country loses almost 40 percent of farm produce because it rots in the field or spoils in transit.

Antiquated institutions. Before modernization began in the 1990s, India was known as the "license Raj" because of the bureaucratic impediments when conducting business. Although the impediments have been reduced, they have not been eliminated. Graft at all levels of Government continues to impose costs of doing business. The national Government recently passed a law requiring some transparency in Government.

Outdated labor laws. Labor laws adopted during the planning years of the 1940s and 1970s have not been modernized. The laws require Government permission when terminating workers and prohibit filling ongoing positions with temporary workers. It can take years to lay off workers.

Although India's Government plans to increase spending on infrastructure, the ability to obtain funding is a problem. India does not generate sufficient domestic savings to finance the anticipated increase, so the balance will have to come from foreign investors.

Sources: "Creaking, groaning", *The Economist*, Dec 13, 2008, p. 11; Steve Hamm, "The trouble with India", *Business Week*, Mar 19, 2007, p. 49; James Lamont, "A critical bottleneck in road to growth", *Financial Times*, Dec 16, 2008, p. 30; Peter Wonacott, "Deadly labor wars hinder India's rise", *Wall Street Journal*, Nov 20, 2009, p. A1.

5. *Monetary freedom* includes central bank independence from the treasury and the rate of inflation.
6. *Investment freedom* includes restrictions on international flows of capital for investment.
7. *Financial freedom* includes independence of financial institutions, particularly commercial banks, from government control, as well as soundness of the financial system.
8. *Property rights* includes the ability of businesses and individuals to use resources without fear of expropriation from the government or other private parties.
9. *Freedom from corruption* includes "bribery, extortion, nepotism, cronyism, patronage, embezzlement" and graft.
10. *Labor freedom* includes the minimum wage, rules concerning working hours, and the ability to hire and fire employees.

Table 4.3 contains the top ten and bottom ten countries according to the 2009 IEF rankings. The top ten countries are all developed economies, although they are not equally free politically. As with similar indices, the bottom ten countries are less developed, without the institutions and policies that would earn them high marks according to the ten freedoms.

Table 4.3   Index of Economic Freedom, 2009

Rank	Country	Score	Rank	Country	Score
	Top 10			Bottom 10	
1	Hong Kong	90.0	170	Solomon Islands	42.9
2	Singapore	87.1	171	Turkmenistan	42.5
3	Australia	82.6	172	Democratic Republic of Congo	41.4
4	Ireland	82.2	173	Libya	40.2
5	New Zealand	82.0	174	Venezuela	37.1
6	United States	80.7	175	Burma	36.7
7	Canada	80.5	176	Eritrea	35.3
8	Denmark	79.6	177	Cuba	26.7
9	Switzerland	79.4	178	Zimbabwe	21.4
10	United Kingdom	79.0	179	North Korea	1.0

Source: http://www.heritage.org/Index/Ranking.aspx.

FREEDOM IN THE WORLD[6]

Freedom House, another think tank, publishes an index of political rather than economic freedom: *Freedom in the World*. The Freedom in the World survey measures freedom of individuals to make political decisions independent of government influence. Unlike the IEF, the Freedom in the World survey does not rank countries. The survey determines a score for each country, and then Freedom House labels each country as Free, Partly Free, or Not Free politically.

Political freedom consists of *political rights*, such as the ability to vote, run for election, and join political parties, and *civil liberties*, such as the rule of law and freedom of association, expression, and belief. Table 4.4 shows the countries receiving the most favorable rating of Free and the countries receiving the most unfavorable rating of Not Free. In this survey, a lower score indicates more political freedom.

There is an ideological bias in the Freedom of the World survey in that Freedom House advocates democratic values and opposes dictatorships. Consequently, a country may receive a low score in this survey because individuals have limited political freedom, but may receive a higher score in the World Bank's Worldwide Governance Indicators because the government is stable and the climate is favorable for investors.

Table 4.4   Freedom in the World, 2009

Free 1.0			Not free 7.0
Andorra	France	Palau	Burma
Australia	Germany	Poland	Equatorial Guinea
Austria	Hungary	Portugal	Libya
Bahamas	Iceland	Saint Kitts and Nevis	North Korea
Barbados	Ireland	Saint Lucia	Somalia
Belgium	Kiribati	San Marino	Sudan
Canada	Liechtenstein	Slovakia	Turkmenistan
Cape Verde	Lithuania	Slovenia	Uzbekistan
Chile	Luxembourg	Spain	
Costa Rica	Malta	Sweden	
Cyprus	Marshall Islands	Switzerland	
Czech Republic	Micronesia	Tuvalu	
Denmark	Nauru	United Kingdom	
Dominica	Netherlands	United States	
Estonia	New Zealand	Uruguay	
Finland	Norway		

Source: http://www.freedomhouse.org/template.cfm?page=475&year=2009.

---

6   http://www.freedomhouse.org/template.cfm?page=475&year=2009.

EASE OF DOING BUSINESS[7]

The World Bank developed an index to measure the ease of doing business in a country. The *Doing Business Index* consists of ten factors that determine a country's ability to enhance or constrain investment, productivity and growth:

1. *Starting a business*: the procedures, time and costs, and minimum capital required.
2. *Licensing*: the procedures, time, and costs of inspections and licenses.
3. *Employing workers*: the difficulty of hiring or firing employees, and rules relating to rigidity of hours.
4. *Registering property*: the steps, time, and cost to register commercial real estate.
5. *Getting credit:* the strength of legal rights, and the depth of credit.
6. *Protecting investors:* the extent of disclosure, director liability, and ease of shareholder suits.
7. *Paying taxes:* the number of tax payments, time to prepare, and taxes as a percentage of profits.
8. *Trading across borders:* the documents, time, and costs for exporting or importing.
9. *Enforcing contracts*: the procedures, time, and costs to resolve commercial disputes.
10. *Closing a business*: the recovery rate in bankruptcy.

Table 4.5 shows the top ten and bottom ten countries according to the Ease of Doing Business Index. These are rankings rather than scores.

Table 4.5   Ease of Doing Business, 2009

Economy	Rank	Economy	Rank
Top 10		**Bottom 10**	
Singapore	1	Niger	174
New Zealand	2	Eritrea	175
Hong Kong, China	3	Burundi	176
United States	4	Venezuela, R.B.	177
United Kingdom	5	Chad	178
Denmark	6	Congo, Rep.	179
Ireland	7	São Tomé and Principe	180
Canada	8	Guinea-Bissau	181
Australia	9	Congo, Dem. Rep.	182
Norway	10	Central African Republic	183

Source: http://www.doingbusiness.org/economyrankings/.

---

7   http://www.doingbusiness.org/economyrankings/.

Summary of Governance

The previous sites have an advantage: they're all free. As I said, there are other surveys, and new ones are added every year. I can't vouch for the currency of the URLs – they probably will be out of date by the time this book goes to press – so if you have difficulty locating the home page, do a search using the name of the index. The indices in this chapter have another advantage: they are updated on a regular basis. Other indices appear occasionally but are not updated regularly.

Several other organizations publish or interpret comparable information for a fee. You can go to each of the locations to read what services the organizations provide, how they compute the rankings, the criteria they use, and the rankings themselves. Some of the organizations use the same surveys that are listed in this chapter. Others develop their own ways of measuring governance, including having access to resources within the country. This list also is by no means exhaustive:

- Business Environment Risk Intelligence http://beri.com/
- Economist Intelligence Unit http://www.eiu.com/index.asp?rf=0
- Euromoney http://www.euromoney.com/default.aspx
- Institutional Investor http://iimagazine.com/
- Political Risk Services http://prsgroup.com/
- Oxford Analytica http://www.oxan.com/Default.aspx

Use whichever of the surveys help you make a decision, whether it is free or costs money. The value of all these surveys is that they help you understand and react to risks. The Washington Consensus helped us understand risks relating to economic indicators. The surveys in this portion of the chapter add to our understanding of governance. Now let's turn our attention to culture.

Why Culture Matters

If you take a moment to think about it, everything in this book is the result of culture. Geert Hofstede defines culture as "the collective programming of the mind that distinguishes the members of one group or category of people from another." Culture determines peoples' attitudes and the institutions people create to perpetuate the culture. Culture can influence performance of employees, attitudes toward the social responsibility of business, willingness to innovate, the structure of organizations, and other aspects too numerous to mention. Religion, language, politics, the legal system, and education are aspects of culture. So are consumer tastes and buying habits, fashion, and attitudes toward saving and investing. Culture cuts a pretty wide swath.

Some cultures believe in the accumulation of wealth, while other cultures focus on other measures of individual or social wellbeing. Some cultures emphasize the individual, while other cultures emphasize the group. As I have pointed out several times already, the Washington Consensus is a view of the world through the cultural lens of Western Europe and the US, so this book is itself based on culture.

Two hundred years ago, the father of modern economics, Adam Smith, wrote two books relating culture to economics: *The Theory of Moral Sentiments*, which focuses on culture and philosophy, and *An Inquiry into the Nature and Causes of the Wealth of Nations*, which focuses on economics. These books are so influential that you frequently find them used as doorstops in offices at the finest academic institutions.

Unfortunately, as economics developed as an academic discipline, economists lost sight of the cultural underpinnings of their field. One problem was that culture was a difficult concept to pin down and an even more difficult concept to quantify so it could be tested. See the article by Guiso, Sapienza and Zingales in the references at the end of the chapter for a good explanation of the problems associated with including culture in economic theory. Fortunately, just as researchers developed methods to measure governance, they also have begun to develop methods to measure culture.

Most of the applications of culture in the business field have been in management and international business, and at the micro level rather than the macro level. Culture has been approached as something managers need to consider when they try to manage across borders. Until recently, culture has not been approached as something that influences investment decisions, the topic of this book. But culture is being used increasingly in business research in fields that previously paid it scant attention: accounting, finance, and economics, for example. This enables us to include culture as one of the factors that influence global investment risk, so we will add it to our arsenal.

HOFSTEDE'S CULTURAL DIMENSIONS[8]

Probably the leading modern theorist on culture is Geert Hofstede, who over the past 30 years has developed a system for classifying cultures. His original work measured culture according to four dimensions; a fifth was added subsequently. Hofstede's work is the most frequently cited in academic literature and increasingly is being used as the basis for academic research into culture's effects on diverse academic disciplines.

Hofstede's original four dimensions are:

1. *Power distance* measures the extent to which the society is stratified into hierarchies reflecting an unequal distribution of power. A high score on the Power Distance Index (PDI) indicates that power is distributed unequally. Power is measured in various ways, such as social status, wealth, laws, and rules protecting those in positions of power. Countries with high PDI scores tend to have more bureaucracy in government because the bureaucracy is a method for perpetuating the status quo.
2. *Uncertainty avoidance* measures the extent that people within the country are willing to tolerate uncertainty. A high score on the Uncertainty Avoidance Index (UAI) indicates that individuals are not willing to tolerate uncertainty or ambiguity, so develop laws, regulations, and controls to avoid uncertainty. Hofstede emphasizes that uncertainty is not the same as risk. Countries with a high UAI score tend to have more regulations because regulations are a way of protecting against uncertainty.
3. *Individualism* measures the relative importance of the individual or the group. A high score on the Individualism Index (IDV) indicates that individualism and individual rights are important, whereas a low score indicates that society tends to favor a collective approach such as through the family and relationships with others. Countries with a high IDV score tend to have laws that protect individual freedoms and property rights.

---

8   http://geerthofstede.nl.

4. *Masculinity* measures the extent to which society values assertiveness, power, and control (characteristics viewed traditionally as masculine) rather than nurturing (viewed traditionally as a feminine trait).

Researchers suggested another dimension, which Hofstede now includes it as part of his approach:

5. *Long-term orientation* measures the extent to which society focuses on the long term rather than the short term. A high score on the Long-Term Orientation Index (LTO) indicates that society values the long term, so has characteristics such as thrift and perseverance.

A country need not rank high according to each dimension, and there is no good or bad associated with the dimensions; they simply describe a culture. Table 4.6 shows the scores for a variety of countries drawn from various regions of the world. Compared to other countries in the sample, the US has a more equal distribution of power, a greater willingness to tolerate uncertainty, a greater emphasis on individualism, a more assertive culture, and an orientation toward the short term. China has a more unequal distribution of power, a greater willingness to tolerate uncertainty, more emphasis on collectivism, a more assertive culture, and an orientation toward the long term.

One innovative way of using Hofstede's dimensions is by looking at the *cultural distance* between countries. Statistical techniques allow us to compute one number that represents the difference between the scores for one country and the scores for another country. We then can compare the difference between the two countries, called the cultural distance. There may be situations where managers in one country will encounter difficulty if the cultural distance is significant because managers may not be familiar with business practices in another country. Or investing in a country that is significantly culturally distant may introduce additional risk into the investment, particularly if it is

Table 4.6   Hofstede's cultural dimensions

Dimension	Power distance	Uncertainty avoidance	Individualism	Masculinity	Long-term orientation
Higher score indicates:	More unequal	Avoid uncertainty	Value individual	More assertive	Long term
Brazil	69	76	38	49	65
China	80	40	20	66	118
Japan	54	92	46	95	80
Sweden	31	29	71	5	33
United States	40	46	91	62	29
Lower score indicates:	More equal	Accept uncertainty	Value collective	More nurturing	Short term

Source: Hofstede, G. (2001) *Culture's Consequences*, 2nd ed., Thousand Oaks: Sage Publications.

foreign direct investment rather than portfolio investment. These are areas that just now are being investigated through academic research.

GLOBE LEADERSHIP SURVEY[9]

Another, more recent approach to understanding how culture relates to leadership and management styles is the Global Leadership and Organizational Behavior Effectiveness Research Program, or GLOBE. As its title implies, the program is oriented toward micro issues such as the characteristics of leaders, the variability of leadership styles among cultures, and appropriate organizational processes and structures. However, the program also relates the cultural dimensions to measures of a country's economic status, such as income, productivity, and human wellbeing. The GLOBE program is the most comprehensive approach to culture yet.

The GLOBE approach involves nine dimensions:

1. *Uncertainty avoidance* measures the extent members of society avoid uncertainty.
2. *Power distance* measures the degree of acceptance of stratification in organizations or government.
3. *Institutional collectivism* measures the extent to which institutions in society favor collective action.
4. *In-group collectivism* measures the extent to which individuals express collectivism in personal relations and the work environment.
5. *Gender egalitarianism* measures the extent to which society promotes gender equality.
6. *Assertiveness* measures the extent of individual assertiveness and aggression.
7. *Future orientation* measures the extent that individuals engage in planning and investing for the future.
8. *Performance orientation* measures the extent that society and organizations use rewards for performance improvements.
9. *Humane orientation* measures the extent of altruism and generosity in society.

If some of these dimensions sound familiar, they should. Many of them are based on Hofstede's dimensions. Some of Hofstede's dimensions were decomposed to provide a more detailed look at culture, while other dimensions were added to provide a more comprehensive measure. One other feature distinguishes the GLOBE survey from Hofstede's research: There are two scores for each dimension because societies sometimes say something is important but reveal in practice that it is not. The GLOBE program distinguishes between what a society thinks is important (the Values survey) and what it actually practices (the Practices survey).

The GLOBE program goes beyond leadership styles and organizational behavior by relating the nine dimensions, which are independent variables, to dependent variables such as GDP per capita, the World Bank's World Development Indicators, the World Economic Forum's Global Competitiveness Index, and other measures of a country's performance. Results of the program indicate that countries generally are more prosperous economically and have higher levels of human development if they distribute power

---

9   http://www.thunderbird.edu/sites/globe/index.htm.

more equally, are more high performance, more gender egalitarian, more assertive, more collective, and more humane.

Table 4.7 shows the scores for the nine GLOBE dimensions for the same countries as in Table 4.6. As expected, the rankings generally agree with the rankings in Hofstede: the US distributes power more equally, accepts uncertainty, tends to be more individualistic both in groups and institutional arrangements, is more assertive, and is oriented more toward the present. We also find that the US tends to reward for performance and is a less humane culture. You can find statistics for the 62 countries included in the GLOBE survey by referring to the book by House.

If you don't have access to the book, you can read summaries of the dimensions and research processes online at a site maintained by a professional who is not part of the GLOBE project: http://www.grovewell.com/GLOBE/. At this time, the only way to obtain the numerical rankings is to find the book.

Box 4.4 explains problems associated with the modernization of Turkey in terms of one of the dimensions use by Hofstede and the GLOBE project.

Summary of Culture

As with measures of governance, there are organizations that provide advice about culture for a fee. In fact, almost any international business consultant will provide advice about handling problems that arise in international management. That brings up one of the problems about culture: most consultants advise about culture's impact on management and organizational behavior rather than on how culture influences a decision to invest in another country.

Studies of culture haven't yet advanced to the stage that they are helpful in providing investment advice, at least to the point of explaining how culture affects the risk of an investment. They're good at providing management advice, but not investment advice. Given the pace of academic research, this will undoubtedly change in a few years.

One thing you'll notice about the Hofstede and GLOBE cultural dimensions is that they don't refer directly to some of the aspects that we think of as culture, such as religion or language. These aspects are included when they influence the distribution of power, preference for the individual or the group, or any of the other dimensions. But because it is difficult to measure concepts such as religion or language, they are not included as specific dimensions.

An attractive feature of both Hofstede's work and the GLOBE project is that they produce scores that can be used to compare countries. The scores have been tested for statistical validity, an important step in academic circles. If the scores can be used reliably to compare countries, we've quantified culture.

Conclusion

The Washington Consensus criteria turned out to be insufficient conditions for economic development. Researchers have added institutions and culture to the criteria. Institutions include governance, regulation, corruption, the legal system, and other formal and informal methods that society uses to govern itself. Everything in this book, including

Table 4.7 GLOBE cultural dimensions: Society practices

Dimension:	Power distance	Uncertainty avoidance	Institutional collectivism	In-group collectivism	Gender egalitarianism	Assertiveness	Future orientation	Performance orientation	Humane orientation
Higher score indicates:	More unequal	Avoid uncertainty	More collective	More collective	Male domination	More assertive	Toward future	Performance oriented	More humane
Brazil	5.33	3.60	3.83	5.18	3.31	4.20	3.81	4.04	3.66
China	5.04	4.94	4.77	5.80	3.05	3.76	3.75	4.45	4.36
Japan	5.11	4.07	5.19	4.63	3.19	3.59	4.29	4.22	4.30
Sweden	4.85	5.32	5.22	3.66	3.84	3.38	4.39	3.72	4.10
United States	4.88	4.15	4.20	4.25	3.34	4.55	4.15	4.49	4.17
Lower score indicates:	More equal	Accept uncertainty	Less collective	Less collective	More equal	Less assertive	Toward present	Not performance oriented	Less humane

Source: House, et al., Culture, Leadership, and Organizations (2004).

Box 4.4   Modernization in Turkey

Turkey is in an exceptional position. Geographically, Turkey lies in both Europe and Asia. More than 99 percent of the population is Muslim, although the Government is secular. Economically and politically, Turkey is more western than other Arab and Middle Eastern countries, largely resulting from reforms initiated in the 1920s by Mustafa Kemal Atatürk, known as the father of modern Turkey.

One major reform made Turkey a representative democracy in which citizens elected the government. Prior to the reforms, Sultans had ruled Turkey for hundreds of years. Another reform separated religion from government, which was achieved by abolishing the Caliphate, a form of religious governance. Turkey became an anomaly in the region: a democracy in which religion and government were independent institutions.

In 2002, an Islamist party won a majority in Parliament. The new Government adopted numerous Washington Consensus policies that changed the country: inflation fell to 10 percent in 2009 from 65 percent in 2000; annual economic growth was more than 6 percent in the six years following the elections compared to less than 3 percent in the six previous years; foreign investment grew to more than $20 billion per year compared to less than $1 billion; exports tripled; many Government-owned firms were privatized; and the bureaucracy was reduced.

Factions in Turkey have accused the new Government not only of violating principles of the Atatürk reforms, but also of attempting to impose an Islamist agenda. When Parliament elected a president from the Islamist party, hundreds of thousands of people protested. The opposition secular party asked the constitutional court to annul the election and ban the Islamist party. The military announced on its home page that it might intervene to support secularism. People on both sides argued whether women should be allowed to wear headscarves at universities and Government offices. The dispute seemed to be whether Turkey should remain a secular country or was becoming an Islamist country.

Another way to view the dispute is to think of it as a manifestation of the Power Distance dimension. For 80 years, a small clique of wealthy families – a secular elite – had run the Government, the military, the courts, and the bureaucracy. The majority of people had neither wealth nor power. The Power Distance Index (PDI) must have been very high due to the stratification of society. The changes instituted by the new Government raised the standard of living and led to an emerging middle class, and in the process threatened the influence of the ruling elite. Faced with a potential loss of power, the ruling elite did whatever it could to maintain their position.

Sources: Andrew Higgins and Farnaz Fassihi, "Muslim land joins ranks of Tigers", *Wall Street Journal*, Aug 6, 2008, p. A1; Guy Chazan, "Ruling party's Islamist past roils politics in Turkey", *Wall Street Journal*, Jun 11, 2007, p. A1; "Turkish Turmoil", *Wall Street Journal*, May 2, 2007, p. A20; Simon Hooper, "Back from the brink", *New Statesman*, Aug 11, 2008, p. 17.

institutions and the economic system, are aspects of culture. In recent decades, researchers have made strides in measuring governance and culture, which enables us to use them as part of our guide to investing.

Further Reading

Beach, W.W. and M.A. Miles (2006) Explaining the factors of the *Index of economic freedom*, http://www.transparency.org.ru/doc/Method_01215_2.pdf, accessed 4/17/08.

Bhardwaj, A., J. Dietz and P.W. Beamish (2007) Host country cultural influences on foreign direct investment, *Management International Review*, 47(1) p. 29.

Friedman, B.M. (2007) Capitalism, economic growth and democracy, *Daedalus*, Summer.

Gat, A. (2007) The return of authoritarian great powers, *Foreign Affairs*, Jul/Aug.

Grove, C.N. (2005) Leadership style variations across cultures: Overview of GLOBE research Findings, http://www.grovewell.com/GLOBE/, accessed 12/31/09.

Guiso, L., P. Sapienza and L. Zingales (2006) Does culture affect economic outcomes? *Journal of Economic Perspectives*, 20(2) p. 23.

Hofstede, G. (2001) *Culture's Consequences*, 2nd ed., Thousand Oaks: Sage Publications.

House, R.J., P.J. Hanges, M. Javidan, P.W. Dorfman and V. Gupta (2004) *Culture, Leadership, and Organizations: The GLOBE study of 62 societies*, Thousand Oaks: Sage Publications.

Kaufmann, D., A. Kraay and P. Zoido-Lobatón (1999) *Governance matters*, World Bank Policy Research Working Paper 2196.

Lopez-Carlos, A., L. Altinger and J. Blanke, The global competitiveness index: Identifying the key elements of sustainable growth, World Economic Forum, http://akgul.bilkent.edu.tr/WEF/2006/chapter_1_1.pdf, accessed 4/15/08.

Loree, D.W. and S.E. Guisinger (1995) Policy and non-policy determinants of US equity foreign direct investment, *Journal of International Business Studies* 26(2) p. 281.

Moustafa Leonard, K., M. Slaubaugh and H.C. Wang (2008) Cultural effects on accounting practice and investment decisions, *Proceedings of American Society of Business and Behavioral Sciences Annual Meeting*, Las Vegas.

North, D.C. (1990) *Institutions, Institutional Change, and Economic Performance*, Cambridge: Cambridge University Press.

Rodrik, D., A. Subramanian and F. Trebbi (2002) Institutions rule: The primacy of institutions over integration and geography in economic development, IMF Working Paper WP/02/189.

Smith, A. (1937) *An Inquiry into the Nature and Causes of the Wealth of Nations*, New York: Modern Library.

Smith, A. (1976) *The Theory of Moral Sentiments*, Oxford: Clarendon Press.

Starling, G. (1988) *Strategies for Policy Making*, Chicago: The Dorsey Press.

Transparency International, Corruption perceptions index, http://www.transparency.org/policy_research/surveys_indices/cpi/2007/methodology, accessed 4/15/08.

World Bank (2007) Ease of doing business, http://www.doingbusiness.org/economyrankings/, accessed 4/15/08.

World Bank (2007) Worldwide Governance Indicators, http://info.worldbank.org/governance/wgi2007/, accessed 4/18/08.

5 *Evaluating Fiscal Policy*

Spending and taxing are two of the most important decisions governments make. Together, they constitute the government's budget, which reflects the government's priorities about its role in society, the services it performs, and the direction of the economy. The budget has important implications for a country's economic performance because the government can use the budget to stimulate or restrain an economy. An outside analyst can develop a feel for the wisdom of a country's decision makers by examining their success in managing the budget.

Learning Objectives

After reading this chapter, you should be able to:

1. explain the sources of government revenue and purposes of government spending;
2. explain the difference between a budgetary surplus and a budgetary deficit;
3. explain the difference between a budget deficit and the national debt;
4. compare and contrast the concepts of tax base and tax rate;
5. explain the incentive effects of taxes and subsidies;
6. explain the economic justification behind government taxation and spending policies;
7. explain measures of government fiscal risk;
8. use budgetary and debt figures to analyze investment risk.

Budget of the United States Government

Like businesses and individuals, governments operate with a budget. A *budget* is an estimate of the receipts and spending over a period of time by an entity such as a government or a business. The budget details how the government will raise funds, primarily through taxes, and how it will spend the funds that it obtains. Unlike businesses and individuals, government budgets are laws, at least in developed countries such as the US. When any level of government – federal, state, or local – taxes its citizens and spends on their behalf, the action requires a series of laws. At the federal level in the US, the laws must be passed by both houses of Congress and signed by the President. Therefore, Congress and the President make all policy decisions relating to the budget: how much revenue the government should collect, who should be taxed and how much, how much the government should spend on behalf of the citizens, and how it is to be spent.

   The budget of the US Federal Government is shown in Table 5.1. Look for several features:

1. In 2000, total receipts were $2,025.2 billion, while total outlays were $1,788.8 billion. Because receipts were greater than outlays, there was a budgetary *surplus* of $236.4 billion.
2. In 2002, total receipts were $1,853.2 billion, while total outlays were $2,011.0 billion. Because outlays were greater than receipts, there was a budgetary *deficit* of $157.8 billion, usually expressed as ($157.8).
3. The primary source of revenue for the Federal Government is taxes on individual incomes. In 2000, individual income taxes accounted for 49.6 percent of federal receipts. In 2002, the percentage was 46.3 percent.
4. Social Security and Medicare accounted for about one-third of federal outlays in 2002. National defense accounted for about 17 percent, and interest payments for about 9 percent.
5. Total spending at the federal level increased each year during the period. In 2000, federal spending was $1.79 trillion, but in two years it grew to $2.01 trillion.

Table 5.1   US Federal receipts and outlays by major category, 2000–2002

	2000	2001	2002
	(billions of US dollars)		
Receipts (on- and off-budget)			
Individual income taxes	1,004.5	994.3	858.3
Corporation income taxes	207.3	151.1	148.0
Social insurance and retirement receipts	652.9	694.0	700.8
Other	160.6	151.8	146.0
Total	2,025.2	1,991.2	1,853.2
Outlays (on- and off-budget)			
National defense	294.5	305.5	348.6
International affairs	17.2	16.5	22.4
Health	154.5	172.3	196.5
Medicare	197.1	217.4	230.9
Income security	253.6	269.6	312.5
Social security	409.4	433.0	456.0
Net interest	223.0	206.2	171.0
Other	239.5	243.4	273.2
Total	1,788.8	1,863.8	2,011.0
Surplus or deficit (-) (on-budget and off-budget)	236.4	127.4	-157.8

Sources: Department of the Treasury and Office of Management and Budget, http://www.gpoaccess.gov/usbudget/.

This presentation of the federal budget is only a summary. You're welcome to find more detail by searching C:\Users\Owner\AppData\Local\Local Settings\Temp\firstgov.gov for spending by agency or receipts by source. However, that level of detail isn't necessary for our purposes, so the detail isn't reproduced here.

I chose the years 2000 to 2002 for a reason, even though they are ancient history by now: there was a presidential election in 2000, so the 2002 budget reflects the priorities of the new administration as well as the behavior of the economy. During the later years of the Clinton administration (1992–2000), the budget was in surplus (receipts exceeded spending), reflecting the economic growth of the 1990s in the US and an agreement in Congress about budgetary processes designed to avoid deficits. After assuming office in January 2001, President Bush advocated legislation that would have the effect of reducing tax receipts. The Economic Growth and Tax Relief Reconciliation Act of 2001 was adopted by Congress and signed by the President in June 2001, showing how quickly (five months is pretty fast in Congressional time) decisions can be made when the President and both houses of Congress are from the same political party. As a result of the Bush tax cuts, spending exceeded receipts and the budget was in deficit.

Fiscal comes from a Latin word, "fiscus," which is the emperor's money basket. "Fiscal" now is a synonym for "budget", so when you see the term "fiscal year" in a corporate or government accounting statement, it means the budgetary year rather than the calendar year. *Fiscal policy* means the set of revenue and spending decisions that determine the government's budget. The fiscal year of the US Government begins on October 1.

REVENUES

Governments collect revenues so that they can pay for the programs and services they provide. In most cases, the major source of revenue for a government is taxes. However, in some countries, the government may own an entity such as an oil exploration and distribution system, a power generation facility, a communications network, or a commercial bank. In these situations, revenues from the entity represent a source of revenue for the government. The oil industry in Mexico, for example, is owned by the Federal Government, as described in Box 5.1.

Like most countries, the US has different levels of government. In the US, the levels are federal, state, and local, and each level usually relies on a different source of revenue. At the federal level, the major source of revenue is taxes on individual incomes, as you saw in Table 5.1. A major source of revenue for most states is taxes on commodities in the form of sales taxes, although 43 of the 50 states also collect taxes on individual incomes. At the local level, property taxes are a major source of revenue.

Although many Americans complain about how heavily they are taxed, in fact the tax burden in the US is one of the lowest of the developed countries. Table 5.2 shows the total tax burden for all levels of government for a selection of countries. At 35.8 percent of GDP, the US had the lowest total tax burden in the table except for Japan. The OECD collects statistics for almost 41 developed countries. If you look at the complete table at the OECD, you'll find only one or two developed countries with tax burdens lower than those in the US.

It's interesting to look at another country such as Sweden and ask yourself "Why does Sweden collect so much in taxes?" Part of the answer is that citizens of Sweden have a different view of the role of government than do citizens of the US: Swedes believe that

Table 5.2   General government revenues and spending, 2000

Country	As percent of GDP	
	Revenues	Spending
Canada	44.1	41.1
Germany	46.4	45.1
Japan	31.5	39.2
Sweden	61.8	56.8
United Kingdom	41.5	37.5
United States	35.8	34.2

Note: General government includes central, state, and local governments plus social security.

Source: Organization for Economic Cooperation and Development, OECD Factbook, http://titania. sourceoecd.org/vl=1515629/cl=47/nw=1/rpsv/factbook/.

Box 5.1   Pemex and Mexico's budget

Pemex [Petróleos Mexicanos] is Mexico's national oil company. The Government expropriated the operations of foreign oil companies in 1938 and citizens felt so strongly about oil's importance that they amended the constitution so that the oil company would always be a national asset that could not be privatized unless the constitution is changed.

Oil accounted for about 16 percent of Mexico's exports in 2006, and most of those exports went to the United States. However, Pemex has not invested in refineries, so Mexico has to import 40 percent of its gasoline from the United States.

Pemex's largest oil field is Cantarell, where oil reserves were discovered in 1971. In the two decades since production at Cantarell began, Pemex produced more than 12 billion barrels of oil, but by 2006 the reserves were beginning to run out.

Most energy experts attribute Pemex's continued depletion of Cantarell and its failure to invest in refining to Mexico's Government. Revenue from the oil industry accounts for 40 percent of the Government's budget. In 2006, Mexico's Government took $79 billion of Pemex's total sales of $97 billion, leaving only the remainder available for improvements in existing facilities or investments in new facilities. Most of what was left was used to increase production at Cantarell so Government revenues could be maintained.

Mexico's President and Congress are responsible for decisions about Pemex's budget, output, and investments. Because the Government relies so heavily on oil exports, it manages Pemex as a cash cow, generating cash to pay for Government services. If it collected less revenue from Pemex, the Government would have to raise taxes elsewhere or reduce services.

Sources: David Luhnow, "Mexico tries to save a big, fading oil field", *Wall Street Journal*, Apr 5, 2007, p. A1; Elisabeth Malkin, "Output falling in oil-rich Mexico, and politics gets the blame", *New York Times*, Mar 9, 2007, p. C1; "Running just to stand still", *The Economist*, Dec 22, 2007; David Luhnow, "Mexico's oil output cools", *Wall Street Journal*, Jan 27, 2007, p. A3.

government should provide more services than Americans do. This difference becomes an issue when viewed through the lens of the Washington Consensus, which advocates a reduced role for government. Obviously, something has to give: either the Swedes should change their culture to adopt a reduced role for government or the Washington Consensus should allow variations in its view of what is good for countries.

In discussing taxes, you'll frequently encounter two concepts: the tax base and the tax rate. The *tax base* answers the question "What does the government tax?" The *tax rate* answers the question "What percentage of the tax base will the government confiscate?" (Confiscate has the word fiscus embedded in it; confiscate means to seize for the public treasury.) These two concepts interact to determine the total amount of tax revenue collected by the government because the tax base multiplied by the tax rate equals tax revenue.

At the federal level, the major tax bases are incomes earned by individuals and corporations. That sounds straightforward, but in fact it is a big leap from the income that a person earns or the revenue that a corporation earns and the taxable income on which the individual or corporation ultimately pays taxes. Between the two are a multitude of exemptions, deductions, and credits that provide ways to shield income from taxation or provide offsets against a tax liability.

It is important to remember that the elements that determine the tax base – exemptions, deductions, and credits – are created through the political process. Most of them were created as a means of addressing some social issue, such as encouraging charitable contributions, education, or alternative forms of energy. How you view these ways to avoid taxes depends on whether you're one of the folks benefiting from them. If you benefit, you view the exemption or deduction as essential for maintaining the viability of your industry or occupation. If you don't benefit, you may view them as loopholes – mechanisms allowing someone else to avoid paying their share of taxes.

Like the tax base, the tax rate is determined through the political process. Unlike the tax base, which determines who should or should not pay taxes, the tax rate applies to everyone at that level of taxable income once the tax base is determined. For personal incomes in the US, there were six tax rates in 2006. They appear in Table 5.3 in the column headed "plus," and are used when calculating the tax to be paid on each increment of income. For example, if your income is less than $7,550, your tax liability is 10 percent of each dollar of taxable income. If your income is above $7,550 but is less than $30,650, your tax liability is 10 percent of $7,550 plus 15 percent of the taxable income in excess of $7,550. Because the rates apply to increments of income, they are called *marginal tax rates*: the tax paid on each additional dollar of taxable income. Each level of taxable income – $0 to $7,550, $7,550 to $30,650, $30,650 to $74,200 – is called a *tax bracket*.

One feature you'll notice about US tax rates is that they increase as income increases, which means that the US tax system is designed to be *progressive*. The argument in favor of progressive tax rates is that people earning higher incomes are able to pay more taxes, so they should shoulder a larger portion of the total tax burden. A system in which tax rates decline as income increases is a *regressive* system. If the tax rate stays the same as incomes increase, the system is *proportional* or a *flat tax*.

But beware! Just because a system is designed to be progressive doesn't mean that it ends up that way. In fact, the US individual income tax is not nearly as progressive as

Table 5.3   US tax rate schedule, 2006

If your filing status is single

If your taxable income is:

Over	But not over	The tax is	plus	of the amount over
$0	7,550	–	10%	$0
7,550	30,650	755.00	15%	7,550
30,650	74,200	4,220.00	25%	30,650
74,200	154,800	15,107.50	28%	74,200
154,800	336,550	37,675.50	33%	154,800
336,550		97,653.00	35%	336,550

Source: IRS Form 1040 Instructions, 2006, http://www.irs.gov/formspubs/article/0,,id=150856,00.html.

intended because of the many ways that individuals can lower their taxable income. A proportional tax such as the sales tax, which may be 5 percent of the purchase price of certain merchandise, actually turns out to be regressive with respect to income, which means that people with lower incomes pay a larger proportion of their income in sales taxes than do people with higher incomes. This occurs because people with lower incomes consume a larger share of their incomes.

How people respond to changes in tax rates and the tax base depends on incentives, one of the most powerful effects of taxation. People have a tendency to try to avoid paying taxes, so imposing taxes leads to changes in behavior. (England imposed a tax on glass in windows in the late seventeenth century, and people responded by boarding up windows or building houses with smaller windows.) Providing a way to avoid taxes, such as through a deduction from income, encourages people to take advantage of the deduction. How people and businesses respond to taxes is important to a country's treasury because taxes are the treasury's source of revenue. The treasury loses revenue whenever Congress approves another deduction, exemption, or credit, and it may lose or gain revenue when tax rates are reduced, depending on how people respond.

This brings up the question "What is a tax cut?" A tax cut doesn't necessarily mean reduced revenues for the treasury, particularly if the effect is considered over a period of years. For example, a cut in tax rates is a tax cut, but it may actually lead to more revenue to the treasury as people respond to the decrease in rates. People may say to themselves "Wow! The government is taking a smaller amount out of each additional dollar I earn. I think I'll work a few more hours to increase my income." This principle derives from what is called "supply side economics" and was the basis of tax cuts in the United Kingdom when Margaret Thatcher was Prime Minister and in the US when Ronald Reagan was President. You can read more about the incentive effect and total tax collections by reading the article by Gwartney in the references at the end of the chapter.

A similar effect occurs in less developed countries. Many governments needed more revenue, so they raised tax rates, but people and businesses responded by simply not reporting income or dealing in cash so that there was no paper trail for revenue agents to follow. Governments discovered that cutting rates allows people and businesses to keep a larger share of what they earn, so they tend to report incomes more willingly. In the process, government tax receipts increase. Box 5.2 contains articles about the interplay between tax rates and the tax base, and the incentive effect of taxes. Try to identify the concepts as you read the articles.

Box 5.2   The interplay between tax rates and tax base

Diageo and US Virgin Islands

Captain Morgan is a brand of rum that became popular in the United States in the early 2000s. Captain Morgan is owned by Diageo, which also owns liquor brands such as Smirnoff vodka and José Cuervo tequila. To encourage Diageo to locate a distillery in the US Virgin Islands, the USVI Government subsidized marketing of Captain Morgan, built a distillery and warehouse and exempted them from property taxes, and reduced Diageo's corporate income taxes.

Source: "Sir Henry's legacy", *The Economist*, Jan 2, 2010, p. 23.

Gordon Brown's last budget

Prior to being elected Prime Minister of the UK, Gordon Brown was in charge of the country's finances as Chancellor of the Exchequer. Mr Brown's last budget as Chancellor in 2006 proposed reducing the corporate income tax rate to 28 percent by 2008; the rate had been set at 30 percent in 1999. The basic rate on personal income taxes would be reduced to 20 percent from 22 percent. At the same time, the budget proposed reducing capital allowances, which would increase the amount of income subject to corporate taxation. The lowest personal income bracket, subject to taxation at 10 percent, would be abolished so that the lowest bracket would be taxed at 20 percent. Some UK executives complained that the UK was uncompetitive in the world market for foreign direct investment compared to countries with more generous tax systems.

Sources: "Gordon's last fling", *The Economist*, Mar 24, 2007; "Britain cuts corporate rate but claws back cost by scrapping allowances", *International Tax Review*, Apr 2007, p. 1.

Tax breaks for Alpacas

Prior to 1984, the United States Government did not allow the import of alpacas. A provision of the Jobs and Growth Tax Relief Reconciliation Act, passed in 2003, allowed owners of small businesses to expense 100 percent of certain newly-acquired assets in one year. Previously, the assets had to be depreciated over a period of years. Since the change in the tax law, the number of alpaca farmers doubled to more than 4,200 in 2007, and the number of alpacas to more than 100,000. An accountant in Hershey, Pennsylvania, who had never owned a farm, reduced his taxable income by more than $40,000 by entering the alpaca farming business. Some alpaca farmers give away the fleece because trying to sell it is not worth the effort. According to one economics professor, "the alpaca industry will never be profitable."

Source: Ianthe Jeanne Dugan, "Backyard bonanza", *Wall Street Journal*, Apr 5, 2007, p. A1.

SPENDING

Government spends to fulfill the objectives of its many stakeholders: the ruler or administration, government agencies, elected representatives, individuals or organizations that try to influence the votes of elected representatives, the voting electorate. Under ideal circumstances, the objectives of all these stakeholders would coincide, and they would all aim toward what is best for a nation, but under real circumstances this seldom happens. Stakeholders are continually jostling for a larger share of the spending pie.

Like taxation, government spending becomes part of a nation's culture, reflecting and reinforcing expectations of citizens about the role of government. Because of these different expectations, governments spend for different purposes. Table 5.4 shows the purposes of spending by the same governments mentioned in Table 5.2. Spending is expressed as a percentage of GDP, so priority is reflected as a larger share of GDP. Compared to other countries, the US spends a larger portion of its GDP on the military, while Sweden spends a larger portion of its GDP on social programs for the elderly, sick, or unemployed. Even the US spends a significant (14.7 percent) portion of its GDP on social programs, which includes Social Security.

Don't be misled into thinking that you could impose one nation's government spending priorities onto another nation's cultural view of the role of government. It can't be done. The US couldn't adopt Sweden's social safety net, for example, because the result would be chaos in the US. It's not part of US culture to rely on government rather than individuals or businesses for the multitude of programs aimed toward social purposes, or even to have programs at all. Similarly, Swedes are amazed that US citizens must rely on the private sector for programs that are provided by the government in their home country. And remember the effect of incentives: some people in the US might take advantage of a government-supported program, while most Swedes might not. Relying on the public sector involves a degree of responsibility that has been engrained into Swedish society over decades but may be absent in the US.

Table 5.4   Spending purposes as percent of GDP, 2003

Country	Military	Social[1]	R&D	Education[2]	Health[3]
Canada	1.1	17.8	2.0	5.9	9.9
Germany	1.4	27.4	2.5	5.3	11.1
Japan	1.0	16.9	3.2	4.8	7.9
Sweden	1.8	29.8	4.0	6.7	9.2
United Kingdom	2.7	21.8	1.9	6.1	7.7
United States	3.8	14.7	2.7	7.5	15.0

Notes: [1] 2001, [2] Canada from 2002, [3] Japan, Sweden, United Kingdom from 2002.

Sources: Organization for Economic Cooperation and Development, OECD Factbook, http://titania.sourceoecd.org/vl=1515629/cl=47/nw=1/rpsv/factbook/; Military spending from Stockholm International Peace Research Institute (SIPRI), http://www.sipri.org/.

When determining the spending side of a budget, governments make two general types of decisions. See if you can tell the difference:

1. Let's spend $50 million building new highways this year. If we need more highways next year, we'll allocate funds at that time.
2. Let's start a program in which the government pays each worker over the age of 65 a yearly pension of $10,000. And we'll even index the payment for inflation so pensioners don't lose purchasing power as a result of inflation.

Obviously, $50 million sounds like more than $10,000, but the total spending in decision #2 depends on the number of people above the age of 65 and how long they live.

The spending that can be changed each year according to budget priorities (type #1) is *discretionary spending*. The discretionary portion of the budget includes spending for defense, national parks, agriculture, the justice system, and many programs that are considered important aspects of federal spending. But discretionary spending accounted for less than half of the federal budget in 2002, and only 40 percent in 2008. The proportion of the US Government budget allocated to discretionary spending is shrinking each year.

Spending that is required because of policy decisions and laws that have been made in the past (type #2) is known as *mandatory spending*. For example, in the US, the Medicare and Medicaid programs provide benefits such as a number of days in hospital or rehabilitative care for everyone who qualifies, and qualification depends largely upon age. Because a greater portion of the population of the US (like other developed countries) is aging, more people qualify for the benefit each year, so spending must increase. The only way that mandatory spending can be curtailed is for elected officials to make choices about eligibility and benefits, and these are politically sensitive decisions for elected officials to make.

The programs leading to mandatory spending are also called *entitlement programs*. To see how rapidly entitlement spending grows, look at the major components of entitlements in the US: Medicaid, Medicare, and Social Security in Table 5.1, plus interest, which depends on the level of the national debt, so is not a discretionary item. In 2002, these four components accounted for 52 percent of total federal spending. In President Bush's budget proposal for fiscal year 2008, they were projected to be 60 percent of federal spending, so spending on these four components has consumed eight percentage points more of federal spending in six years. Because of population demographics in the US, entitlement spending will crowd out nondefense discretionary spending by 2020 at current spending growth rates unless decisions are made about eligibility and benefits.

BORROWING

When a government spends more than it collects through taxes, it has two choices: it can obtain the funds by borrowing, or it can create new money. We pursue the idea of creating new money in the next chapter on central banking. Right now we discuss the borrowing alternative.

As the treasury or finance ministry collects revenue and spends on behalf of the government, there may be periods when inflows of revenue are not sufficient to finance outflows of spending. This may happen simply because of timing: spending may occur regularly throughout the year but tax receipts may be collected only on certain dates, for example. When this happens, the treasury can borrow on a short-term basis and repay the borrowing when receipts are collected. At other times, the shortfall of revenue may occur because policy makers have adopted a budget that is in deficit; they intend for the government to spend more than it collects in revenue. In this situation, the government typically borrows on a longer-term basis.

The treasury or finance ministry of the country has the responsibility for borrowing on behalf of the government. It usually borrows by issuing securities that promise to pay a specified amount (called the principal) at some time in the future (called the maturity) and sometimes pay periodic interest (called the coupon rate) in the meantime.

Government securities have different names in various countries: in the US they are called Treasury Bills, Notes and Bonds; in France they are called OATs and BTANs; in Japan they are called JGBs; in the UK they are called gilts. All these securities have similar characteristics:

1. Short-term securities typically are issued for less than one year because they are the primary means of managing short-term fluctuations in the treasury's cash flows. In cases, these securities do not pay interest. Investors get a return by paying less than the principal amount when they purchase the security. When the security matures, the investors receive the principal, so they receive an amount higher than they paid, and in this way they earn a return on the investment. In the US, these securities are called Treasury Bills.

2. Longer-term securities typically pay interest until the security matures two, five, ten or more years in the future. Investors earn interest on the security and at maturity receive the final interest payment plus the principal. In the US, these securities are called Treasury Notes (maturing in two to five years) and Treasury Bonds (maturing in ten or more years).

Government securities are almost always the least-risky form of debt in a country because the government can use its taxing power to obtain funds necessary to pay interest and principal. Individuals and businesses that are interested in safety purchase securities issued by the government. For example, the safest investment for a UK investor is gilts because the Government of the United Kingdom has never defaulted on its borrowing and the Government has a taxing power that corporate or individual borrowers do not have. Sometimes investors from one country purchase securities issued by another country, such as when Japanese insurance companies purchase US Treasury securities. They may do this because lending to the US Government is safer than lending to their domestic government, or they may do it as a means of diversifying their portfolio of investments. But when investors purchase securities issued by the government of another country, they face the risk of fluctuation in the value of the currency, so the investment is no longer without risk.

Unfortunately, safety has a down side: investors reflect their perceptions of risk by adjusting the interest rate they are willing to accept. Riskier investments provide higher returns, while safer investments provide lower returns. Therefore, an investor in US Treasury securities can be assured that the investment is safe, but the investment also provides a lower return than other investments, such as in corporate bonds.

Not every government is equally safe, of course. Governments of some countries are more reliable about repaying debt and have never defaulted on their obligations. Governments of other countries may not pay in a timely manner or may have a history of default. Governments that are perceived as riskier must pay higher interest rates to borrow compared to governments that are perceived as safer, as you will read in Box 5.3.

Box 5.3   Japan's Government bond rating

In November 2002, Japan's Government submitted a budget that would lead to 5 trillion yen in new Government borrowing. On November 21, 2002, Fitch Ratings announced that it would give a lower rating to Japanese Government bonds that were denominated in yen. Fitch attributed the downgrade to a decade-long slump in Japan's economy, continuing deflation, and the Government's budget deficit and national debt. Japan's banks also have trillions of yen in bad loans because of the economic slump.

Fitch lowered the rating to AA-minus, which makes Japanese bonds the lowest rated of the seven major industrial countries: Canada, France, Germany, Italy, the United Kingdom, and the United States.

The next day, another major rating agency, Moody's Investors Service Inc., announced that it would not downgrade Japan's bonds. Moody's had already downgraded Japan's Government debt rating in May, so Japan was already the lowest-rated of the seven countries.

The downgrade will cause Japan's Government to pay higher interest rates when it borrows.

Sources: "Fitch lowers Japanese government bond rating", *Kyodo News Service*, Nov 21, 2002; "Moody's not to change Japan rating for now", *Jiji Press English News Service*, Nov 22, 2002, p. 1.

National Debt

The surplus and deficit figures in Table 5.1 represent yearly amounts: they record whether revenues exceeded (surplus) or fell short of (deficit) spending in any one budget year. Consequently, the deficit figures show the amount of new borrowing that must occur in any fiscal year. What if there is a deficit this year and there was a deficit the previous year, and the year before that? When we accumulate the deficits and subtract the surpluses from one year to the next, we derive the total amount of government borrowing, or the *national debt*.

Table 5.5 shows the national debt of the US during a ten-year period. You'll see that the gross debt increased each year in dollar terms. The astute readers among you will be tempted to go back to Table 5.1 to find the yearly deficit or surplus, then add the deficit to or subtract the surplus from the yearly gross debt figures in Table 5.5 to see if they equal the next year's total. Generally speaking, a yearly budgetary deficit should increase the national debt by that amount, while a yearly budgetary surplus should decrease the national debt by that amount. Unfortunately, the process doesn't work that easily in practice because of subtle differences between the treasury's cash flow and the

Table 5.5   US Federal debt at end of fiscal year

Year	Gross debt	Held by Federal Government accounts	Held by public
		(millions of dollars)	
1995	4,920,586	1,316,208	3,604,378
1996	5,181,465	1,447,392	3,734,073
1997	5,369,206	1,596,862	3,772,344
1998	5,478,189	1,757,090	3,721,099
1999	5,605,523	1,973,160	3,632,363
2000	5,628,700	2,218,896	3,409,804
2001	5,769,881	2,450,266	3,319,615
2002	6,198,401	2,657,974	3,540,427
2003	6,760,014	2,846,570	3,913,443
2004	7,354,673	3,059,129	4,295,544
2005	7,905,300	3,313,088	4,592,213

Source: Federal debt at end of year, 1940–2012; http://www.whitehouse.gov/omb/budget/fy2008/hist.html.

government's need to borrow. If you're afraid you may lose sleep unless you understand why the figures don't match, I invite you to read pages 248–250 of the publication by the Office of Management and Budget listed among the references at the end of this chapter. I guarantee that you will fall asleep without difficulty.

Who owns the national debt of the US? This is the same as asking who lends to the US Government by purchasing securities issued by the Treasury. The answers are shown in Table 5.6:

- Some of the gross debt is owned by other federal agencies, particularly the Social Security Administration. By law, the Social Security Trust Fund must invest in the safest securities, so the Fund purchases US Treasurys.
- Another portion of the debt is owned by the Federal Reserve System, the central bank of the US. The next chapter explains why the Federal Reserve purchases Treasury securities and what are the effects on the economy when that happens.
- That leaves about $4 trillion worth of securities to be purchased by the public, whether domestic or foreign. About half of this total – slightly more than $2 trillion – is owned by foreign investors: Japanese insurance companies, the central bank of China, the royal family of Saudi Arabia, and so on.
- The remaining $2 trillion that is owned domestically is owned by individuals, state, and local governments and a variety of financial institutions: banks, pension funds, and insurance companies.

Box 5.4 discusses a question that many Americans ask: "Who owns the national debt?"

Table 5.6   Who owns the US debt?

	December 31, 2005 (billions of dollars)
Total debt	8,170.4
Owned by:	
Federal reserve and other government agencies	4,199.8
Depository institutions	117.2
US Savings bonds	205.1
Pension funds	310.6
Insurance companies	160.4
Mutual funds	252.2
State and local governments	456.2
Foreign	2,036.0
Other	432.8

Source: Table OFS.2 Estimated ownership of US Treasury securities; ../../../../../AppData/Local/Temp/ Local Settings/Temp/fms.treas.gov/bulletin/b2007-1ofs.doc.

Economics of the Budget

There is more to the budget than just the accounting concepts. The budget also plays an important role in the performance of the economy. For about 200 years, political economists and social philosophers have argued about the proper role of government in society. At one extreme were those who thought that government should perform only limited functions, leaving the private sector to act with a minimum of interference by the public sector. At another extreme were those who argued that government should play a positive role in society, particularly in areas such as regulating business activity and directing or even owning the productive resources of a nation.

The Great Depression of the 1930s seemed to bring an end to the argument. The depth (almost 25 percent of the labor force of the US was unemployed) and breadth (the recession was a worldwide phenomenon, although it occurred at different times in various countries) of the Depression appeared to tilt the scale toward the argument favoring government intervention. It was apparent, at least to them, that the private sector by itself could not be relied upon to improve the welfare for all of a nation's citizens. The pendulum appeared to swing in favor of a larger role for government.

A British economist, John Maynard Keynes, proposed a theory that government should intervene in economic decisions in some circumstances. For example, when the level of economic activity in the private sector does not lead to full employment, government can purchase more goods and services, which would stimulate economic activity and in doing so, would help to increase employment. Using the government's budget to stimulate or contract a nation's economy is called *fiscal policy*. In a situation

---

Box 5.4   Who owns the United States Government debt?

A frequent question is: "Who owns the debt of the United States Government?" If we look at the Treasury statements for fiscal year 2009, which ended on September 30, public debt securities outstanding were $11.9 trillion. Of the total, $4.3 trillion, or 35 percent, was owned by United States Government accounts, particularly the Social Security Trust Fund. The Federal Reserve, the United States central bank, owned $895 million, or about 8 percent of the debt.

So private individuals, businesses, and governments other than the Federal Government owned about 57 percent of the national debt, or $6.6 trillion. Slightly less than half of this total was owned domestically and slightly more than half by foreign investors, so people, businesses, and governments around the world own as much of the federal debt as United States investors do. That shouldn't be too surprising, given that the rest of the world accounts for about 75 percent of the world's GDP.

Two countries own the lion's share of the debt. China owns about $799 billion and Japan owns about $752 billion, so those two countries own about 44 percent of the debt that is held by foreigners. At $249 billion, the United Kingdom is a distant third, followed by a group of oil exporting countries, some that are members of OPEC and others that are not. China has increased its purchases of United States Government securities; China's ownership grew from $350 billion three years earlier.

Official organizations such as central banks and treasuries of foreign countries own $2.4 trillion of the $3.5 trillion held by foreign investors.

Sources: "Major foreign holders of Treasury securities", "Estimated ownership of US Treasury securities", *Treasury Bulletin*, Dec 2009.

---

of unemployment, government should run an *expansionary fiscal policy* by incurring a budgetary deficit, meaning the government should spend more than it brings in through taxes. In this way, government creates more incomes through hiring or purchasing than it takes out of incomes through taxes.

The opposite situation was an overheated economy in which there was a high rate of inflation. In this situation, government should run a *contractionary fiscal policy* by incurring a budgetary surplus, meaning the government brings in more tax revenue than it spends. In doing so, the government takes more incomes out of the economy through taxes than it creates through hiring or purchasing.

Even today, these principles are the theoretical basis for government intervention in economic decisions. Modern economic theory has refined the Keynesian approach, but the basic reasoning still applies: government should run a budgetary deficit when it wants to expand the economy and run a budgetary surplus when it wants to slow down the economy.

Through the years, Keynes' idea that government should intervene only under specific circumstances was co-opted by politicians into the idea that government intervention was justified in most circumstances. It was also co-opted by economists who thought they would be able to manage an economy through the periods of boom and bust that typically occur during a business cycle. The result was an increasing role for government in the economies of most developed countries. Over the 40 years from the 1930s through the 1970s, government spending, taxes, and deficits increased around the globe.

In the 1970s, a group of economists gained increased visibility by arguing that government played too large a role. Government spending was too high, as were the taxes necessary to finance the spending. These economists argued that a nation would be better off if tax policies were changed, and that government needed to play a smaller role in national spending. The high levels of government spending and the taxes necessary to support the spending were actually disincentives for people to work or businesses to invest. The economists proposed that governments cut tax rates, arguing that people would respond by working more and businesses would respond by expanding production, and in this way the economy would grow.

The reason relates back to marginal tax rates. If you work another few hours each week to earn an extra $100, how much of the $100 do you get to keep? The amount of your gross income that you keep is your *disposable income* – the amount you have available to spend or save after taxes have been taken out of your gross income. If the government takes $70 out of the extra $100 (the marginal tax rate is 70 percent, which is what it was in the US back in the 1970s), you might not be willing to work the additional hours. But if the government takes only $35 out of the extra $100 (the marginal tax rate is 35 percent, which is what it was changed to in 1986), you might react differently. If enough people respond to the lower tax rates by working more hours, the economy benefits from the additional incomes. The same reasoning applies to business decisions.

You'll recognize the reduced role for government and the reduction in tax rates as two pillars of the Washington Consensus. The reforms were implemented first in the United Kingdom by the Government of Prime Minister Margaret Thatcher, then in the US during the presidency of Ronald Reagan. As a result of the Thatcher and Reagan revolutions, the pendulum seemed to swing in the direction of a reduced role for government.

Then, in 2008 and 2009 much of the world experienced a recession, and the pendulum again appeared to swing in favor of government intervention. Many governments around the world used fiscal policy to stimulate their economies in 2009. They reduced taxes or increased spending in an attempt to increase employment and return to a growing economy. Table 5.7 shows the stimulus packages as a percent of GDP for selected countries. Some packages, such as China's, are spread over more than one fiscal year.

Box 5.5 illustrates the two opinions about how fiscal policy should be used to fight recessions. The box also illustrates Keynes' point that governments should save when the economy is growing and spend when the economy is suffering, a lesson that Chile apparently has learned.

Budget Process in the United States

In the US, the President submits a proposed budget to Congress each February, detailing the administration's estimates of revenues and spending by the various departments within the administration. Then the political skirmishing begins. Throughout US history, Congress and the President have disputed their relative roles in the taxing/spending debate:

Box 5.5   Two stories about fiscal policy

Before the depth of the latest economic collapse became known, officials in many countries debated the wisdom of using fiscal policy to combat recessions. In the 1930s, John Maynard Keynes advocated fiscal stimulus as a technique for helping to grow an economy experiencing significant unemployment.

In 2005, Portugal's budget deficit grew to 6 percent of GDP, about twice the 3 percent level permitted by the European Central Bank. Officials from the European Union (EU) threatened Portugal with fines, so Portugal's government raised taxes and cut spending to cut the deficit to the allowable 3 percent. As a result, economic growth declined to 1.3 percent. EU officials encouraged other member countries to balance their budgets by 2010, but this was in early 2008 before the economic crisis worsened. Once the depth of the crisis became apparent, even countries that had advocated fiscal prudence instead adopted stimulative fiscal policies.

A contrasting approach occurred in Chile. Earlier in the 2000s, Chile's economy benefitted from the high price of copper, Chile's main export. The Finance Minister decided to save money generated by the Government's budget surpluses. Although some people advocated increasing spending, the Finance Minister took the unpopular route and continued to save.

When the worldwide economic crisis occurred in 2008, Chile used the savings to stimulate the economy by creating jobs through infrastructure improvements and providing tax reductions for businesses. As a percent of GDP, Chile's stimulus plan was larger than that of the United States, and it was accomplished entirely by spending previous savings rather than by incurring more debt.

Sources: Sudeep Reddy, "The new old big thing in economics: J.M. Keynes", *Wall Street Journal*, Jan 8, 2009, p. A10; Adam Cohen, "The Portugal study: How EU rules curbed growth", *Wall Street Journal*, Mar 10, 2008; Matt Moffett, "Prudent Chile thrives amid downturn", *Wall Street Journal*, May 27, 2009, p. A1.

---

1. Those in favor of a strong President argue that the budget reflects the President's estimate of the cost of operating the Government of the US. It is Congress's responsibility to provide the means of financing those operations.
2. Those favoring a strong Congress argue that the budget reflects Congress' desires for taxing and spending. It is the responsibility of the President to implement those desires without refusing to spend for purposes the Congress has appropriated.

Viewed in this way, the budget becomes a vehicle for carrying out political priorities, and the winner of the budget battle becomes a function of power. The budget is the link between politics and economics and is one of the reasons that economics formerly was termed "political economy."

Of course, members of the Senate and the House of Representatives, the two branches of Congress in the US, have their own priorities about how funds are to be raised and how the funds should be spent, so there are political battles between and within the two branches. The next several months after the President presents the budget are spent discussing bills in committees, then on the floors of each branch of Congress before the adopted bills are submitted to the President for signature. The budget document that eventually passes thus reflects work by the Executive branch (the President and administrative staff) and the Legislative Branch (members of the House and Senate and their staffs). The question of whose priorities ultimately are reflected in the budget depends as much on power and politics as it does on economics and national priorities, but that is a fact of life with governments. When a decision must go through the political process, the outcome reflects political realities.

Once the budget is approved by Congress and the President, responsibility for administering the budget passes to the Executive Branch because the President is the Chief Executive Officer of the US Government. The President delegates responsibility for administering the budget to the various departments of the Executive branch. The Department of the Treasury collects taxes on behalf of the Government and spends to carry out the myriad activities of the Government, from purchasing office supplies and military equipment to operating national parks and the federal court system.

Believe it or not, the concept of budgeting for governments in the US did not exist until early in the twentieth century. Prior to that time, federal agencies submitted funding requests directly to Congress, so the President had no effective control over spending by the administration. It wasn't until the Bureau of the Budget (under the office of the President, and now called the Office of Management and Budget, or OMB) was created by Congress in 1921 that budgeting was adopted at the federal level. The act also had the unintended result of increasing the power of the President relative to Congress, because now the President controlled the Government's purse.

Not only did the President control the purse, but the President also controlled the information flows relating to Government administration: estimates of tax revenues, economic growth, inflation, the number of people employed and their earnings, how businesses and individuals would react to taxes; and estimates of spending, eligibility for and participation in federal programs, and how people would react to these programs. Through the years, this information began to take a bias toward the priorities and public relations needs of the Executive Branch.

Table 5.7   2009 Fiscal stimulus as percent of GDP for selected countries

Country	New 2009 spending as % of GDP
China	12%
Germany	3%
Japan	4%
Korea	2%
United States	5%
United Kingdom	1%

Sources: Rowley, A., "Japan to ratchet up financial stimulus by 10 trillion yen", *Business Times*, Singapore, 4/7/09, Baek, S-g., "More aggressive economic policy needed", *Korea Times*, 2/27/09, UK Pre-budget report, 11/24/08, *Times Online*, http://business.timesonline.co.uk/tol/business/economics/pbr/article5224823.ece.

To counteract this bias, Congress created the Congressional Budget Office (CBO) in 1974. The CBO takes the President's budget proposal but uses its own economic and estimating techniques that are presumed by the CBO staff to be more realistic than those coming from the Executive Branch. Thus, in any budget debate there are two sets of figures: those from the administration and those from Congress. When listening to news during the annual budget battle, it is important to consider not only the content of the news but also its source. Many people consider the budget figures from the CBO to be more unbiased than those from the OMB.

Measuring Government Risk

Just as people and businesses can borrow too much, a government can too. A government that borrows too much may encounter difficulty repaying the debt, so investors monitor indicators of a government's borrowing. In practice, the ratios will already be calculated for you. However, this section shows how the ratios are calculated so you'll understand the reasoning behind them.

GOVERNMENT SPENDING RATIO

The *government spending ratio* measures government spending as a percentage of a country's GDP so that the analyst has an idea about the impact of government in the economy. Using data from Table 5.8 containing the US Government portion of the National Income and Product Accounts (NIPA), which typically are available for most countries, the government spending ratio is:

$$Government\ spending\ ratio = \frac{Total\ government\ spending}{GDP} \quad \frac{1,721.6}{9,817.0} = 17.5\%$$

This means that 17.5 percent of the final goods and services purchased in the US during the year 2000 were purchased by various levels of government.

However, you'll notice that the figures for Federal Government spending in Table 5.8 are not the same as those listed as outlays by the Federal Government in Table 5.1 (go ahead and look; there's a difference of only $1.5 trillion!). The difference is that the government figures in the National Income Accounts (Table 5.8) consider only government consumption of final goods and services. Government outlays for intermediate goods, for capital projects, and for transfer payments are not included in the NIPA figures because of the way GDP and its components are calculated. For example, as we found earlier, a significant portion of the US Federal budget consists of transfer payments such as Social Security, in which the government collects revenues but transfers the to individuals so they make the decisions about how to allocate their incomes. T ents are not recorded as government consumption in National Income Acc o not show up in the government spending ratio calculated above. Conse the government spending ratio on the government portion of the National Income Accounts underestimates the role of government in the economy. It's a fine distinction, but it amounts to billions of dollars of difference.

Table 5.8   US GDP components, 2000 to 2002

	2000	2001	2002
	(billions of dollars)		
GDP	9,817.0	10,128.0	10,469.6
Personal consumption expenditures	6,739.4	7,055.0	7,350.7
Gross private domestic investment	1,735.5	1,614.3	1,582.1
Net exports of goods and services	(379.5)	(367.0)	(424.4)
Government consumption expenditures	1,721.6	1,825.6	1,961.1
Federal	578.8	612.9	679.7
State and local	1,142.8	1,212.8	1,281.5
Government consumption/GDP	17.5%	18.0%	18.7%

Source: http://www.bea.gov/national/nipaweb/TableView.asp#Mid, accessed 4/9/07.

The international comparisons in Table 5.9 are more meaningful because the OECD uses total government outlays rather than government purchases of final goods and services. Notice that the trend for all the countries is for government outlays to decrease as a percent of GDP. Of the six countries, only Japan showed an increase during the period, and that was only 0.5 percent of GDP. Even Sweden, which we identified earlier as a society that expects government to play a large role, has experienced a decline of more than 10 percent of GDP. This trend is in keeping with the Washington Consensus view that government should play a smaller role in the economy, and the trend is occurring even in Sweden.

A good analyst would view the government spending ratio in light of the administration and any political priorities at the time. For example, government as a percent of GDP declined in the US during the later years of the Clinton administration (1992–2000) but increased during the early years of the Bush administration (2001–2005). This might surprise many people who cast Clinton as a liberal Democrat who prefers to spend and Bush as a conservative Republican who prefers a smaller role for government.

However the government spending ratio is defined, it does not include other government constraints on individual and business behavior. Laws and regulations frequently influence behavior even when there is no budgetary impact from the law or regulation. Social mores, many of them influenced by governments, help establish the civil society in which people form a nation. Therefore, governments play a role in society beyond the simple purchasing of goods and services.

According to the Washington Consensus, global investors typically prefer a less intrusive government, so prefer a lower government spending ratio. This bias reflects the belief that in a market economy, individuals and business, rather than governments, should be the major influences on economic behavior.

Table 5.9   Government outlays as percent of GDP for selected countries, 1995 to 2005

	Canada	Germany	Japan	Sweden	United Kingdom	United States
1995	48.5	48.3	36.5	67.1	44.9	37.0
1996	46.6	49.3	36.9	64.8	43.1	36.5
1997	44.3	48.3	36.0	62.5	41.6	35.4
1998	44.8	48.1	37.3	60.3	40.4	34.7
1999	42.7	48.2	38.8	59.8	39.8	34.3
2000	41.1	45.1	39.2	56.8	37.5	34.2
2001	42.0	47.5	38.7	56.5	40.9	35.3
2002	41.2	48.0	39.0	57.9	42.0	36.3
2003	41.2	48.4	38.5	58.2	43.6	36.7
2004	39.9	47.3	37.3	56.7	43.8	36.4
2005	39.3	46.8	37.0	56.3	44.9	36.6

Note: General government includes central, state and local governments plus social security.

Source: Organization for Economic Cooperation and Development, OECD Factbook, http://titania. sourceoecd.org/vl=1515629/cl=47/nw=1/rpsv/factbook/.

BUDGET DEFICIT RATIO

As you learned earlier in the chapter, governments frequently spend more than the revenues they generate through taxes, creating a budget deficit. Other times, governments spend less than the revenues generated through taxes, creating a budgetary surplus. The *budget deficit ratio* measures the size of the government surplus or deficit expressed as a percentage of the country's GDP. In the US, the ratio for 2000 was:

$$budget\ deficit\ ratio = \frac{budget\ surplus\,(deficit)}{GDP} = \frac{236}{9,817} = 2.4\%$$

This positive result indicates a budgetary surplus; a budgetary deficit would lead to a negative result.

The budget deficit ratio reflects the government's ability to spend within the tax revenues it generates, which global investors interpret as sound fiscal policy. Just like the government spending ratio, the budget deficit ratio may be for only the central government or for all levels of government added together. The ratio above was calculated for only the central government. As you see in Table 5.10, the US experienced an improving ratio throughout the last five years of the Clinton administration, which ended in 2000, but since then the ratio has become increasingly negative under the Bush administration.

Similar data are available from the OECD, but for all levels of government – federal, state, and local in the US. Comparing the deficit as percent of GDP in Table 5.11 to deficit as percent of GDP in Table 5.10 reveals that during 1995, 1996, and 1997, when the Federal Government was running budgetary deficits, other levels of Government were running budgetary surpluses so that the ratio for general Government was positive. The same is true in 2003 through 2005: the combined Government deficits as percent of GDP are less negative than the figures for the Federal Government only, indicating that state and local governments ran budgetary surpluses.

Because government's total impact on the economy is measured by the combined taxing and spending of all levels of government, the broader indicator of general government's surplus or deficit is more appropriate. However, it frequently is difficult to obtain timely information about all levels of government, and it certainly is difficult to evaluate decision making in all states and municipalities. For that reason, more attention is focused on behavior of decision makers at the central government level, so measures of the sort in Table 5.10 are more common.

Table 5.10   US budget receipts and outlays, 1995 to 2005

	Receipts	Outlays	Surplus (Deficit)	GDP	Surplus (Deficit)	Surplus (Deficit)
	(millions of US dollars)			(billions of dollars)	(% of GDP)	(% of outlays)
1995	1,351,932	1,515,884	-163,952	7,325.8	-2.2%	-10.8%
1996	1,453,177	1,560,608	-107,431	7,694.1	-1.4%	-6.9%
1997	1,579,423	1,601,307	-21,884	8,182.4	-0.3%	-1.4%
1998	1,721,955	1,652,685	69,270	8,627.9	0.8%	4.2%
1999	1,827,645	1,702,035	125,610	9,125.3	1.4%	7.4%
2000	2,025,457	1,789,216	236,241	9,709.8	2.4%	13.2%
2001	1,991,426	1,863,190	128,236	10,057.9	1.3%	6.9%
2002	1,853,395	2,011,153	-157,758	10,377.4	-1.5%	-7.8%
2003	1,782,532	2,160,117	-377,585	10,805.5	-3.5%	-17.5%
2004	1,880,279	2,293,006	-412,727	11,546.0	-3.6%	-18.0%
2005	2,153,859	2,472,205	-318,346	12,290.4	-2.6%	-12.9%

Source: http://www.gpoaccess.gov/usbudget/fy07/sheets/hist01z1.xls   and   http://www.gpoaccess.gov/usbudget/fy07/sheets/hist01z2.xls.

A variation on the budget deficit ratio that is not used as frequently is to divide the budget surplus or deficit by total outlays. This indicates how much of government spending is financed by borrowing rather than by taxes, so it is another measure of the extent to which the government lives within its means. The ratios for the US appear in the right column of Table 5.10, where you see that almost 11 percent of government outlays

Table 5.11 General government surplus or deficit as percent of GDP, 1995 to 2005

	Canada	Germany	Japan	Sweden	United Kingdom	United States
1995	0.4	(0.3)	(3.8)	(5.5)	(2.7)	0.4
1996	2.5	(0.4)	(3.8)	(1.2)	(1.1)	1.2
1997	5.0	0.2	(2.7)	0.8	1.1	2.4
1998	4.9	0.8	(4.4)	3.2	3.1	3.5
1999	5.9	1.3	(6.0)	3.6	3.7	3.6
2000	6.0	4.0	(6.2)	5.8	6.4	4.1
2001	3.6	0.3	(4.9)	3.2	2.9	1.9
2002	2.5	(1.2)	(6.7)	0.5	–	(1.7)
2003	1.5	(1.5)	(6.6)	(0.1)	(1.6)	(2.9)
2004	2.1	(1.3)	(4.9)	1.4	(1.5)	(2.7)
2005	2.5	(0.9)	(3.9)	2.4	(1.4)	(1.6)

Note: General government includes central, state and local governments plus social security.

Source: Organization for Economic Cooperation and Development, OECD Factbook, http://titania. sourceoecd.org/vl=1515629/cl=47/nw=1/rpsv/factbook/.

were borrowed in 1995. By 2000 the budgetary surplus amounted to more than 13 percent of government outlays, but by 2004 the deficit had grown to 18 percent of outlays.

Until the recession of 2009, most countries were reducing budget deficits. To offset the drop in personal and business spending due to the recession, many countries expanded their deficits in 2009 by spending more and taxing less. Box 5.6 describes India's efforts to reduce its budget deficit.

DEBT RATIO

Another indicator of the government's ability to run sound fiscal policy is the *debt ratio*, in which the country's national debt is compared to its GDP. Remember that the national debt is the accumulation of all the previous deficits, less any surpluses. The debt shows the country's obligation to repay, while the GDP shows the country's ability to generate economic activity that will lead to government revenues that can be used to pay the debt. Of course, global investors prefer a lower ratio or a ratio that is declining.

The debt and GDP figures for the US are in Table 5.12. The ratio for the US in 2000 was:

$$debt\ ratio = \frac{national\ debt}{GDP} = \frac{5,629}{9,710} = 58\%$$

Box 5.6 India's budget deficit

India is one of the BRIC nations (Brazil, Russia, India, China) – the large, rapidly growing and emerging economies in the 2000s. But at almost 8 percent of GDP, India's budget deficit is the worst of the four economies. India's public debt also is the worst of the BRIC nations – more than 80 percent of GDP in 2007.

The deficit for the state and central governments is about 6 percent of GDP, but the Government also subsidizes enterprises that don't appear on the budget, which adds another 2 percent to the deficit.

Government officials, with support from the IMF, are taking steps to decrease the deficit. Part of the problem is generous tax exemptions for certain activities. Eliminating exemptions would broaden the tax base and help make the tax code more fair. Another aspect of the deficit is India's extensive subsidization of Government-owned enterprises, which account for about 24 percent of the budget deficit.

Authorities caution that the budget deficit could affect India's ability to attract investment and could prevent the Government from investing in the infrastructure improvements necessary to keep the economy growing.

Sources: "India on fire", *The Economist*, Feb 3, 2007, p. 69; Shalini S. Dagar, "What will Chidambaram do?", *Business Today*, Feb 11, 2007, p. 112; "IMF for continuing reforms to ensure higher growth", *Businessline*, Jan 27, 2007; "India: Asia's new giant emerges", *Euromoney*, Jan 2007, p. 1.

Table 5.12 US Federal debt as percent of GDP, 1995 to 2005

	Gross debt (millions of dollars)	GDP (billions of dollars)	Gross debt as % of GDP
1995	4,920,586	7,325.8	67.2
1996	5,181,465	7,694.1	67.3
1997	5,369,206	8,182.4	65.6
1998	5,478,189	8,627.9	63.5
1999	5,605,523	9,125.3	61.4
2000	5,628,700	9,709.8	58.0
2001	5,769,881	10,057.9	57.4
2002	6,198,401	10,377.4	59.7
2003	6,760,014	10,805.5	62.5
2004	7,354,673	11,546.0	63.9
2005	7,905,300	12,290.4	64.4

Source: Federal debt at end of year, 1940–2012; http://www.whitehouse.gov/omb/budget/fy2008/hist.html.

What circumstances would cause changes in the debt ratio? A country that slows its rate of borrowing will experience a decline or a slower rate of growth of debt, the numerator of the fraction. Also, a country's economy may grow faster than the government's debt grows, which means that the denominator grows faster than the numerator, so the ratio will decline. The ratio also will decline if the government runs budgetary surpluses, because it can use the surplus to pay off the national debt. Japan has a very high national debt as a percent of GDP, as you see in Table 5.13.

Now that you know the difference between deficits and debt, you should understand two of the criteria for admittance into the European Monetary Union (EMU) that are described in Box 5.7. Because Greece did not meet the criteria in time for its admittance into the EMU, Greek officials created numbers of their own.

Table 5.13 General government gross debt in percent of GDP

	Canada	Germany	Japan	Sweden	United Kingdom	United States
1995	121.3	55.1	92.2	77.5	51.6	72.6
1996	121.6	57.9	99.3	77.1	52.0	72.3
1997	117.5	59.1	105.8	75.2	50.3	69.9
1998	114.8	59.3	117.8	72.9	47.2	66.2
1999	111.6	59.6	131.1	65.6	44.6	62.8
2000	101.5	58.7	139.3	57.7	41.6	57.1
2001	100.3	57.9	148.8	50.6	38.4	56.6
2002	97.4	59.6	158.4	48.9	37.9	58.7
2003	91.9	62.8	164.7	50.0	39.3	60.6
2004	87.9	64.5	169.2	49.0	41.1	60.7
2005	83.0	67.7	174.4	49.0	42.5	60.9

Source: International Monetary Fund, World Economic Outlook.

EXTERNAL DEBT

There is another concept relating to a country's borrowing capacity: its external debt. Individuals, businesses, and governments of one country borrow from many lenders. Some of the lenders are domestic, and some of the lenders may be from other countries. The total borrowing by businesses, individuals, and governments in one country from lenders in another country is called the country's *external debt*. Borrowing by governments is public sector debt, while borrowing by businesses and individuals is private sector debt. Thus, total borrowing consists of public and private sector borrowing combined.

External debt is a subtotal of a country's total debt, which includes borrowing from domestic as well as foreign sources. Individuals, businesses, and governments borrow from abroad for a variety of reasons, and not all of them are bad. It may be cheaper to

---

Box 5.7   Greece and the Maastricht Convergence Criteria

The European Monetary Union (EMU) developed several criteria that countries must meet to become members. The criteria, which were adopted in 1991, apply to current as well as prospective members. Because they were adopted at Maastricht, Netherlands, they are known as the Maastricht Convergence Criteria.

The policies relating to fiscal policy are:

- Deficits should be no more than 3 percent of GDP
- National debt should be no more than 60 percent of GDP

Greece was admitted to membership in the EMU based on its economic performance in 1999. In 2004, the EU's statistics agency, Eurostat, discovered that the figures Greece submitted about its 1999 economic performance were inaccurate.

Greece reported a budget deficit of 1.8 percent of GDP for 1999 when the actual figure was 3.4 percent. Similar misstatements were made about 1998 (2.5 percent reported, 4.1 percent actual) and 1997 (6.4 percent actual, 4.0 percent reported). In other words, Greece actually violated a condition of the Maastricht Convergence Criteria but submitted numbers showing that it met the criteria.

The Governor of the Bank of Greece argued that the methods for preparing figures had changed, and was quoted as saying "I don't think the people of Greece and Europe were misled." When the discrepancy was discovered in 2004, the Government attributed the error to the previous administration, which was from a different political party.

The discrepancy led to two major results: 1) The European Commission began legal action against Greece that could lead to fines; 2) Standard and Poor's lowered Greece's credit rating, making it only the second country to have its credit rating lowered since the euro was launched in 1999. Greece has the highest debt of any country in the eurozone. The downgrade increased the spread between yields on Greek Government bonds compared to bonds issued by other eurozone countries, creating a loss for owners of Greece's Government bonds.

Greece's fiscal situation did not improve through the years. By 2009, the budget deficit was 12.7 percent of GDP and all three credit rating agencies further downgraded Greece's credit rating.

Sources: David Cocker, "European Union", *International Financial Law Review*, Oct 1995, p. 51; Ralph Atkins, Kerin Hope, George Parker, "Greece escapes expulsion from single currency", *Financial Times*, Nov 16, 2004, p. 7; Charles Batchelor, Kerin Hope, Paivi Munter, "Greece suffers credit rating downgrade", *Financial Times*, Nov 18, 2004, p. 48; George Parker, Ralph Atkins, "Greece faces court action over false deficit figures", *FT.com*, Nov 30, 2004, p. 1; Brian Blackstone, "Trichet rejects 'Special' ECB help for Greece", *Wall Street Journal*, Jan 15, 2010, p. A8.

---

borrow abroad because interest rates are lower than domestic rates. It may be helpful to borrow because of international trade flows. Borrowing abroad may be necessary when the domestic pool of savings is not sufficient to satisfy the investment needs of the country. Foreign investors may be anxious to enter the domestic market, so provide capital.

External debt also includes borrowing from large global organizations such as the World Bank or the International Monetary Fund. These loans usually arise because the country needs to develop or because it is experiencing a financial crisis, so debt owed to the WB or IMF could have a negative connotation.

Sometimes foreigners refuse to lend in the domestic currency because its value is unstable and they don't want to assume the risk. Instead, foreigners may lend only in a currency other than the country's domestic currency so they don't assume the currency risk. However, not all external debt is denominated in a foreign currency. The most recent accounting definitions of external debt at the IMF and WB show that it is not required that an external debt be denominated in a foreign currency.

Here is an example to illustrate external debt from the WB's web site:

A Government of Brazil debt to Citicorp (New York) is an external debt, because the creditor institution is a resident of the US. It is immaterial whether the debt is denominated in US dollars or in Brazilian currency. A government of Brazil debt to the Banco do Brasil (a major Brazilian commercial bank) in Rio de Janeiro that is denominated in US dollars is an internal debt, not an external debt, even when the debt is repayable in foreign currency. A government of Brazil debt to the London branch of the Banco do Brasil, however, is an external debt. The currency of repayment (probably US dollars or pounds sterling) is not the deciding factor because the creditor is located in the United Kingdom.[1]

Be careful not to confuse external debt with the national debt. The national debt is owed by the Federal Government, and a portion of the debt may be to foreigners, so that portion counts as external debt. But external debt also includes borrowing by businesses and individuals, which are not part of the government's debt. External debt and national debt both try to measure the borrowing exposure of the country, but the national debt relates only to government, while external debt includes individual, business, and government borrowing from lenders outside the country.

DEBT TO EXPORTS RATIO

Regardless of how external debt is defined, there is one overriding aspect: the funds to repay the debt owed to foreigners have to come from somewhere. Because the funds will flow out of the country when they are repaid, it is beneficial that the funds be generated through sales of goods and services to foreigners. That way, funds inflows will be used to repay funds outflows. Sales of goods and services to foreigners are termed exports, so we have another measure of debt coverage: external debt as a percent of exports. We'll call this the *debt to exports ratio*. As of December 2005, the US had gross external debt of $9,476 billion (remember, this is both public and private debt). Exports in 2005 were $1,303 billion, so the debt to exports ratio for the US in 2005 is:

$$debt\,to\,exports\,ratio = \frac{external\,debt}{exports} = \frac{9,476}{1,303} = 727\%$$

---

1   http://web.worldbank.org/WBSITE/EXTERNAL/DATASTATISTICS/EXTDECSTAMAN/0,content MDK:20877026~menuPK:2648159~pagePK:64168445~piPK:64168309~theSitePK:2077967,00.html.

This means that external debt was seven times the inflows that generate the financing for the external debt. Although this sounds like a high number, it is not unusual for developed countries, which have a variety of sources of export earnings. By itself, this number is difficult to interpret. We must compare it to the ratios of other countries or to the same ratio over time in the US.

The debt to exports ratio itself is a little misleading because it looks only at the stock of external debt: $9.5 trillion. What really matters are the cash flows that occur due to payments of principal and interest on the debt, because these represent the amounts that must be paid each year from the funds generated through exports. However, it is much more difficult to find the details concerning principal and interest payments, so at least we have the broader measure of total debt.

DEBT TO GROSS NATIONAL INCOME RATIO

An alternative view of the debt load is provided by the *debt to gross national income ratio*, which expresses external debt as a percentage of the country's gross national income (GNI). We haven't discussed national income previously, but you can think of it as the sum of incomes earned by all of the economic agents in the economy: businesses, individuals, and governments. GNI is only a few accounting adjustments different from GDP, which we have discussed, and the amounts for GNI and GDP turn out to be fairly close to each other, at least in the US.

The external debt to GNI ratio is conceptually similar to the national debt to GDP ratio: it is an attempt to measure the debt relative to the country's capacity to generate incomes that will repay the debt. If we use the same figure for US external debt that we used previously, $9,476 billion, and divide it by US GNI in 2005, $12,810 billion, the debt to GNI ratio is:

$$debt\ to\ GNI\ ratio = \frac{external\ debt}{gross\ national\ income} = \frac{9,476}{12,811} = 74\%$$

This means that the external debt was 74 percent of the country's yearly income-generating capacity. As with the debt to exports ratio, it would be better to have the principal and interest payments rather than the total debt, but those figures are as difficult to obtain here as they were before. So we'll go with what the major data-gathering agencies such as the WB and the IMF use.

As with most measures of risk, global investors are more comfortable when a country is not so highly leveraged, meaning it hasn't borrowed too much. Just as a business generates revenues from selling products and uses those revenues to pay its financial obligations, so does a country generate revenues from selling exports and use those revenues to pay obligations such as debt payments to foreigners. Investors prefer a low debt ratio or a ratio that is declining over time because it indicates that debt is declining relative to the ability to generate funds to repay the debt. For many years, Brazil has been notorious globally for the size of its external debt. The statistics used in the two ratios are from a variety of sources.[2]

---

2   Debt: http://www.treas.gov/tic/deb2ad05.html, Exports and GDP: Economic Report of the President, Table B1, http://www.gpoaccess.gov/eop/tables07.html, GNI: World Bank, World Development Indicators, http://ddp-ext. worldbank.org/ext/DDPQQ/member.do?method=getMembers&userid=1&queryId=135.

Using data from a variety of sources creates potential difficulties: data may be from different time periods or use different accounting approaches in preparing the numbers. It would be nice to find all the data in one place to be sure of consistency, but it doesn't always happen.

Table 5.14 shows the external debt ratios for a variety of countries, including Argentina and Brazil, two of the world's most heavily indebted countries. Try to decide which countries have improved from 2000 to 2006 and which have gotten worse.

Table 5.14 External debt ratios for selected countries

	Argentina		Brazil		India		Mexico	
	2000	2006	2000	2006	2000	2006	2000	2006
External debt (US$ billions)	144.1	122.2	241.6	194.1	99.1	153.1	150.9	160.7
Exports (US$ billions)	30.9	53	64.3	156.5	60.9	202.4	180	267.9
GNI (US$ billions)	275.6	201.3	673.7	892.7	458.1	914.7	500.9	815
Debt/Exports (%)	466%	231%	376%	124%	163%	76%	84%	60%
Debt/GNI (%)	52%	61%	36%	22%	22%	17%	30%	20%

Source: World Bank, World Development Indicators, http://ddp-ext.worldbank.org/ext/DDPQQ/member. do?method=getMembers&userid=1&queryId=135.

Conclusion

Governments play an important role in a country's economy. They can influence individual behavior by changing the tax base or the tax rate, and by providing subsidies. Governments also can influence the national economy by changing spending relative to taxation, a process known as fiscal policy. A fiscal stimulus can be provided by spending more and taxing less, leading to a deficit in the government's budget.

Attitudes toward the appropriate role for government differ from country to country and have been developed through generations. People in some countries expect a larger role for government, so are willing to pay higher taxes in exchange for more government programs. In several countries where government has provided a high level of service, government spending as a percentage of GDP has decreased over the decades. This may be in response to the preference of the Washington Consensus for a smaller role for government and a larger role for the private sector.

Government spending that is not financed through taxes or other revenue leads to budgetary deficits, and deficits create risk that the government will not be able to repay its borrowing. Therefore, risk measures include the surplus or deficit as a percent of GDP, the national debt as a percent of GDP, and external debt relative to either exports or GNI.

Further Reading

Birnbaum, J.H. and A.S. Murray (1987) *Showdown at Gucci Gulch*, New York: Random House.

Bronchi, C. and F. de Kam (1999) The income taxes people really pay, *OECD Observer*, http://www.oecdobserver.org/news/fullstory.php?aid=77, retrieved 3/12/07.

Brook, D. (2004) How Sweden tweaked the Washington Consensus, *Dissent* 51(4) Fall, p. 24.

Crippen, D.L. (2002) Informing legislators about the budget: the history and role of the US Congressional Budget Office, http://www.cbo.gov/showdoc.cfm?index=3503&sequence=0, retrieved 2/7/07.

Federation of Tax Administrators (2007), State individual income taxes, http://www.taxadmin.org/FTA/rate/ind_inc.html, retrieved 4/15/07.

Gardner, H.S. (1988) *Comparative Economic Systems*, Chicago: Dryden Press.

Lowenstein, R. (2006) Who needs the mortgage-interest deduction? *New York Times*, http://www.nytimes.com/2006/03/05/magazine/305deduction.1.html?ex=1299214800en=e789e97b669d2f3fei=5088partner=rssnytemc=rss&pagewanted=print, accessed 3/9/07.

Office of Management and Budget (2006) Analytical perspectives, Budget of the United States Government, Fiscal year 2006, http://www.whitehouse.gov/omb/budget/fy2006/pdf/spec.pdf, accessed 5/15/06.

Riedl, B. (2006) Discretionary spending trends: past, present and future, Heritage Foundation, http://www.heritage.org/Research/Budget/tst021606a.cfm, accessed 3/13/07.

Schick, A. (2000) *The Federal Budget: Politics, Policy, Process*, Washington, DC: Brookings Institution Press.

Slivinski, S. (2005) Bush beats Johnson: comparing the presidents, Cato Institute, October, http://www.cato.org/pubs/tbb/tbb-0510-26.pdf, accessed 3/13/07.

Skousen, M. (2001) *The Making of Modern Economics*, Armonk: M.E. Sharpe.

6 *Evaluating Monetary Policy*

Besides the government, the other major institution influencing economic conditions in a country is the central bank. Each nation's government defines the objectives of the central bank, but generally a central bank is responsible for controlling the rate of inflation, which it accomplishes by influencing monetary conditions such as the level of interest rates. A central bank also may be responsible for influencing the level of employment, the value of the nation's currency on the international currency market, and safety of the financial system, among other functions.

In most cases, you can identify a nation's central bank by filling in the blank in Bank of _____ with the name of a country: Bank of England, Nippon Ginko (Bank of Japan), Banque de France, or Banco Central do Brasil. In some countries, the central bank is called a reserve bank for reasons we discuss in this chapter: Reserve Bank of India, Reserve Bank of Australia, or Federal Reserve System in the US. When several of the countries of Europe decided to adopt a single currency, the euro, it was necessary for the countries to create a central bank, the European Central Bank.

Learning Objectives

After studying this chapter, you should be able to:

1. explain what money is and how it is created;
2. explain the purpose of a nation's central bank;
3. explain how a central bank influences interest rates in an economy;
4. discuss the economic conditions that would cause a central bank to adjust interest rates upward or downward;
5. explain the consequences of a central bank adjusting interest rates upward or downward.

What is Money?

At first, the answer to this question seems obvious: money is what you buy things with. But in a developed country such as the US, people buy things with currency, checks, debit cards, credit cards, traveler's checks, PayPal accounts, electronic transfers, and numerous other methods. In a less developed country or in other circumstances, people might buy things with shells, tobacco, or rice, all of which served as money in the American colonies before the US was created. This ability to buy things is the first characteristic of money:

money is a medium of exchange in that it can be traded for goods and services or even other forms of money.

Economists are more precise about what constitutes money: the coins and currency that we carry around in our pockets, plus the checkable deposits we maintain in the banking system. (They're called checkable deposits because we can write a check to transfer ownership of the funds to someone else, just like we can give currency to someone else as payment; the official name is "demand deposits.")

Techniques that we use to pay for things aren't always money. A debit card is a way you provide instant transfer from your checking account to another party. The balance in your account is money; the debit card is simply a means of providing access to it. A credit card isn't money, it's a way to defer payment for a month or more until you ultimately make an electronic transfer or write a check drawn against your checking account balance. The balance in your checking account is money; the credit card is a means of borrowing. Like a debit card, an electronic transfer is another process for transferring money from your checking account to someone else. In your mind, separate the means of payment – writing a check, using a debit or credit card, making an electronic transfer – from the funds you have in your pocket or in your account. Money is what's in your account, not the process you use to transfer it to someone else.

Economists call this basic definition of the money supply M1: currency in circulation, traveler's checks, and demand deposits in financial institutions. At the end of 2007, the quantity of M1 in the US was about $1.36 trillion. About half that, $758 billion or 55 percent of the total, was currency; the rest was demand deposits and traveler's checks. You and I could live comfortably on that, but remember that this money was used to purchase all the goods and services that were produced and consumed in the US during 2007, and that was about $14.1 trillion, more than ten times the amount of M1. Obviously, money gets spent many times during the year.

There's one other thing that money isn't: it isn't the same as income. We're in the habit of saying "how much money do you earn?" when we should ask more precisely "what is your income?" Or we say "the government took 20 percent of my money last year" when we should say more precisely "the government took 20 percent of my income in the form of taxes last year." It's important to distinguish money from income to avoid confusion. In fact, if you glance back at the chapter on fiscal policy, which focused on incomes and taxes, you'll find the word "money" used only three times: once in the definition of the emperor's money basket and twice when introducing the government's ability to create money, which is the subject of this chapter. (Go ahead and check; I used the computer to search the chapter.) The chapter on fiscal policy covered concepts such as income, taxes, spending, and borrowing, but didn't mention the word money in the process. In this chapter, because we're discussing money, you'll find the word mentioned frequently.

If we take a slightly broader perspective of money and include everything in M1 plus various forms of saving, such as savings accounts, certificates of deposit, and money market mutual funds, we have M2. The reason for taking a broader perspective is that people and businesses can draw on some types of savings relatively quickly if they wish to spend more. Some types of saving are relatively liquid in that they can be converted into cash quickly and at low cost. That's another characteristic of money: it's the ultimate liquid asset. Other assets may be valuable, but they can't always be liquidated or exchanged for money in a short period of time without losing some of the asset's value, as you'll read in Box 6.1.

Box 6.1   Auction rate securities aren't money

Investors search continually for ways to earn a return on idle cash while still having the ability to convert an asset into cash quickly and at low cost. Wall Street is very good at inventing new investment vehicles to satisfy those criteria. One vehicle invented over the past couple of decades is the auction rate security.

Auction rate securities pay interest that is determined each time the securities are auctioned, which typically occurs every seven or 28 days. Investors like the securities because they pay interest, which cash does not, and because they can be liquidated at the next auction. The market for the securities grew to $330 billion in early 2008, 20 years after they were created.

In February 2008, during the United States financial crisis, investors who owned auction rate securities found that they could not liquidate their investments. Approximately $60 billion of the securities were to be auctioned, but there were not enough bids for that volume of securities. Many investors found out that the securities were not as liquid as they thought. In coming months, the lack of bidders continued.

The lack of a market led investors to bring lawsuits against some of the firms selling auction rate securities, arguing that they were misled about the liquidity of the securities.

It is not uncommon for financial markets to freeze when investors become panicked. Similar situations have occurred in the market for commercial paper, and occasionally in the market for common stocks.

Sources: Robert Frank, "Debt crisis hits a dynasty", *Wall Street Journal*, Feb 14, 2008, p. A1; Jane J. Kim, Shefali Anand, "Some investors forced to hold 'auction' bonds", *Wall Street Journal*, Feb 21, 2008, p. D1; Rebecca Buckman, "Auction-rate securities snag start-ups in credit crunch", *Wall Street Journal*, Mar 14, 2008, p. C1.

When we add savings accounts to M1, we find that M2 was about $7.4 trillion at the end of 2007. Now the percentage that is currency is only 18 percent of the total for M2. That's why you hear sometimes that currency is only a small portion of the nation's money supply. Notice the difference in the number of times M2 turns over – only about twice per year – compared to M1, which turns over ten times per year. Economists call this turnover the velocity of money, and velocity varies according to which measure of the money supply you use. Why do you think there is such a difference between the velocities of M1 and M2?

One interesting feature is that the supply of money ebbs and flows constantly, both in the short and long runs. In the short run, meaning within the year 2007, the M2 money supply of the US changed from a low of less than $7.1 trillion to a high of $7.4 trillion, a difference of $300 billion. In the long run, meaning over a decade or so, not only does the amount fluctuate, but the components of the money supply evolve. For example, money market mutual funds, a component of M2 that was almost $1 trillion in 2007, didn't exist until the 1970s. That means that in a space of three decades, a totally new component of the money supply was created and grew to almost a trillion dollars. Pretty impressive! Why and how the money supply changes are the subject of this chapter.

For most of the rest of this chapter, when we talk about money we assume we're discussing M1: currency and checkable deposits. That's what most people think of when they spend a few spare moments contemplating the definition of money. In the US, when we ultimately decide to pay for something, we deliver cash (either physically, or electronically in the form of a debit card) or write a check, so we're dealing with M1.

One feature of money is that it does not always have the same value over time in terms of the goods and services it can purchase. When it takes more money to purchase a given amount of goods and services, you're experiencing inflation. Inflation has been a characteristic of economies for thousands of years, so it isn't going away. The best hope is to control the rate of inflation to a manageable amount. When inflation gets out of control, all kinds of ills begin to beset the economy.

The US experienced a bad spate of inflation during the late 1970s into the early 1980s. We compensated for inflation by inventing ways to adjust to it:

- Cost of Living Adjustments (COLAs) became part of labor agreements and numerous pension agreements, particularly Social Security.
- Adjustable rate mortgages (ARMs) were developed by lending institutions because they were lending money at lower rates than the rate of inflation, which meant they were losing purchasing power with every loan.
- Inflation-adjusted bonds were offered by the US Treasury during the 1990s as a vehicle for protecting investors against inflation.
- People in other countries also have adopted habits to compensate for inflation, such as spending money quickly before it loses purchasing power, lending only for short periods of time, and charging extremely high interest rates when lending.

A Brief History of Banking

Now that we know what money is, let's discuss banking. When people began to use banks as a safe place to deposit gold and silver coins, bankers gave customers receipts for their money in the form of bank notes, which subsequently were used to purchase goods and services. Bankers noticed that many of the coins just sat in the bank after they were deposited. Some customers might withdraw a portion of their coin deposits, but there remained in the bank plenty of coins deposited from other customers. The actual coins stayed on reserve in the bank while the notes circulated throughout the economy; the notes were used to purchase things, just as the coins were.

With a reserve of coins they were holding, bankers soon realized they could lend money to other clients by giving them bank notes on loan, even when the client had not deposited coins into the bank. Like the original bank notes, these bank notes were spent throughout the community, generating commerce and economic growth. But notice what had happened. The original coins that were on reserve as deposits were still there, but now there were more bank notes outstanding: the original notes given to depositors plus the new notes out on loan. The bank actually kept hard money (coins) that was only a fraction of the value of the bank notes that were outstanding, a process that became known as fractional reserve banking.

These principles were developed by banks in trading centers such as Venice, Genoa, and Amsterdam 500 years ago and continue to be the basis of modern banking. Banks have on reserve only a portion of the money people think is in the bank. As a result, banks never have enough money to satisfy all the claims against the money. In banks 500 years ago, there were never enough coins to give people if they came in to redeem their bank notes all at once. In modern banks, there is never enough cash to give people if everyone with a deposit in the bank wants to withdraw their cash at one time. It's the wonder and the danger of fractional reserve banking. In the words of Charles Dickens in *A Christmas Carol*, "This must be distinctly understood, or nothing wonderful can come of the story I am going to relate."

Some bankers are more conservative than others. In the old days, a cautious banker would keep on reserve in the form of cash or coins a higher proportion of the outstanding bank notes. A more speculative banker would lend liberally, creating lots of bank notes or deposits through the lending process. Everything in the banking system would be fine until something happened to cause depositors to try to withdraw their funds all at once. If that happened, even conservative banks did not have cash sufficient to meet all depositor withdrawals. The attempt by depositors to withdraw cash all at once is known as a *run* on a bank.

In the US in the 1800s, banking was a largely unregulated industry. Any bank could issue notes, and state and federal governments frequently issued notes to pay for the goods and services they purchased. Galbraith tells the story of one bank in Massachusetts that issued $500,000 of notes, but had on deposit coinage valued at only $86.48. That's hardly conservative banking!

In the US of the 1700s and 1800s, people and businesses accepting bank notes learned to compensate for the perceived risk of the bank by adjusting the value of the notes they would accept. They didn't always deliver $1 worth of goods for $1 worth of bank notes. Notes issued by banks in New England, which had reputations as being more reliable, generally traded at par, meaning you could purchase $1 worth of goods for $1 of bank notes. Notes from New York banks were discounted 10 percent, meaning you would receive only $0.90 worth of goods for $1 of bank notes. Notes issued by banks in the Appalachians were discounted as much as 50 percent because they were perceived as being more risky.

The situation became confusing and frustrating for citizens and businesses trying to conduct interstate commerce. Bank notes came from a variety of issuers, some familiar, others less so. A merchant holding notes from different banks was never sure about the true value of the notes because they were not always worth their face values. It became apparent to some people that the country needed a uniform currency that would have the same value throughout the country.

Another trend that developed during the 1800s was that people began to accept deposits in the bank rather than bank notes when borrowing from the bank. In other words, they were content with a bookkeeping entry that said they had a deposit in the bank and didn't require a physical commodity in the form of a bank note to prove it. They would access their deposits by writing a check payable to the party from which they were purchasing something. Now, when a bank wished to lend to a customer, it didn't even have to issue new bank notes. Instead, the bank simply made a bookkeeping entry that increased the borrower's deposit balance with the bank. In addition to bank notes serving as money, deposit balances also became money. The nation's money supply would increase whenever bank notes were printed, but it could as easily increase through the creation of deposits through a bookkeeping entry at the bank. This was the beginning of M1, although it didn't have a name at the time and the amount of currency and bank deposits were not yet measured.

When viewed from the perspective of the national economy rather than from the perspective of individual banks or depositors, the 1800s were tumultuous. When times were good, banks would lend liberally, creating lots of deposits or bank notes, and thus increasing the money supply. Two results occurred: first, the level of national economic activity would increase as people and businesses purchased more goods and services with the newly-created money; second, prices would increase due to the pressure of everyone wanting to purchase more. These were known as booms; good times looked like they would go on forever.

But booms do not continue forever. Businesses overestimate the amount of goods or services they will sell, builders overestimate the need for housing or commercial buildings, owners of stocks overestimate the value of their shares and find that they cannot sell at higher prices, consumers borrow too much and find they can't repay the loans. Any number of things can cause booms to end, as they eventually do. The downturn isn't always kind. Sellers lower prices in an attempt to liquidate their positions as quickly as possible, but the pressure to sell causes prices to decline even further. Some people can't get out of a position without a significant loss in value because some assets are less liquid than others. When the boom stalls, everyone wants to have cash rather than the other assets they invested in.

The rush to have cash eventually moves to the banking system. People want cash rather than a statement saying they have money in the bank because with cash, they don't have to worry about the bank failing. People rush to banks to withdraw their funds, where they encounter the downside of fractional reserve banking. Each bank has to tell people that it does not have cash sufficient to meet all the withdrawals, but doing so causes even more people to rush to the bank. Panic sets in. When the bank can't meet the demands of depositors, the bank fails and remaining depositors face the prospect of losing everything. Even banks able to weather the storm of panic withdrawals begin to curtail lending in an effort to conserve cash. People and businesses otherwise deserving of credit find that they cannot borrow. The boom becomes a bust, leading to economic contraction and unemployment.

Thus was the history of the 1800s in the US: periods of overspeculation followed by panic. Boom and bust cycles occurred like night and day. Economists studied business cycles – how long they lasted, what caused the turns, what should be done to counteract the cycles – but were unable to agree on the details. Even today, there is evidence that business cycles exist. What do the years 1970, 1981, 1991, 2001, and 2009 have in common? They are the years of recessions in the US, and the periods are roughly equal to the length of business cycles 100 years earlier.

Despite the efforts of financial authorities, bank runs continue to the present day. Runs occur in all types of financial institutions, not only commercial banks. Insurance companies, investment banks, and savings associations are all subject to rapid withdrawals of cash by depositors or lenders. The financial crisis that emerged in 2007 led to loss of depositor confidence in banks in the UK and US, as described in Box 6.2.

Box 6.2   **Bank runs in the United States and United Kingdom**

A financial crisis began in the United States in 2007 when the rate of defaults on home mortgages increased. The "subprime market" consisted of low-income borrowers who were unable to make payments of principal and interest on loans they had borrowed to purchase a house. The scale of defaults created alarm in the United States as well as in the United Kingdom.

In the United States, the first big panic occurred at a Los Angeles bank, IndyMac Bancorp in late June 2008. Bank executives realized that the bank faced loan defaults, so began taking steps to improve profitability. When depositors found out the bank was in difficulty, they began withdrawing money from their accounts. Depositors "stampeded tellers and demanded their money" according to the New York Times. Depositors withdrew $100 million daily for almost two weeks, a classic bank run.

On Friday, July 12, the Federal Deposit Insurance Corporation took control of IndyMac, the first step toward liquidating the bank. IndyMac became the second-largest bank failure in United States history. In 2009, 140 banks failed in the United States.

A similar situation occurred in the United Kingdom a few months before. The financial problems in the United States made it difficult for banks around the world to obtain financing for their operations due to what is known as a "credit squeeze." One bank affected by the credit squeeze was Northern Rock, a large lender for home mortgages.

Once depositors learned of the operating problems at Northern Rock, they began withdrawing money, another bank run. Over a period of about a week, depositors withdrew £2 billion, equal to approximately $4 billion. The bank had to increase the bandwidth on its web site because so many customers accessed their accounts electronically.

There was so much demand for money in the banking system that the overnight lending rate increased 1 percent in a few hours, a dramatic change. Only when the Bank of England began to lend more to the banking system did the rate subside.

Sources: Saskia Scholtes, "IndyMac admits deposit run at 'elevated levels'", *Financial Times*, Jul 9, 2008, p. 25; Louise Storey, "Regulators seize mortgage lender", *New York Times*, Jul 12, 2008, p. C5; Julia Werdigier, "Official assurances fail to stem rush of withdrawals at British bank", *New York Times*, Sep 18, 2007, p. C3; Julia Werdigier, "British central bank adds more funds in credit crisis", *New York Times*, Sep 19, 2007, p. C5.

The United States Central Bank

The Federal Reserve System (the Fed), the central bank of the US, was created in 1913 partially in an effort to break the boom-bust cycle. But creating a central bank with powers concentrated in a political center such as Washington, DC or in a financial center such as New York City was a controversial concept in the US of the day, where many people distrusted the concentration of power. The compromise was a system with a central framework but with 12 district banks distributed throughout the US. Each of the district banks was responsible for economic conditions in its region, while some decisions were reserved for the central bank in Washington, DC. Over time, the division of powers has been changed so that all decisions are centralized. The 12 district banks now are an anachronism, although they continue to operate.

Creating a central bank addressed several problems: first, the Fed would be responsible for issuing all currency and bank notes throughout the US, which would promote commerce; second, the Fed would establish a minimum amount that commercial banks would be required to hold as reserves against their deposits, which would promote safety throughout the banking system; third, the Fed would lend money to banks experiencing unanticipated withdrawals, which would forestall the liquidity crises that accompanied panics. There were other arguments for creating a central bank. In fact, two previous attempts at creating a central bank in the US had failed.

You can read more about the history of the Federal Reserve by visiting its home page or referring to one of the books at the end of the chapter. It's always interesting to read the official perspective, which is factual but without drama, then compare it to an outsider's interpretation to find out what really happened, complete with the warts and blemishes. You might be surprised by the history of banking in the US.

The US was a relatively late entry into the central banking arena. The Bank of England was originally chartered in 1694. Although it began as a commercial bank, the Bank of England was the Government's bank, and it eventually gained the trust of other banks so that it was able to perform many of the functions of a central bank even before it was designated as such.

This brings up an important point: central banking is an evolutionary process. The duties, functions, and powers of a central bank in 2009 are not the same as they were 50 years earlier, whether in the US or another country. The objectives and powers of a central bank change according to political priorities, and the framework in which central bankers make decisions change as economic theory evolves. Hopefully, we know more about how the world operates (or should operate) now than we did 50 years ago, so the practice of central banking should improve.

What does a Central Bank do?

One basic function of a central bank in all circumstances is to influence the amount of money in circulation in a country. Remember that money in the US is either M1 (currency plus checkable deposits) or M2 (M1 plus some savings accounts), so what we're saying is that the Fed tries to influence the amount of M1 or M2. That sounds straightforward, but the key word is "influence." The Fed can't dictate the amount of M1 or M2 because those amounts depend on the accumulation of millions of individual decisions by people, businesses, and financial institutions. Instead, the Fed uses a set of policy tools to influence the decisions. It's not an exact science by any means.

Any central bank has some basic tools at its disposal, although the efficacy of each tool varies from country to country. For example, central banks in developed countries have a broader palette, so are able to use all these tools if they wish. Central banks in less developed countries without a sophisticated financial system don't have the broad range of tools at their disposal.

The basic tools are:

1. Adjusting the amount of cash that a financial institution must keep on reserve relative to the amount of deposits that are claims against the cash reserves. Remember that bankers who lend liberally will want to create more deposits relative to the amount of cash, so the central bank may wish to curtail this tendency by requiring banks to keep more on reserve. In the US, we call this rule about how much cash reserves are necessary relative to the bank's deposits the *reserve requirement*.
2. Adjusting the interest rate that it charges banks desiring to borrow from the central bank. Financial institutions may want to borrow from central banks for two main reasons: first, the institution may have a profitable lending opportunity, and borrowing from the central bank could provide a low-cost source of funds; second, the institution may be in financial distress, so borrowing from the central bank is a source of emergency funds. Central banks in different countries have different attitudes about lending to commercial banks. In some countries, lending to commercial banks is common, while in other countries it is discouraged. Before the Fed was created in 1913, for example, banks in the US relied on other banks for help during a financial crisis. In modern Japan, the Bank of Japan encourages banks to help one another solve a financial crisis, and to rely on the central bank only as a last resort. When banks borrow from the central bank, they pay interest on the borrowing. In the US, we call the interest rate on borrowing from the Fed the *discount rate*.
3. Buying securities from or selling securities to the public or the banking system. When a central bank purchases securities, it acquires securities (which are not money) and puts cash or deposits into the public's hands (which is money). In this way it increases the money supply directly. The opposite occurs when a central bank sells securities: the central bank takes money out of circulation and sells to the public securities, which are not money. In the US, we call this technique an *open market operation* because the Fed purchases or sells securities on the open market rather than dealing directly with the issuer of the securities. In other countries, the central bank may purchase securities directly from the issuer of the securities, which frequently is the government. Lately, the technique also has been called *quantitative easing*.

The tools are used with different frequency, as you'll notice when you're aware of them over a period of time. The Fed buys and sells securities daily or weekly, for example, while the reserve requirement changes perhaps once in a decade under ordinary circumstances. The tools also have different degrees of effectiveness. For example, changing the reserve requirement only slightly leads to dramatic changes in bank lending and consequently in the performance of the economy. All these tools have the effect of influencing credit conditions by raising or lowering interest rates throughout the economy. Credit conditions are the ability or tendency to lend or borrow, a practice we have turned into a national obsession in the US. The same tools are available in other countries, although they frequently have different names.

The three tools can be used to implement monetary policy, the desire of the central bank to influence economic conditions such as unemployment, inflation, or the foreign exchange value of the nation's currency. When people don't have jobs or businesses are not selling as much as they wish, the central bank may pursue an easy money policy by making more money available through the banking system. When the rate of inflation is

---

Box 6.3 Different economic conditions, different bank policies

Central bank policies depend on economic and financial conditions in the home country. This became evident about the time of the Northern Rock crisis described in Box 6.2. In September 2007, three major European central banks adopted three different policies regarding easing credit conditions.

Swiss officials worried that the economy was growing too rapidly and creating inflationary pressure. They decided to raise interest rates by slowing growth of the money supply, which would make credit tighter. The Swiss National Bank allowed the short-term interest rate to increase by 0.25 percent to 2.75 percent. This was accomplished by refusing to provide reserves through purchases of securities.

The Bank of England faced the threat of additional bank failures after the run on Northern Rock. Officials at the Bank of England eased credit conditions by providing additional reserves through the purchase of additional securities on the open market. The Bank of England also changed reserve requirements so that banks were able to lend more.

The European Central Bank faced a dilemma. According to one set of data, inflation was increasing in the EU. Other statistics indicated that economic growth might be slowing. Because of the conflicting data, the European Central Bank did not take any action, deciding to wait until it had a clearer view of unfolding economic conditions.

Sources: "Europe's central banks on different paths", *Wall Street Journal*, Sep 14, 2007, p. A2; Haig Simonian, "Swiss raise interest rates", *Financial Times*, Sep 14, 2007, p. 6; Julia Werdigier, "Bank of England eases money policy", *New York Times*, Sep 20, 2007, p. C10; Ralph Atkins, "Eurozone inflation jump is headache for bank", *Financial Times*, Sep 28, 2007, p. 4.

---

high, the central bank may pursue a tight money policy by making money more difficult to obtain. Using the three tools to influence the right amount of money in an economy is a delicate task. This is the *central bankers' dilemma*: striking the balance between too much money, which causes inflation, and too little money, which causes recession. Box 6.3 describes how three central banks viewed the dilemma in mid-2007. Box 6.4 explains the dilemma facing the Fed shortly after a new chairman was appointed.

How do the Policy Tools Work?

The policy tools work in different ways to make money easier or more difficult to obtain. The focus is on *bank reserves*, the money that banks keep so they can meet withdrawals by depositors.

RESERVE REQUIREMENT

Because banks have a tendency to keep as little cash as possible on reserve, the central bank frequently sets a lower limit on how much money banks must keep on reserve by

---

Box 6.4   Use of the federal funds rate

The Fed manipulates credit conditions primarily through the federal funds rate, the rate on overnight lending between banks. When it wants to tighten credit, the Fed raises the federal funds rate by making fewer reserves available for lending. When it wants to make credit easier to obtain, the Fed lowers the federal funds rate by making more reserves available for lending. Two situations over the past few years illustrate use of the Fed funds rate.

In March 2006, Ben Bernanke became the new Chairman of the Federal Reserve Board at a time when United States economic growth threatened to lead to higher inflation. At his first meeting, the Board decided to increase the federal funds rate to 4.75 percent, the fifteenth consecutive rate increase. Some economists thought that the rate was close to neutral, the rate where there was no pressure for inflation or recession. According to *The Economist*, "Now the central bankers must decide how much higher rates should go. Stop too soon and inflation could become a problem. Raise rates too far, and the consequences for America's unbalanced, debt-laden economy could be calamitous." It was the classic central banker's dilemma, which the Fed resolved by increasing the Fed funds rate. At the same meeting, the Fed raised the discount rate to 5.75 percent.

By December 2008, credit condition had changed drastically – the United States was in the midst of its worst recession for almost 30 years. At the December meeting, the Fed decided to reduce the Fed funds rate to 0.25 percent. It accomplished the reduction by purchasing about $1.1 trillion of securities on the open market. The Fed signaled that it would go beyond purchasing Treasury securities and was willing to purchase mortgage-backed debt, consumer debt, and debt issued by Fannie Mae and Freddie Mac.

Sources: "Bernanke ponders his course", *The Economist*, Mar 25, 2006, p. 77; Greg Ip, "Fed raises rates by ¼ point, hints more may come", *Wall Street Journal*, Mar 29, 2006, p. A1; Edmund L. Andrews, Jackie Calmes, "Fed cuts key rate almost to zero", *New York Times*, Dec 17, 2008, p. A1; "Ground zero", *The Economist*, Dec 20, 2008, p. 120.

---

using the reserve requirement. For example, a reserve requirement of 10 percent means that a bank must keep at least 10 percent of its customer deposits on reserve as deposits in the central bank. The 10 percent lower limit is called the *reserve requirement* and the reserves are called *required reserves*. The bank can't do anything with the required reserves, and the bank doesn't profit from them because the Fed doesn't pay interest on deposits of commercial banks. Consequently, banks have an incentive to minimize the amount of money they keep on reserve because it is a nonearning asset. Banks would much rather use the reserves to invest in securities or lend because these uses generate interest income, a major source of revenue for the bank.

If the central bank wants to slow growth of the money supply, it can raise the reserve requirement, which means that banks must cease lending and instead keep cash idle in the bank or on deposit at the central bank. This also means reduced profits for the bank, of course, because it is not earning interest through loans or investments. When this happens, banks have to find a way to allocate credit, so they stop lending or lend only to their best customers. Because loans are more difficult to obtain, interest rates increase. Higher interest rates are a characteristic of a tight money policy.

The same principle works in reverse. If the central bank wants to grow the money supply, it can reduce the reserve requirement, which means that commercial banks do not have to keep as much money on reserve in the central bank. Now the commercial bank has *excess reserves* – reserves in excess of the amount required – that it can invest or lend. Credit is easier, and interest rates decrease because of the easy money policy.

You see that there is almost a direct link between the reserve requirement and the amount of lending by banks. But there is one slight kink in the process. Raising the reserve requirement decreases bank lending and causes interest rates to increase. When faced with a higher reserve requirement, banks don't have any choice other than to curtail lending.

You would think that decreasing the reserve requirement would work as well in reverse, but it doesn't. Decreasing the reserve requirement makes it possible for banks to lend more money because now they have excess reserves. Unfortunately, that doesn't mean that banks will suddenly lend or people will suddenly borrow more. People and businesses borrow for a variety of reasons, and just because more money is available to be borrowed, it doesn't mean that they suddenly will borrow more. They may have gotten frightened because of what happened the last time they borrowed too much. Even when banks have more money available to lend, it doesn't mean that they will suddenly lend it. Bankers may be cautious about lending because they experienced problems during some recent episode of liberal credit.

Someone made an analogy that monetary policy is like a string. When there is too much lending and the economy is getting too far ahead of where it should be, the central bank can slow it down by pulling on the string. But when the economy is lagging and more lending is called for, the central bank can't push on the string to force lending to increase. That's a pretty good way to look at monetary policy. Box 6.5 describes use of the reserve requirement by China's central bank, the People's Bank of China.

Box 6.5   China's reserve requirement

In December 2007, officials at China's central bank, the People's Bank of China (PBC), learned that inflation in November had been almost 7 percent, the highest rate in 11 years. Inflation had increased despite the Bank's efforts to control it.

The PBC decided to raise the reserve ratio yet again. The Bank had increased it ten times over the past year, but inflation continued. This time, it raised the ratio by a full percentage point, to 14.5 percent. Previous increases had been only half a percentage point. Officials expected the full percentage point increase to serve as a signal to banks to reduce lending.

Because it was not introduced until 1984, the reserve ratio was a relatively recent tool for the central bank. The central bank also raised interest rates five times during the past year as part of the attempt to stem inflation.

Sources: J.R. Wu, "Again, Beijing raises banks' reserve ratio", *Wall Street Journal*, Dec 10, 2007, p. C3; "China lifts deposit reserve ratio for 10th time since 07 start", *SinoCast China Business Daily News*, Dec 25, 2007, p. 1; Richard McGregor, "China inflation at new high", *Financial Times*, Dec 12, 2007, p. 1.

DISCOUNT RATE

Sometimes, financial institutions such as commercial banks experience problems with liquidity: they don't have cash available when they need it. A typical example is that the bank may need cash because depositors suddenly desire to withdraw their deposits. These withdrawals can be expected (such as the need for more cash before the Christmas shopping season) or unexpected (such as a financial panic). Another example is that at the end of the day, a bank may not have reserves sufficient to meet the reserve requirement. In situations where banks need cash, they may go to the central bank to borrow it.

Some central banks may encourage banks to borrow from other banks before attempting to borrow from the central bank. In this situation, the bank borrowing cash must pay interest to the lending bank. The interest rate for borrowing or lending through the interbank market in the US is called the *federal funds rate*. The loans typically are for overnight use; if a bank wishes to borrow for a longer period, it must renegotiate the interest rate each day. This is the ultimate in short-term borrowing.

If a bank is unable to borrow through the interbank funds market, it may ask to borrow from the central bank. The central bank becomes a lender of last resort, meaning that the commercial bank was unable to obtain funds from other sources, so it went to the central bank because there weren't any alternatives. When this happens, borrowing from the central bank acquires a negative connotation: It means that the commercial bank was such a poor credit risk that no one else would lend it money, so the central bank became a last resort.

When the central bank lends to commercial banks, it charges an interest rate called the *discount rate*. If the central bank wants to make it easier for commercial banks to borrow money, it will lower the discount rate. Even when banks don't actually borrow from the central bank, lowering the discount rate signals that the central bank is more willing for bankers to lend freely because if they get into trouble, the central bank won't charge as much interest. The discount rate also serves as a signal because it is one of the basic interest rates in the US economy. When the discount rate declines, other interest rates frequently follow. Of course, the same caveat about the string applies here. The central bank can slow the economy by pulling on the string (raising the discount rate), but it can't push the string (force banks to lend or people to borrow by lowering the discount rate).

In Box 6.6, you read that the Fed not only lowered the discount rate, but also allowed other financial institutions to borrow in an attempt to make borrowing easier for banks during the financial crisis of 2008.

OPEN MARKET OPERATIONS

The interest rate that is most frequently mentioned in media reports, at least in the US, is the federal funds rate. Sometimes you hear it described as the Fed's "benchmark" rate or "basic lending" rate. In media reports, analysts say that the Fed is making money more difficult to obtain by raising the fed funds rate, or making money easier to obtain by lowering the fed funds rate. How does the Fed manipulate the fed funds rate?

The answer lies in the Fed's ability to manipulate bank reserves. When the Fed wants the fed funds rate to decline, it puts reserves into the banking system. By now, we know that whenever banks have extra reserves, they will try to earn interest by lending them,

---

Box 6.6 The Fed's discount window

The severity of the United States financial crisis led the Federal Reserve to adopt two practices related to lending through its discount window. One practice was a typical attempt to provide liquidity, but the second practice had not been used for 70 years.

The normal practice during a recession is to lower the discount rate. The Fed lowered the discount rate twice during October 2008, to 1.25 percent. It also encouraged borrowing through the discount window to the point that borrowing reached a record of $430 billion by mid-October. Although lending through the discount window is normal practice, two features stand out. First, the Fed met twice during the month, which is unusual; normal practice is for the Board to meet every four or five weeks. Second, it is unusual for the Fed to encourage borrowing, which traditionally was viewed as a sign of a bank's weakness.

The practice that had not been used for 70 years was to allow institutions other than member banks to borrow from the Fed. Traditionally, the Fed lent only to commercial banks that were members of the Federal Reserve System. The Fed expanded the list of allowable borrowers to include investment banks, primary securities dealers, and insurance companies, provided they became a bank holding company by purchasing a bank; there was a subsequent rush to purchase small banks.

The Fed also announced that it would accept collateral other than United States Treasury securities when lending. It agreed to accept commercial paper, corporate stocks, and investment-grade corporate bonds as collateral.

Sources: Meena Thiruvengadam, Brian Blackstone, "Crisis on Wall Street: Direct borrowing from the Fed leaps", *Wall Street Journal*, Oct 10, 2008, p. C4; Steve Sloan, "Firms jump on the bank bandwagon", *Bank Loan Report*, Oct 20, 2008; Steve Sloan, "Drops for Bear assets, discount window", *American Banker*, Oct 24, 2008, p. 20.

---

even if only for one night. The extra reserves cause banks to try to lend more, which causes interest rates to decline.

In the reverse situation, the Fed wants the fed funds rate to increase, so it takes reserves out of the banking system. When banks don't have so much money to lend, they must allocate credit and interest rates will increase.

The question you're dying to ask is: "How does the Fed put reserves into or take reserves out of the banking system?" The answer is that when the Fed wants interest rates to decline, it purchases securities. It doesn't really matter who the Fed purchases securities from – people, businesses, or financial institutions. Because they wanted cash to spend rather than securities to hold, whoever gets the cash from the Fed will put it into a bank in order to write checks against the deposit. Now the bank has more cash to lend, and we're back in the situation where the fed funds rate will decline.

Because it doesn't matter from whom the Fed purchases securities, the securities are purchased on the open market, hence the name *open market operation*. It also turns out that it doesn't make too much difference what securities the Fed purchases. The process works equally well if the securities were issued originally by the US Treasury, by the State of California, or by General Electric Corporation. The key is that before the transaction, the Fed had money and investors owned securities, but after the transaction the Fed owns securities and the investors have money. There is more money circulating out there in the economy; that's the important part. That's why the process also is known as quantitative easing: the quantity of money increases when the Fed purchases securities.

(Here is a quick aside relating to the previous paragraph. By tradition, the Fed purchases only securities issued by the US Treasury, and almost always Treasury Bills, which are short-term securities. Back in the glory days of the late 1990s, the Treasury was running budgetary surpluses, which means the quantity of Treasury securities was shrinking. There were only about $5 trillion worth outstanding. The concern among economists and Wall Street experts was that the Fed would run out of Treasury securities to purchase, so would have to find other securities through which to conduct open market operations. That concern quickly evaporated once George W. Bush was elected President, because the Treasury soon resumed running budgetary deficits and the quantity of Treasury securities increased. How times change!)

Of course, the same process works in reverse. When the Fed wants the federal funds rate to increase, it takes reserves out of the banking system by selling securities on the open market. The Fed ends up with cash and the public ends up with securities, so there isn't as much money circulating through the financial system.

The Fed uses open market operations to fine-tune the economy by influencing the fed funds rate. The Fed selects a fed funds rate it thinks is appropriate for economic conditions, then enters the securities market to buy or sell securities in an attempt to adjust the actual fed funds rate to the target. When things are going well in the economy, the Fed doesn't have to work too hard to maintain the target rate. But when things aren't going well, such as during the monetary crisis that began in late 2007, the Fed is constantly pumping money (reserves) into the economy to provide liquidity and drive down the fed funds rate.

Unlike changes in interest rates, central banks seldom announce to the public that they are undertaking open market operations. Instead, you must read behind the actions to see that the central bank is purchasing or selling securities. Box 6.7 describes open market practice at the Bank of Japan.

What Happens at the Fed?

So far, we've examined the effect of monetary policy on the banking system. In this section we'll examine what happens at the Federal Reserve to create the monetary policy. Of course, the Fed consists of people who are trained in the theory of monetary economics, so they have a better idea of what they're doing than the average person you meet on the street. They may, however, disagree on the economic conditions underlying the need for a policy.

The Fed can change the discount rate or the reserve through simple edicts; the Fed announces what the new discount rate or reserve requirement will be, and that's it. There's not much drama involved. But the Fed can't dictate the fed funds rate, since that is determined in the market for borrowing and lending bank reserves. The interesting point to examine is: where does the Fed get the money it uses to purchase securities on the open market?

Box 6.7   Japan's quantitative easing

Japan faced persistent deflation in the 1990s and early 2000s. Deflation occurs when prices decline, which would be fine if your salary remained the same. But deflation also causes salaries to decline, as well as prices of assets such as houses.

To counteract the trend toward deflation, the Bank of Japan began a practice it called "quantitative easing," in which it provided reserves to the banking system by purchasing securities. The thinking was that the excess reserves would encourage banks to lend, which would stimulate the economy and promote price increases. The massive injection of reserves caused interest rates to fall to zero. As *Sunday Business* said, "The Bank conducts open market operations to control the money supply and the level of long-term interest rates. It buys government bonds, printing additional money whenever it wants to boost the money supply."

The Bank of Japan is a major purchaser of government bonds. It purchases about two-fifths of the government's bonds issued each month, a practice that in most countries would lead to massive inflation. However, in Japan it has done little to counteract deflation.

In 2006, the Bank of Japan decided to cease the practice of quantitative easing because it was doing little to solve the problem and there were faint stirrings of inflation in Japan. Even interest rates as low as 0.05 percent were not effective in stimulating lending. Some analysts attribute the problem to the Japanese tendency to save rather than borrow, making it a cultural phenomenon characteristic of many Asian countries.

Sources: "After the flood", *The Economist*, Mar 11, 2006, p. 63; "BoJ to cut excess bank liquidity over 3 months from April", *Jiji Press English News Service*, Mar 27, 2006, p. 1; Allister Heath, "Tokyo claims deflation now under control", *Sunday Business*, Mar 12, 2006, p. 1.

Remember that back in the 1800s, people learned to accept a bookkeeping entry rather than physical notes whenever they received a loan from a commercial bank. As long as they could write checks against the bookkeeping entry, people believed they had money in their account; it wasn't necessary for them to receive physical cash. In the process, the commercial bank added to the nation's money supply. You could say that money was created via a bookkeeping entry rather than via a printing press, but it was created nonetheless.

Central banking works much the same way. When a central bank purchases a security from a commercial bank, the central bank simply tells the commercial bank that there now is more in the commercial bank's reserve deposit with the central bank. The commercial bank then has excess reserves, which it then can lend out at interest. The commercial bank delivered securities (which are not money) to the Fed, and the Fed added to the bank's reserves (which are money) in the Fed. New money was created through a bookkeeping entry.

It's the wondrous thing about central banking. Whenever a central bank wants to create money, all it has to do is make an electronic entry creating more reserves in the form of commercial bank deposits, then use the reserves it created to purchase securities from the banking system. We live in a *fiat* currency world. A central bank adds to the money supply by saying (electronically) *fiat currency*, which means "let there be currency."

One remarkable feature is that when the Fed injects additional reserves into the system, the money supply increases by a multiple of the amount injected. Because of the fractional reserve principle, a bank keeps on reserve only a portion of the deposits it can issue against those reserves. The balance of the reserves is available for lending, so if the Fed wants to grow the money supply by $100 billion, it needs to purchase only perhaps $10 or $15 billion of securities. The amount of the multiple depends on factors such as commercial banks' willingness to lend rather than hold onto the reserves, or on borrowers' willingness to borrow. The inability to predict the multiple is what makes central banking as much an art as a science.

Confidence

It boils down to this: a central bank can create money whenever it wants. It is only necessary for the central bank to print more currency or even easier, to make an electronic entry putting money into a commercial bank's reserve account.

It wasn't always like this, however. In the early days of banking, a central bank's ability to create new money was constrained by the amount of gold it owned. More gold in the central bank meant more money, while less gold meant less money. It was a strict way of regulating a nation's economic performance, and it had some disadvantages. Sometimes the economy was in recession, so needed a monetary stimulus to get it growing. If this occurred at the same time the central bank's gold reserves were shrinking, the spark couldn't be provided by monetary authorities. In the reverse circumstance, monetary authorities might want to constrain inflation, but if gold was flowing into a country, it led to more money, which contributes to the inflation the central bank is trying to constrain. The gold standard wasn't all it was cracked up to be.

But those days haven't existed since the 1930s, when major countries around the world abandoned the gold standard (the US left the gold standard in 1933). Now a nation's currency is backed by only one thing: confidence. On the US Federal Reserve Notes (the official name for the US currency), is the statement "This note is legal tender for all debts, public and private." If you believe this, you have confidence in the US currency.

Maintaining confidence is one of the important responsibilities of a nation's central bank, but sometimes people lose confidence in the central bank. When that happens, people lose faith in the banking system. They withdraw cash because they want something physical rather than that electronic bunkum telling them they have a deposit in the bank. Then when they get cash, they may spend it as quickly as possible, whether on goods, gold, or even another nation's currency. The loss of confidence in a central bank has dire consequences for a nation.

One of the factors that helped instill confidence in the US banking system was creation of deposit insurance in the 1930s. Even after the Federal Reserve System was created in 1913, monetary crises continued, and during the 1920s thousands of banks failed, costing depositors hundreds of millions of dollars. The situation was so bad that when Franklin D. Roosevelt became President in 1933, the first thing he did was close ALL the banks in the US for a week. Roosevelt delivered his first "Fireside Chat" that weekend in an effort to restore the public's confidence in the banking system. A few months later, Congress created the Federal Deposit Insurance Corporation (FDIC), which promised to reimburse depositors if they lost their deposits due to bank failure. Through the years, the FDIC has had a calming effect on bank depositors in the US.[1]

The FDIC is one of the enduring legacies of the Roosevelt administration. The FDIC is an insurance fund that collects premiums from national banks, based on the level of deposits. The insurance fund accumulates cash that can be used to reimburse depositors in the event that a bank fails. Creating the FDIC has promoted confidence in the banking system by reducing the incentive for depositors to rush to the bank to remove cash.

Box 6.8 describes the loss of confidence in the banking system following the financial crisis of 2008. The ultimate loss of confidence in a nation's central bank is for the nation to abandon its currency altogether, do away with the central bank, and adopt another nation's currency. This is what happened in two Latin American countries. Ecuador and El Salvador had such bad experience with monetary policy that they adopted the US dollar as their currency, which means that their economic performance depends on what happens in the US.

Box 6.8   Central bank credibility

In the modern world, the only thing backing the money of a country is trust – trust that the central bank will execute policies that make the currency worth holding. In the 1980s and 1990s, most central banks did a pretty good job earning trust by containing inflation. In fact, controlling inflation is one of the ways you can tell whether a central bank is doing its job well.

Beginning with the credit crunch of 2007, the spotlight on central bank credibility shifted to maintaining soundness of the financial system. Bankers lost confidence and refused to lend to one another through the interbank market, leading to bank failures. When the public became aware of the problem, they lost confidence and began to withdraw money from the banking system, leading to more bank failures.

Central bankers reacted to the crisis by bailing out banks, even banks that had pursued risky lending practices. The public had another reason for losing confidence in central bankers, who were viewed as playing favorites by protecting their friends in the financial sector. *The Economist* suggests that "Steelworkers and coalminers have to face grim economic reality; bankers, it seems, do not." Confidence was undermined further by the large bonuses earned on Wall Street and other financial centers, leading to the argument that central bankers were bailing out the rich.

The Federal Reserve Bank of St Louis warns that "It is a terrible thing if policymakers lose their credibility. Restoring credibility takes time. It took well over a decade to completely restore low inflation in the United States after the inflation of the 1970s, and in the process the economy experienced the worst recession, in 1981–82, since the Great Depression."

It probably will take time to restore central bank credibility after the current financial crisis.

Sources: "The faith that moves Mammon", *The Economist*, Oct 18, 2008, p. 88; "Restoring confidence", *Central Banking*, Aug 2009, p. 1; "The year of living dangerously", *The Economist*, Aug 9, 2008; William Poole, "Understanding the Fed", *Federal Reserve Bank of St Louis Review*, Jan/Feb 2007, p. 7.

---

1   If you'd like to hear or read the Fireside Chat on banking, go to http://xroads.virginia.edu/~ma02/volpe/newdeal/banking.html. The Fireside Chat is a great summary of this chapter, a lucid statement of banking principles, and a testimony to Roosevelt's leadership.

How does the Central Bank Relate to the Treasury?

The government of each nation determines the relationship between the nation's central bank and the government's treasury. You'll recall that the treasury is the organization that borrows on behalf of the government; it is an arm of the government because it implements decisions made about the government's budget. The central bank is a slightly different situation. Because it is the organization responsible for the quantity of money in an economy, it may be desirable to separate its decisions from decisions made by the treasury. Here's why:

When a government wants to spend, it has two choices: it can raise revenue through taxes, or it can borrow. Taxing is seldom popular, so governments frequently run budgetary deficits and must borrow the amount that spending exceeds tax revenues. This is one of the issues that were covered in the chapter about fiscal policy.

When a treasury borrows, it must find someone willing to purchase its securities. But if the government tries to borrow too much, investors may not be willing to purchase the securities, or may require higher interest rates than the treasury is willing to pay. If that happens, it is tempting for the treasury to ask the central bank to purchase the securities. Now the relationship between the treasury and the central bank becomes important.

If the central bank is part of the treasury and does not have the ability to make independent decisions about policy, the central bank doesn't have much choice. In this situation, we say that the central bank lacks independence from the treasury. The central bank is unable to make policy decisions on its own. If the treasury says "buy these securities," the central bank buys them.

At the other end of the spectrum, the central bank may be independent of the treasury in that it is free to follow its own policies, regardless of treasury influence. In this situation, when the treasury requests that the central bank purchase securities, the central bank has the power to refuse.

What's the problem with a central bank not being independent of the treasury, you ask. The problem is that when the central bank purchases the treasury's securities, it creates new money to do so. It's a process that economists call "monetizing the debt," and it can be a dangerous practice when used to excess. Remember that new money can lead to inflation, so a treasury that controls a central bank is likely to rely on the central bank for new money to finance the treasury's borrowing.

All central banks purchase treasury securities to some extent, because it's the way central banks influence the amount of money in circulation. In December 2007, the Federal Reserve owned $780 billion of approximately $9 trillion of outstanding securities issued by the US Treasury, so the Fed owned less than 10 percent of the total. But in countries where the central bank lacks independence from the treasury, the proportion owned by the central bank may increase drastically, to half or two-thirds of the treasury's debt. In these cases, there is a great probability of inflation.

Central bank independence is important because independence frees central bankers from political influence in policy decisions. Politicians tend to like easy money and low interest rates, but you've learned that these are prescriptions for inflation. There are times when it may be necessary for the central bank to adopt a tight money policy, but that tends to be politically unpopular.

Economists have investigated the relationship between the degree of a central bank's independence from the treasury and the rate of inflation in the country. In a famous 1993 study, analysts found that countries with a greater degree of central bank independence experienced lower rates of inflation.

Although central bank independence isn't mentioned as one of the points of the Washington Consensus, independence is one of the factors that influence the rate of inflation. Over time, governments throughout the world are granting central bank independence from their treasuries. For example, in 1997, the Bank of England was given ability to adopt policies independent of the Chancellor of the Exchequer. The Bank of Japan gained independence from the Ministry of Finance in 1998. The Fed was created independent of the Treasury in 1913, although its independence was seriously tested in the 1950s and again in 2009. The trend toward central bank independence is likely to continue. Box 6.9 covers central bank independence in Japan and in the US, where Congress is considering the extent of the Fed's independence.

Box 6.9   Central bank independence

Closely related to the concept of central bank credibility is central bank independence from the government. Central banks of most developed countries are independent of the government in that they are free to make policy decisions without political interference. The global trend has been for governments to grant central banks independence.

Some governments questioned the degree of central bank independence following the financial crisis of 2008. Since then, politicians have threatened the autonomies of the Bank of Korea, the Bank of Japan, the European Central Bank, and the Federal Reserve, among others. The most frequent charge was the central banks did not execute adequate supervision over the financial system.

The danger of political control over central banking is that central bankers will be forced to adopt policies that are politically acceptable rather than policies that are good for the economy even though they are unpopular. For example, governments always prefer low interest rates because governments borrow. But a policy of promoting low interest rates leads to inflation. In Japan, the government over the past decade has opposed even small increases in interest rates proposed by the Bank of Japan.

In the United States, politicians have proposed legislation that would limit the Fed's independence, arguing that the Fed did not regulate the financial system sufficiently. The Fed kept some banks alive because they were too big to fail, but politicians were responsible for the legislation creating large banks and allowing them to conduct nontraditional banking activities. Politicians also created the atmosphere of deregulation.

If you want to see what happens when a central bank loses independence from the government, look at the economy of Zimbabwe.

Sources: "Policy punchbags", *The Economist*, Jan 16, 2010, p. 25; Michiyo Nakamoto, David Turner, "BoJ seen bowing to political pressure", *Financial Times*, Jan 18, 2007, p. 1; "The value of bank independence", *Financial Times*, Aug 3, 2009, p. 6; Henry Kaufman, "The real threat to Fed independence", *Wall Street Journal*, Nov 11, 2009, p. A21; Michael Wines, Zimbabwe's prices rise 900%, turning staples into luxuries, *New York Times*, May 2, 2006, p. A1.

Measuring Central Bank Risk

INFLATION

Measuring success of a central bank is pretty straightforward: look at the rate of inflation. The sure sign of whether the central bank is doing its duty is whether the rate of inflation is low, or at least decreasing. A rate of inflation that is high or is getting worse is a sure sign that the central bank doesn't have control of the situation.

Look at the countries in Table 6.1 and decide which countries improved from 2000 to 2006 and which countries got worse. Inflation declined in Canada, Germany, and the US. Although inflation increased slightly in Japan and China, the levels of inflation in 2006 were not extraordinarily high; it would be hard to fault their central banks. Zimbabwe is a basket case. The President of Zimbabwe, Robert Mugabe, has been quoted as saying that people shouldn't worry about the Government of Zimbabwe running out of money; it can always print more.

Bear in mind that a rate of inflation that looks like an improvement to citizens of one country may look like catastrophe to citizens of another country. For example, when inflation in the United States was extraordinarily high in the early 1980s, the rate was in the neighborhood of 13 percent to 15 percent; those rates were high relative to inflation of 4 percent or 5 percent in previous years. But those same rates of 13 percent to 15 percent inflation would seem like a blessing to citizens of Zimbabwe, where inflation in 2006 exceeded 1,200 percent. So inflation is relative to what you experienced previously.

Table 6.1   Yearly change in consumer price index, selected countries

Country	2000	2006
Canada	3.1%	1.3%
China	0.9%	2.0%
Germany	2.2%	1.4%
Japan	-0.5%	0.3%
United States	3.4%	2.6%
Zimbabwe	55.2%	1,281.1%

Source: International Monetary Fund, World Economic Outlook Database, April 2008.

One difficulty is that measuring inflation is a retroactive measure of the central bank's performance; we're looking backward to see what the rate of inflation was. We would rather have an indicator that will help us evaluate the central bank's policies as they occur.

Because growth of the money supply contributes to inflation, the temptation is to look simply at yearly changes in the money supply. However, one could get the wrong impression by focusing solely on money supply growth because a growing economy needs to have a growing money supply. Therefore, a better measure is to compare growth of the money supply to growth of the economy. If the money supply is growing faster than the economy, there will be pressure for prices to increase. If the money supply is growing slower than the economy, it could retard economic growth.

Which measure of economic growth is appropriate? Our old friend real GDP is a viable candidate because it measures the output of goods and services produced in the economy. Table 6.2 shows growth rates of each indicator for the US from 2000 to 2006. As you see, the money supply grew faster than did real GDP during the period, so we expect moderate inflation in the US.

Developing a relationship between growth rates of real GDP and the money supply is filled with statistical issues, so the table is simply a demonstration. One issue is which measure of the money supply to use: M1, M2, or perhaps another that we haven't discussed. The Fed performs studies about which money supply indicator correlates better with price changes, and M2 appears to be most appropriate in the US. Another issue is the time lag between when a change in the money supply has an effect on either prices or the output of goods and services. Evidence indicates that the economy begins to slow about six months after the Fed tightens monetary conditions, and inflation starts to slow after about a year has passed. A third issue is that money supply data is collected monthly but GDP data is collected quarterly, so it is necessary to adjust for the difference. In other words, deriving a simple statistical relationship isn't nearly as easy as it sounds.

Table 6.2   Comparison of growth rates of money supply to real GDP

	M2 growth	Real GDP growth
2000	6.1	3.7
2001	10.4	.8
2002	6.4	1.6
2003	5.1	2.5
2004	5.8	3.6
2005	4.2	3.1
2006	5.1	2.9
average	6.2	2.6

Source: Economic Report of the President, 2008.

Conclusion

Money performs important functions in an economy, and it is tempting to think that the solution to many problems is simply to inject more money into the economy. Unfortunately, it is not that easy. More money frequently leads to higher inflation, which is not popular with global investors and violates one of the principles of the Washington Consensus.

The quantity of money is the responsibility of a nation's central bank, which can use several policy tools to inject money into or withdraw money from the economy. The policy tools affect the level of interest rates, which in turn affect the amount of borrowing and lending.

One of the policy tools involves purchasing securities. In some situations, the central bank may purchase securities issued by the treasury. If the central bank is not independent of the treasury, there is a greater chance of abuse through issuing more securities that are financed by money creation. The result is higher inflation.

Further Reading

Alesina, A. and L.H. Summers (1993) Central bank independence and macroeconomic performance: Some comparative evidence, *Journal of Money, Credit and Banking*, 25(2), p. 151.

Friedman, M. and A.J. Schwartz (1963) *A Monetary History of the United States*, Princeton: Princeton University Press.

Galbraith, J.K. (1975) *Money*, New York: Houghton Mifflin Company.

Grant, J. (1992) *Money of the Mind*, New York: Farrar Straus Giroux.

Greider, W. (1987) *Secrets of the Temple*, New York: Simon and Schuster.

Meltzer, A.H. (2003) *A History of the Federal Reserve*, Chicago: University of Chicago Press.

Quispe-Agnoli, M. and E. Whisler (2006) Official dollarization and the banking system in Ecuador and El Salvador, *Economic Review*, 91(3), p. 55.

7 *Evaluating International Transactions: The Balance of Payments*

People have traded for thousands of years, and they have traded across borders since countries have existed. However, the practice of recording international transactions from a country perspective is a more recent development. It wasn't until National Income Accounting was developed during the first half of the twentieth century that a systematic approach to organizing and recording domestic and international transactions was created.

The *Balance of Payments (BoP)* is the accounting record of transactions between a country and other countries. As with all accounting systems, judgments must be made about defining terms, classifying transactions, and standardizing results. The International Monetary Fund leads the effort toward standardizing accounting practices for international transactions. The IMF periodically issues guidelines and encourages countries to conform to the guidelines, but because individual countries prepare the raw data, the data are only as reliable as the individuals and governments preparing them.

BoP accounting is an evolutionary process. The standards that apply today are not the standards that applied two decades ago, and they probably will not be the standards that will apply two decades hence. In fact, the IMF proposed standards in the early 1990s that are just now being implemented in each nation's national accounting system, so there is a possibility of overlap and confusion when discussing accounting aspects of the BoP. Fortunately, interpreting the results is not as fluid as the underlying data, so there is some degree of consistency in interpretation. If you'd like to find out more about the concepts, definitions, classifications, and conventions in all their excruciating detail, refer to the IMF manual in the references at the end of this chapter.

As you see in Table 7.1, exports and imports of most countries have increased from 1980 through 2000, reflecting the growth of world trade. Sound economic policy depends on knowing a country's international experience, and a country's BoP position influences the riskiness of investing in a country. Therefore, we need to know how to interpret BoP figures.

Learning Objectives

After studying this chapter, you should be able to:

1. compare and contrast the Current, Financial, and Reserve Accounts;
2. explain the implications of a Current Account surplus or deficit;

3. explain measures of BoP risk;
4. analyze risks facing a country using BoP figures.

Table 7.1 International trade in selected countries, 1980 and 2000

		Exports (X)	Imports (M)	GDP	(X+M)/GDP
United States (billions of US dollars)	1980	279.7	293.8	2,771.5	20.7%
	2000	1,103.8	1,466.9	9,810.2	26.2%
Chile (billions of pesos)	1980	245.4	290.1	1,075.3	49.8%
	2000	12,031.0	11,629.4	37,774.7	62.6%
China (billions of yuan)	1980	34.4	35.6	451.8	15.5%
	2000	2,314.3	2,075.3	8,940.4	49.1%
France (billions of francs)	1980	587.5	657.8	2,882.2	43.2%
	2000	2,640.7	2,510.6	9,214.7	55.9%
Japan (trillions of yen)	1980	32.8	35.0	243.2	27.9%
	2000	55.3	47.9	513.5	20.1%
Nigeria (billions of naira)	1980	14.8	9.6	50.3	48.5%
	2000	2,186.4	1,714.7	4,178.2	93.4%
Singapore (billions of S dollars)	1980	54.0	56.1	25.1	439.0%
	2000	286.1	256.8	159.0	341.4%

Source: World Bank, World Tables, selected years.

The Importance of Reserves

Three hundred years ago, European powers such as France, England, and Spain followed an economic system called *mercantilism*. The objective of mercantilism was to acquire the most gold. The winner of the game was the country with the biggest pile. Countries established colonies that they could exploit, particularly if the colony had natural resources such as gold or silver. The governments would even pay privateers and pirates to raid the ships of other countries in hopes of grabbing a share of the loot.

Mercantilism was long ago discredited as an economic theory, but the concept of increasing a country's pile is a convenient way of thinking about the BoP. The economic activities of a country in the international arena lead to either an increase or decrease in a country's pile, and that's what we will refer to as we discuss the BoP.

Of course, economists have a more sophisticated term than "pile," The correct term is *reserve assets* or *reserves*, which consist of gold, foreign currency, and certain assets at the IMF. Reserves are important because they are assets that can be used to pay for international transactions. Through the processes of international trade and investment, reserves flow into or out of a country.

What causes a country to gain reserves? A country that produces goods or services that it can sell to other countries gets foreign currency in exchange, so its reserves increase. Another way a country gains reserves is when people or businesses from another country invest in it. The foreign business sends money to purchase assets such as stocks or bonds, so the host country's reserves increase.

So here is how the game works. A country gains reserves when it: sells more goods or services to foreign countries than in buys from foreign countries, and follows policies that make it an attractive place for foreigners to invest. Doesn't that last phrase sound like the theme of this book? A country loses reserves when it: buys more on the international market than it sells to the market, and follows policies that make it unattractive as a place to invest. The country's pile of reserves goes up or down depending on how successful it is according to those two dimensions: trade and investment.

It is possible for a country to run out of reserves by pursuing bad policies, so we'll watch for that as a danger signal to help us measure risk. Countries do, in fact, run low on reserves, so a country in that position experiences a crisis. Let's cover the BoP in more detail.

Accounts in the Balance of Payments

Three accounts are necessary to keep track of the Balance of Payments:

1. The *Current Account*, which focuses on trade activities such as exports and imports of goods and services. An *export* is the sale of a good or service produced domestically to someone in a foreign country. Exporting leads to an increase in reserves. An *import* is the purchase of a good or service that was produced in a foreign country. Importing leads to a decrease in reserves.
2. The *Financial Account*, which focuses on investment activities such as purchases and sales of equity and debt securities, plus the means of payment for imports and exports. When someone from a foreign country invests in the host country, it increases the host country's reserves. When someone from the host country invests in a foreign country, it decreases the host country's reserves. Investments can be either *direct investment*, representing a lasting interest in an enterprise, or *portfolio investment*, representing a temporary interest.
3. The *Reserve Account*, which measures the increase or decrease in reserves belonging to the Treasury or Central Bank of a country. Any reserves belonging to the banking system, such as the foreign currency earned from exports or used to pay for imports, is reflected in the Financial Account.

So that's it. As long as you understand the factors that lead to changes in reserves, you can sort them into either the Current or Financial Account. In an ideal world, the Current and Financial Accounts are mirror images of one another because one account records the goods and services while the other records the financial transactions that pay for them. We'll find out later than the world isn't always ideal. The sum of flows in the Current Account plus flows in the Financial Account equals the change in the Reserve Account.

Let's make up an example to see how the accounts interact. Suppose our country exports $110 of goods and $70 of services during the year. At the same time, we import $90 of goods and $80 of services. Citizens and business from our country make $85 direct investments and $40 portfolio investments abroad, and our country attracts $75 in direct investments and $40 in portfolio investments from foreign investors.

Table 7.2 shows one way of displaying the flows from the previous paragraph. Before you look at the table, try it on your own to see what results you obtain.

Did you come up with an addition to reserves of $0? The Current Account led to an increase in reserves of $10, while the Financial Account led to a loss of reserves of $10, so the net change in reserves is $0. Our country generates $10 in extra income by selling to foreigners. We use that extra income to invest in foreign enterprises. One of the luxuries of having a surplus in the Current Account is that you can use the surplus to finance investments in other countries.

Those are the basics of the BoP. If you understand them, you're halfway home. But there is more to the interplay between the accounts. First, notice that our country in Table 7.2 sold more goods and services abroad than we imported from abroad. The Current Account is in *surplus*, meaning exports exceed imports, leading to a net inflow of reserves from trade activities. Second, notice that outflows exceed inflows in the Financial Account. There is a *deficit* in the Financial Account, meaning outflows of reserves exceed inflows of reserves.

Table 7.2   Illustration of Current, Financial and Reserve Accounts

Current Account	Exports of goods	110		
	Imports of goods	90		
	Balance		20	
	Exports of services	70		
	Imports of services	80		
	Balance		-10	
	Current account balance			10
Financial Account	Direct investment inward	75		
	Direct investment abroad	85		
	Balance		-10	
	Portfolio investment inward	40		
	Portfolio investment abroad	40		
	Balance		0	
	Financial account balance			-10
Reserve Account	Net change in reserves			0

Third, notice that the Current and Financial Accounts have opposite signs, indicating that a surplus in the Current Account (a net inflow of reserves) is offset by a deficit in the Financial Account (a net outflow of reserves). This is almost always the case in the BoP except when there are errors somewhere in the system or when a government acquires or disposes of reserves so that the Reserve Account changes. A country losing reserves due to trade activities (which would occur if there was a Current Account deficit) must obtain those reserves from abroad (which would lead to a Financial Account surplus). It's not a hard and fast rule, but things generally work out this way.

Accounting Enters the Picture

If only life were this simple. An unfortunate fact is that the world is never as precise as the example we made up. We need to revise our approach to include two additional possibilities. First, some events may occur that don't fit into the trade or investment accounts. For example, a country might forgive or adjust a debt that a foreign entity owes or an entity might transfer assets to an entity in another country. This is an accounting adjustment that is not caused by a flow of gold or foreign currency. To record these types of transactions, accountants create the *Capital Account*, which is almost always small relative to the Current and Financial Accounts.

The second problem is that accountants are a demanding group. Accounting systems consist of terms such as "debits" and "credits," and in a double entry accounting system, the debits must equal the credits. When recording international transactions, debits seldom equal credits, so accountants create an adjusting account called *Errors and Omissions* to balance the accounts. Sometimes the Errors and Omissions entry is large, and sometimes it is a debit entry while other times it is a credit entry. There's no rule; it's just a matter of making the cheese come out equal with the crackers.

Now look at Table 7.3, which shows the BoP for the US. You'll recognize the Current Account and Financial Account, but you'll also see the Capital Account and Errors and Omissions. If you add the amounts in the accounts for the year 2000, you'll see that they total .30, which should be the increase in reserves: -444.69 +.68 +443.58 +.73 = .30. But the entry in Table 7.3 for Reserves and Related Items is -.30, the opposite sign of what we expect.

The explanation also lies in accounting. When a double entry accounting system is presented in a single entry format, which occurs in Table 7.3, an increase in cash shows up as a negative number. A decrease in cash shows up as a positive number. It's counter-intuitive, but that's the way in turns out when accountants get their hands on the checkers.

The logic behind the BoP identity is the same as the logic behind the corporate accounting identity that Assets plus Equities equal zero. As with any accounting system, there is a relationship between the accounts, known as the Balance of Payments identity:

Current Account + Capital Account + Financial Account + Errors and
Omissions + Reserve Account = 0   (1)

According to Equation (1), the sum of all the accounts must be zero:

CurA + CapA + FinA + ErO + ResA = -444.69 + .68 + 443.58 + .73 – .30 = 0.

But if we move the Reserve Account to the other side of the equation, the result conforms to what we expect:

CurA + CapA + FinA + ErO = – ResA

-444.69 + .68 + 443.58 + .73 = + .30

Now we see that the changes in the other accounts lead to a change in reserves, which seems to be the point of the whole process.

The identity in equation (1) implies that a positive Current Account (exports greater than imports) must lead to a negative Financial Account (investments abroad greater than investments at home) or one of the other adjusting accounts. A negative Current Account (imports greater than exports) must lead to a positive Financial Account (inbound investments greater than outbound investments) or one of the other adjusting accounts. This confirms what we learned earlier about the accounts being mirror images of one another.

In BoP accounting, a credit entry records an inflow, while a debit entry records an outflow. Inflows (credit entries) are given a positive sign, while outflows (debit entries) are given a negative sign. When summing accounts, if inflows exceed outflows the account is said to be in surplus and will have a positive sign. If outflows exceed inflows the account is said to be in deficit and will have a negative sign. In 2000, the US Current Account was $-444.69 billion, indicating that the US lost reserves as a result of trading activities; there was a Current Account deficit. The Financial Account was $443.58 billion, indicating that the US gained reserves as a result of financing activities; there was a Financial Account surplus. This again confirms the reasoning in the simplified example.

To summarize, the BoP is divided into five accounts:

1. The *Current Account*, which focuses mainly on trade activities such as exports and imports of goods and services. A few other activities are included: income received and paid, and current transfers.
2. The *Capital Account*, which records transfers of certain types of assets and accounting adjustments such as forgiveness of debt. The Capital Account is small relative to the Current and Financial Accounts.
3. The *Financial Account*, which focuses on investment activities such as purchases and sales of equity and debt securities, plus the means of payment for the exports and imports from the Current Account.
4. *Errors and Omissions* is an accounting entry whose purpose is to bring the BoP into balance. Otherwise, the debit entries would not equal the credit entries and accountants would have a conniption.
5. The *Reserve Account*, which measures the increase or decrease in official international reserves resulting from the flows in the Current, Capital, and Financial Accounts. Reserves consist of assets that the Central Bank of a country can either retain or use to settle international transactions. Reserves consist primarily of foreign exchange (the currency of another country) and gold, but also of certain accounts in the IMF.

Table 7.3   Balance of Payments, United States, 1999 and 2000

		1999	2000
		(billions of US dollars)	
A.	**Current Account**	**-324.39**	**-444.69**
	Goods, exports f.o.b.	686.86	774.86
	Goods, imports f.o.b.	-1,029.98	-1,224.43
	Balance on Goods	-343.12	-449.57
	Services: credit	270.54	290.88
	Services: debit	-189.27	-217.07
	Balance on Goods and Services	-261.85	-375.76
	Income: credit	285.32	352.90
	Income: debit	-298.94	-367.68
	Balance on Goods, Services, and Income	-275.47	-390.54
	Current transfers: credit	9.27	10.24
	Current transfers: debit	-58.19	-64.39
B.	**Capital Account**	**-3.50**	**.68**
	Capital account: credit	.49	.68
	Capital account: debit	-3.99	...
	Total, Groups A Plus B	-327.89	-444.01
C.	**Financial Account**	**367.93**	**443.58**
	Direct investment abroad	-155.41	-152.44
	Direct investment in United States	301.02	287.68
	Portfolio investment assets	-131.22	-124.94
	Equity securities	-114.39	-99.74
	Debt securities	-16.83	-25.20
	Portfolio investment liabilities	354.75	474.59
	Equity securities	112.34	193.85
	Debt securities	242.41	280.74
	Financial derivatives	...	...
	Other investment assets	-159.23	-303.27
	Monetary authorities	...	...
	General government	2.75	-.94
	Banks	-76.27	-138.49
	Other sectors	-85.71	-163.84
	Other investment liabilities	158.01	261.96
	Monetary authorities	24.59	-6.80
	General government	-.97	-.55
	Banks	67.19	93.75
	Other sectors	67.19	175.56
	Total, Groups A Through C	40.03	-.43
D.	**Net Errors and Omissions**	**-48.77**	**.73**
	Total, Groups A Through D	-8.73	.30
E.	**Reserves and Related Items**	**8.73**	**-.30**
	Reserve assets	8.73	0.30
	Use of Fund credit and loans	...	...
	Exceptional financing	...	...

Source: International Monetary Fund, Balance of Payments Statistics Yearbook, 2001; p. 944.

CURRENT ACCOUNT

We can examine the Current Account in more detail to discover the reason for the deficit. First, look at exports and imports. The US exported $774.86 billion of goods to other countries, but imported $1,224.43 billion of goods from other countries. *Goods* are physical items such as steel, computers, aircraft, and cherries. Sometime you may see a reference to these items as merchandise, referring to the physical nature of the product. In 2000, the US had a Balance on Goods or *merchandise balance* deficit of $-449.57 billion, leading to a loss of US reserves.

During the same period, the US exported $290.88 billion of services to other countries, but imported $217.07 billion of services from other countries. *Services* are activities such as engineering, shipping, tourism, and banking. The US had a surplus in the services account equal to $73.81 billion, indicating a net flow of reserves into the US due to services transactions. When exports and imports of goods and services are added together, the result is the Balance on Goods and Services, or the *balance of trade*. The US had a balance of trade deficit of $-375.76 billion, indicating that the US lost reserves as a result of trading activities with the rest of the world.

Income is the amount received or paid as earnings on investments between countries and the amount paid to citizens of one country working in another country. US individuals and businesses that previously invested abroad earn interest or dividend income from their investments. US citizens who work abroad also earn income. Because the income earned for either purpose leads to an increase in US reserves, they are listed as a credit entry. In 2000, US citizens working abroad and US investors earned a total of $352.90 billion. At the same time, foreign businesses and individuals who previously invested in the US earn income on their investments, and foreign citizens working in the US earn incomes. Because the income paid to foreign workers and investors leads to a decrease in US reserves, this amount is listed as a debit entry. In 2000, the US paid $367.68 billion to foreign workers and investors as income for their investments in the US. The running total, the Balance on Goods, Services, and Income is $-390.54, indicating that reserves flowed out of the US.

Notice that income represents only the earnings on investments. It does not represent the investment itself. Investments between countries are recorded in the Financial Account, but earnings on the investments are recorded in the Current Account. Both activities must be recorded, but they are recorded in different accounts.

One other item appears in the Current Account: *Current Transfers*. Sometimes individuals, businesses, or governments of one country send cash or in-kind services to other countries as gifts. For example, the US Government has foreign aid programs; nongovernmental organizations (NGOs) such as the Red Cross, the Ford Foundation, or the Bill and Melinda Gates Foundation make grants to overseas entities; individuals working in the US send a portion of their earnings to support families in another country. All of these activities are recorded under Current Transfers.

Table 7.3 shows that $10.24 billion flowed into the US, while $-64.39 billion flowed out due to Current Transfers in 2000. Although Current Transfers are minor in the US compared to other entries in the Current Account, this is not necessarily true for other countries, particularly less developed countries. Workers from many countries come to the US and send a portion of their earnings home. These workers' remittances can be an important source of US dollars for the foreign country, representing foreign exchange that can be used to purchase imports from other countries. Box 7.1 discusses the importance of workers' remittances to the world economy.

Box 7.1   Importance of worker's remittances

In the 1970s, the President of the Philippines encouraged Filipino workers to work abroad. By 2006, one in every ten Filipino workers worked abroad, and they sent home more than $17 billion in 2009, accounting for more than 12 percent of the country's GDP. Almost half of the remittances sent to the Philippines originate in the United States.

In fact, workers' remittances play an important role throughout the world. Spain attracts laborers from Africa; Russia attracts workers from Armenia and Tajikistan; and the Persian Gulf countries import workers from South Asia. The exchange benefits both directions. Host countries benefit from the services performed by foreign workers, and the foreign countries benefit because workers send home a significant portion of their earnings.

In dollar terms, the three countries receiving the most money from workers abroad are India, China, and Mexico. However, these countries are large, so remittances account for less than 3 percent of GDP for all of those countries. Remittances make up a much larger proportion of GDP in smaller countries. For example, remittances constituted more than 20 percent of GDP for Jamaica, Jordan, Lebanon, and a few other countries in 2007.

Remittances to developing countries worldwide totaled $301 billion in 2006, which exceeded the amounts that the countries received from foreign aid ($104 billion) and even from foreign direct investment ($167 billion). Remittances were almost seven times the level of 1990, a mere 16 years earlier. Even the labor force is becoming globalized.

Sources: Richard C. Paddock, "Overseas workers are lifeline for poor Filipinos", *Orlando Sentinel*, Apr 20, 2006, p. A12; "Trickle-down economics", *The Economist*, Feb 21, 2009, p. 76; "Migrant worker blues", *Business Asia*, Jan 12, 2009, p. 4; Susan Ferriss, "Foreign workers worldwide send billions home", *McClatchy-Tribune Business News*, Nov 25, 2007; Richard Lapper, "Globalization exiles keep the home fires burning", *Financial Times*, Aug 28, 2007, p. 7.

The sum of all the flows reveals a Current Account deficit of $-444.69 billion, indicating that the US lost that amount of reserves to the rest of the world as a result of trading goods and services, income flows and Current Transfers. This is the amount that must be financed by activities in the Financial Account.

CAPITAL ACCOUNT

The Capital Account records mainly accounting adjustments such as debt forgiveness, and transfers of certain assets. Look in the IMF's *Balance of Payments Manual* for a more complete discussion of the Capital Account if you need to know. Table 7.3 shows that $.68 billion of reserves flowed into the US as a result of activities recorded in the Capital Account.

FINANCIAL ACCOUNT

Citizens and businesses have invested in other countries for years. Sometimes the investments take the form of physical investments, such as erecting facilities for manufacturing or distributing products. Other times, investments take the form of securities issued by governments or businesses: government bonds, corporate bonds, and stocks. In addition, all the goods and services recorded in the Current Account have to be paid for; the means of payment are recorded in the Financial Account. The Financial Account in Table 7.3 shows that the United States gained $443.58 billion of reserves from investing activities in 2000. What were the sources of these funds?

Direct investment (sometimes called *Foreign Direct Investment*, or *FDI*) represents ownership of businesses in another country, so this account records investments primarily in corporate stocks. The result of the investment may be a new physical facility or it may be a change in ownership of an existing company. The key issue is ownership. In 2000, businesses and individuals from the US invested in other countries, leading to an outflow of reserves of $-152.44 billion. During the same period, businesses and individuals outside the US invested in the US, leading to inflow of reserves of $287.68 billion.

Portfolio investment is investment in stocks or bonds. The difference is that portfolio investment is not for the purpose of acquiring controlling interest in a firm. The bonds may be issued by corporations or by governments, such as the US Government. Portfolio Investment Assets are US investments abroad, while Portfolio Investment Liabilities are foreign investments in the US. In 2000, the US invested an additional $-124.94 in foreign assets. During the same period, businesses and individuals outside the US invested an additional $474.59 billion in US assets.

Other investment includes short-term assets and liabilities such as loans, accounts receivable and payable, trade credits, bank deposits, and foreign currency. The vast majority of these are the means of payment for the goods and services that were recorded in the Current Account. The Other Investment account includes short-term methods of financing, whereas direct investment and portfolio investment include long-term methods of financing. Other investment assets show that the US lent an additional $-303.27 billion abroad, while Other investment liabilities show that foreigners lent an additional $262.96 billion to the US.

NET ERRORS AND OMISSIONS

As with other accounting systems, the BoP is a double entry system. At the end of the accounting period, the debits should equal the credits. However, in international trade this seldom happens. One reason is that the numbers in the various accounts come from different raw data. For example, in the US, exports and imports are reported through customs documents but means of payment flow through the banking system. An account termed *Errors and Omissions* adjusts for the imbalance between debits and credits at the end of the accounting period. At times the discrepancy may be substantial, such as in 1997 when balancing the accounts required a debit entry of $-132.01 billion, or in 1998 when balancing required a credit entry of $71.84 billion. In 1999, balancing required a debit entry of $-48.77; in 2000, the amount was a credit entry of only $0.73 billion – enough for you and me to live on, but a minor amount compared to other BoP accounts.

RESERVES AND RELATED ITEMS

In the IMF's presentation, the *Reserve Account* records the change in the amount of gold and foreign exchange held by the country's central bank, and the country's position in the IMF (its contribution to capital and any access to the Fund's borrowing).

An increase in the Reserve Account will have a negative sign because of the presentation of a double entry accounting system in a single entry format. In 2000, $.30 billion of reserves was added to the accounts of the US Federal Reserve, although this appears in the IMF statements as $-0.30 billion.

That's a lot of accounting detail, and perhaps more than you wanted to know. By now you should be able to make sense from reading articles about the BoP in business periodicals. Box 7.2 describes China's reserve position and what it does with the foreign exchange.

Box 7.2   China's reserve position

China accumulates foreign reserves at a rapid rate. Foreign reserves increased more than $453 billion in 2009, to a total of $2.4 trillion, the largest in the world. The reserves result mostly from China's trade surplus and from inbound foreign direct investment. Funds from these activities are deposited in commercial banks. The central bank then requires that a portion of those funds be deposited with it, so the funds end up as official reserves.

However, Chinese authorities think that another source of the inflow may be from speculators betting that China will allow its currency to appreciate. If that happens, investors owning Chinese assets will be able to sell their investment for more of the foreign currency. Speculators are purchasing stocks and bonds in China, creating the potential for a speculative bubble. The risk facing China is that the speculators can liquidate their investments quickly if they become spooked by events or lose confidence in the country. Investments of this type have earned the name "hot money" because it seeks the highest return around the globe.

One problem facing Chinese authorities is what to do with the $2.4 trillion reserves. For many years, the Government purchased securities issued by the United States Treasury. While these securities are safe, they provide a low return to investors.

In 2007, the Chinese Government invested in a United States-based private equity firm, Blackstone Group, which in turn invests in businesses and securities in the United States. Analysts believe that the Government did this in part to earn higher returns on its investments. Since then, the Government has purchased minority interests in other institutions.

Another reason that China invested in Blackstone is an attempt to deflect criticism that might arise due to China purchasing United States companies. China previously faced negative public reaction when it tried in 2005 to invest in a large United States oil company, Unocal. Owning a minority interest in Blackstone allows China to acquire United States assets without the negative publicity.

Sources: Jamil Anderlini, "China's foreign reserves increase sharply", *Financial Times*, Jan 16, 2010, p. 7; Richard McGregor, "Capital influx pushes China's foreign reserves past $2,000bn", *Financial Times*, Jul 16, 2009, p. 1; Kate Linebaugh, Henny Sender, Andrew Batson, "China puts cash to work in deal with Blackstone", *Wall Street Journal*, May 21, 2007, p. A1; "Bogus fears send the Chinese packing", *Economist.com*, Sep 6, 2005, p. 1.

Balance of Payments as Flows

The BoP statement is based on flows rather than stocks, so all of the amounts shown in Table 7.3 are changes that occur during the year. Exports and imports are a country's sales and purchase of goods and services during a year, a flow concept. The Financial Account shows how much new investment from the US flowed overseas during a year, or how much new investment from overseas flowed into the US, two more flow concepts.

The Financial Account does not show the total accumulated amount of investments that US individuals and businesses own overseas or that foreign individuals and businesses own in the US. These are stock concepts. For example, at the end of 2000, accumulated US investments abroad totaled about $6.2 trillion, as shown in Table 7.4. At the same time, total foreign investment in the US was more than $7.5 trillion. The US was a net debtor to the rest of the world in the amount of $1.3 trillion.

The table also shows that the US owned official reserves of $128.4 billion at the end of 2000. These were about one-ninth of the reserves owned by China in 2000.

Table 7.4   US international investment position, end-of-year 2000

	2000 (Billions of US dollars)
Assets:	6,238.79
Direct investment abroad	1,531.61
Portfolio investment	2,425.53
Other investment	2,153.25
Reserve assets	128.40
Liabilities:	7,569.42
Direct investment in US	1,421.02
Portfolio investment	4,035.35
Other investment	2,113.05
Net international investment position	-1,330.63

Source: Bureau of Economic Analysis, International Investment Position.

Economic Implications of the Balance of Payment Figures

The explanations up to now have been accounting: in which boxes should items be placed and how do the numbers add up? But what does it all mean? What are the implications for a country that has a deficit in the Current Account? Where do businesses and consumers in a country get the financial ability to purchase imports?

One way to think about the Current Account is to consider it in the same terms one would think of a business. Businesses purchase raw materials and labor services, then sell final products. The selling of the final product generates the cash flow that allows the business to hire labor and purchase raw materials. Parallel reasoning for a nation is to think of exports as equivalent to sales by a business. Exports generate incomes for a nation as workers produce the goods and services for export. In fact, the income for a nation can be described as the sum of income generated through domestic sales plus income generated through foreign sales, which are exports:

National income = domestic income + exports

Imports are the opposite – they represent the portion of a nation's income that is spent on products and services of other countries. A nation's total spending can be described as the sum of domestic spending plus spending for foreign goods and services, which are imports:

National spending = domestic spending + imports

In National Income Accounting, the domestic portions of each equation are equivalent because domestic spending creates domestic income. Therefore, when we combine the two equations we are left with:

National income – National spending = exports – imports (2)

This means that when a country exports more than it imports (it has a Current Account surplus), it earns more income than it spends as a nation. The extra income the nation earns can be invested abroad, which will be reflected in the Financial Account.

On the other hand, when a nation imports more than it exports (it has a Current Account deficit), it spends more than it generates in income as a nation. The extra spending must be financed somehow. The spending may be financed through borrowing, such as when the US Treasury sells securities that are purchased by insurance companies in Japan or the central bank in China. The spending also may take the form of selling a nation's assets, such as when Germany's Daimler Benz purchases Chrysler Corp. or China's Lenovo purchases IBM.

This is the danger of a Current Account deficit: a nation is at the mercy of foreign investors. If something happens to cause foreign investors to lose confidence in the nation, they stop lending to it or investing in it. This means that the nation doesn't obtain financing for all the spending it wants to do. A country that runs a persistent Current Account deficit is at the mercy of global investors.

Economic theory textbooks frequently present the income/spending equation in an alternative format focusing on the relationship between saving and investment:

Saving – investment = exports – imports (3)

A country that is a net exporter also is a net saver, sending capital to the rest of the world. Whether the focus is on income/spending or on saving/investment, a country with a Current Account surplus sends capital outside the country.

Is it possible for a country to run out of reserves? Yes. Countries sometimes run persistent BoP deficits, don't have reserves on which to draw, and do not attract reserves through investment. In this situation, the country finds that it does not generate foreign exchange sufficient to purchase imports, so it is unable to conduct international transactions. Crises such as this occurred in Mexico in 1994–1995, in many Asian countries in 1997–1998, and in Argentina in 2002.

International authorities created the IMF at Bretton Woods to help countries experiencing BoP problems. A country experiencing a BoP crisis can borrow reserves from the IMF. The IMF lends at interest and expects to be repaid. The loan comes with conditions to help assure a country's ability to repay the loan.

Measuring Balance of Payment Risk

CURRENT ACCOUNT RATIO

The broadest and most frequently used measure of BoP risk is the *Current Account ratio*: the Current Account surplus or deficit as a percentage of the country's GDP. In 2000, the US Current Account deficit in Table 7.3 is $-444.69 billion. US GDP for the same year was $9,817.0 billion, so the ratio is:

$$Current \ \ account \ \ ratio = \frac{Current \ \ Account \ \ surplus \ (deficit \ )}{GDP} = \frac{-444.69}{9,817.0} = -4.5\%$$

There is no magic number representing a "bad" or "good" ratio, although investors may begin to sweat when the ratio deteriorates beyond -5.0 percent. Investors generally prefer a positive number, indicating a Current Account surplus, but every country can't have a Current Account surplus. If there is a deficit, investors prefer to see the ratio improving, which means it should be approaching zero. Box 7.3 discusses implications of the Current Account deficit in the US.

Let's have a quiz. Before looking at Table 7.5, cover the names of the countries so you're looking only at the numbers for Current Account surplus or deficit. Then decide which countries fit these descriptions:

- three countries experienced financial crises within a year after the last period of data;
- one country is a large supplier of financing to other countries.

Table 7.5   Current account surplus (deficit) as percent of GDP for selected countries, 2002–2006

	2002	2003	2004	2005	2006
China	2.4	2.8	3.6	7.2	9.5
Hungary	-7.0	-7.9	-8.4	-7.5	-7.5
Iceland	1.6	-4.8	-9.8	-16.1	-25.3
India	1.4	1.5	0.1	-1.3	-1.1
Thailand	3.7	3.4	1.7	-4.3	1.1
United States	-4.3	-4.7	-5.3	-5.9	-6.0

Source: International Monetary Fund, World Economic Outlook Database, October 2009.

Box 7.3 The United States Current Account

The United States has run a deficit in the Current Account every year but three since 1977. According to *The Economist*, "Americans spent some $857 billion more than they produced in 2006, the equivalent of 6.5 percent of GDP, a new record." Two issues that have intrigued economists are: 1) Where does the United States get the money that enables it to spend more than it earns, and 2) Can the United States continue to spend more than it earns?

The first question is easier to answer than the second. Countries that are net savers provide funds to the United States, which is a net borrower. During the 2000s, developing countries – led by China, Russia, and India – have provided a larger share of the pool of savings. To most economists, the surprising feature is that funds are flowing from poorer countries to richer countries such as the United States. For example, China, Russia, and India have per capita incomes that are less than one-twentieth of United States incomes, yet they are subsidizing the United States buying habit.

Until recently, economic theory argued that a country couldn't continue to spend more than it earns, so the answer to the second question should be "No." In fact, the United States violates two economic principles by running persistent Current Account deficits accompanied by persistent government budget deficits. According to theory, the United States eventually will have to reduce borrowing from abroad and lower its standard of living.

For two alternative explanations of why traditional economic theory may not apply, see these articles, both of which are available online: Dooley, M., D. Folkerts-Landau, P. Garber (2003) "An essay on the revived Bretton Woods System", NBER Working Paper 9971, http://www.econ.puc-rio.br/gfranco/Dooley_Landay_Garber_Bretton%20Woods.pdf; Bernanke, B. (2005) "The global savings glut and the US Current Account deficit", http://www.federalreserve.gov/boarddocs/speeches/2005/200503102/default.htm.

In a prescient article, *The Economist* argued that the United States Current Account deficit was "excessive and dangerous. Left alone, it could end in a global recession, rampant protectionism, and even a disastrous financial crash." The article appeared in 2005, about two years before the global recession and financial crisis led governments to adopt protectionist policies to ensure economic survival.

Sources: "Sustaining the unsustainable", *The Economist*, Mar 17, 2007, p. 79; Michael Kouparitsas, "Is the US Current Account deficit sustainable?", *Chicago Fed Letter* #215, Jun 2005; Eduardo Porter, "Another drink? Sure, China is paying", *New York Times*, Jun 5, 2005, p. 3; "Rebalancing act", *The Economist*, Sep 24, 2005, p. 27.

How did you do on the quiz? The three countries that experienced financial crises are Hungary, Iceland, and US. The country that is a big supplier of financing is China. In these examples, it should be easy for you to spot the problems. It's never that easy in reality, as you probably guessed.

As with any general ratio, there are hidden dangers in the Current Account ratio. One is that it ignores the issue of what goods or services were imported. If imports were consumer goods to satisfy the appetites of a greedy populace wishing to consume today and tomorrow be damned, that's a bad sign. But if imports were capital goods such as machinery or technology that promote improvements in the nation's production capacity, that's a good sign. To find the answer to that question requires examining the trade accounts in more detail, and the information frequently is difficult to find.

Another consideration is the economy of the nation running the deficit. Developed countries such as the US, the UK, or Germany have diversified economies compared to less developed countries such as Thailand, Ghana, or Turkmenistan. Developed countries have more developed capital markets, allowing investors to spread the risk of investing. Developed countries also don't rely heavily on any one import or export, so are not as vulnerable to a shock to the economy from changes in price or availability of the import or export. Therefore, a Current Account deficit doesn't have the same implications for a developed country that it has for a less developed country.

Still another issue is the return investors earn in a country compared to the risk of investing in the country. The US is known for the safety of US Treasury securities, so investors from around the world may have a greater tolerance for supplying capital to the US even when it runs Current Account deficits. After allowing for risk, the US may be a safer place to invest than other countries, even when the US Current Account is in deficit. The US frequently is a "safe haven" because whenever there is a crisis around the world, investors park their money in the US.

DEBT SERVICE RATIO

A more informative ratio, the *debt service ratio*, compares the country's debt service to its exports of goods and services. Debt service consists of the principal and interest payments that the country makes on its external debt: the money it owes to nonresidents and is payable in a foreign currency. For many countries with external debt, the country has borrowed from the IMF or the World Bank.

Interest is the cost of borrowing money. Principal is the portion of the original loan that is required to be repaid during the period. Figures for debt service sometimes are difficult to find, but they usually are available through the WB, and they may be available through the home page of a country's treasury or central bank.

Where does a country obtain the foreign exchange reserves needed to repay interest and principal? From the foreign exchange it generates through exports of its goods and services. The debt service ratio is stated as debt service divided by exports of goods and services, so a lower number indicates that a country does not have much debt service relative to its ability to generate the means of payment. A ratio greater than 100 indicates that a country paid more in interest and principal than it generated through export sales.

Here is the debt service ratio for Argentina in 2000:

$$Debt\ service\ ratio = \frac{debt\ service}{exports\ of\ goods\ and\ services} = \frac{27.3}{26.4} = 103.4$$

Other things being equal, investors would begin to shy away from Argentina due to the perceived lack of ability to service its debt. As a matter of fact, Argentina defaulted on its foreign debt the next year.

Table 7.6 shows debt service ratios for several countries in 2007. The low debt service ratios reflect the improved financial positions of most indebted countries as the decade progressed. Exports grew as countries grew, but many countries reduced their external debt.

Table 7.6   External debt and debt service ratios for selected countries, 2007

	External debt (billions of US$)	Debt service ratio (%)
Argentina	128	13.0
Brazil	237	27.8
China	374	2.2
India*	123	13.2
Indonesia	141	10.5

Note: * Data for India is from 2005.

Source: World Bank, Country Profiles.

Managing the Balance of Payments

IMPLICATIONS OF A CURRENT ACCOUNT DEFICIT

Economic theory is unambiguous about the consequences for a country that runs a persistent Current Account deficit. The Current Account deficit will create pressure for the country's currency to depreciate in the world currency markets. What happens next depends on the country's policy toward its currency.

1. If the country has a policy of letting its currency *float* on the currency markets, the persistent Current Account deficit will cause the country's currency to depreciate relative to the currencies of its trading partners. This happens because currency traders end up with more of the country's currency relative to other currencies (remember, the country is buying more goods and services than it is selling). Traders begin to bid down the value of the country's currency, causing it to depreciate. The depreciation eventually causes exports to be less expensive on world markets and imports to be more expensive in the country. Therefore, over time other countries will purchase more exports and domestic residents will purchase fewer imports, causing the Current Account deficit to improve. Thus, the international currency markets act as an automatic adjustment mechanism that prevents countries from running persistent Current Account deficits, as long as nothing interferes with the mechanism's operation.
2. If the country has a policy of trying to *fix* or peg the value of its currency relative to the currency of another country, the persistent Current Account deficit will cause the country eventually to run out of reserves. As before, traders will exert downward pressure on a country's currency by trying to sell it. The only way to offset this pressure

is for the country's central bank to intervene in currency markets by purchasing its currency. This upward pressure on value offsets the downward pressure resulting from the Current Account deficit. Where does the central bank get the money to purchase its currency? It uses accumulated reserves of foreign currencies. However, a country can only play this game for a limited time before the central bank runs out of reserves. When it does, the country is no longer able to conduct international transactions such as purchasing imports or making debt service payments in foreign currencies.

The other thing a country can do in a pegged system is to raise interest rates in an effort to attract foreign investors. As with intervention in the currency markets, higher interest rates have the effect of increasing the price of the country's currency, which offsets the pressure toward depreciation caused by the Current Account deficit. Unfortunately, higher interest rates have the effect of slowing down the economy, so are unpopular with domestic consumers and businesses.

The point of both these examples is that a country cannot run a persistent Current Account deficit without bearing the consequences. Either currency markets will cause the country's currency to depreciate or the country will exhaust its ability to conduct global transactions.

Between these two poles of floating or fixed currencies, the world is filled with countries trying to manage the BoP to achieve some national objective. Let's examine ways to influence some of the underlying variables.

Exports depend on the demand in other countries for your country's products and services. It is difficult to influence foreign demand, at least in the short run. Producers can lower prices, which will cause prices of exports to decline relative to prices in the other countries. Beyond that, demand depends on incomes and economic growth in the other country, on marketing, on tastes for your country's goods and services, and on barriers to trade. Sometimes exports are a matter of negotiation between countries, as when the US tries to gain access to the Japanese market or when the US negotiates voluntary imports of Japanese automobiles. Box 7.4 describes some of the drivers of exports.

Imports are different. Imports depend on the demand for foreign-produced goods and services in the local economy. A country can reduce the demand for imports by using any of the tools to contract the domestic economy: increasing taxes, decreasing government spending, running a tight monetary policy. Unfortunately, these tools don't work only against imports; they curtail demand for all goods and services, including those produced domestically. Consequently, taking steps to slow imports may have undesirable consequences for the domestic economy.

TRADE RESTRICTIONS

Countries occasionally attempt to restrict imports through other means. A *tariff* is a tax on imported goods or services that raises their prices relative to prices of domestic goods. Higher prices cause consumers to purchase fewer of the imported products relative to domestic products, so that imports decline.

A *quota* is a limit on the quantity of a product that can be brought in from another country. Because of the limited quantity, prices of the imported goods increase relative to domestic goods, causing consumers to purchase fewer imports. Box 7.5 describes two interesting examples of tariffs and quotas that took place recently in Europe.

Box 7.4   What drives exports?

Because the United States economy is the world's largest and because it is a net importer, United States growth frequently drives world economic growth. But when the United States slows down, it must count on demand from other countries to stimulate United States exports. Such was the case in 2005 and 2006.

In 2005, the United States economy performed better than did the economies of most of its trade partners. Although growth in Asia continued, most Asian countries are not big markets for United States exports. Canada and Mexico account for more than 30 percent of United States exports. Europe and Japan account for another 20 percent. Growth of those four areas was expected to increase in 2006, which would stimulate United States exports.

By 2009, China overtook Germany as the world's largest merchandise exporter. The world recession of 2008 and 2009 affected German exports more than Chinese exports. Although exports from both countries declined in 2009, German exports declined more than 25 percent, compared to a 20 percent decline in Chinese exports. China's exports had been growing more than 20 percent per year for the previous decade.

One official at BGA, the German Chamber of Industry and Commerce, said that China represented a good market for German goods. "Our biggest competitor is also our most dynamic customer." China imports high-tech machinery from Germany, then uses the machinery to produce manufactures for export.

Sources: James C. Cooper, "The export engine is shifting into high gear", *Business Week*, Jan 16, 2006, p. 23; John W. Miller, Marcus Walker, "China dethrones Germany as top goods exporter", *Wall Street Journal*, Jan 6, 2010, p. A6; Ralph Atkins, "China to overtake Germany as biggest exporter", *Financial Times*, Jan 9, 2010, p. 6.

One of the objectives of the World Trade Organization is to decrease the use of trade restrictions such as tariffs and quotas globally. In fact, tariffs on industrial goods have fallen from an average of 40 percent in 1945 to an average of 4 percent in 1995.

MANAGING THE CLIMATE FOR INVESTING

Policy makers also can manage the Financial Account. If a country finds that it needs to attract capital, officials can take steps to make the investing climate more attractive. In the short run, they can increase domestic interest rates to encourage global investors to invest in the country. However, this has the negative side effect of slowing the domestic economy, so even though it is attracting capital, the country may suffer the consequences of tight money. In the long run, policy makers can take other steps such as adopting the principles of the Washington Consensus: relaxing restrictions on the outflow of capital, allowing increased foreign ownership, improving the legal environment, and fostering private property rights.

A mechanism used frequently for adjusting Current Account imbalances is to change the value of a country's currency. To encourage exports, policy makers will take steps to depreciate a country's currency. A depreciated currency causes world prices of exports to decline relative to competing products, so consumers worldwide purchase more of the

---

Box 7.5   Two tales of tariffs and quotas

Countries frequently are accused of "dumping," a practice of selling exported goods at artificially low prices in an effort to gain market share or get rid of surplus production. Two responses to alleged dumping occurred in Europe in 2005.

Shoe tariffs

The EU accused China and Vietnam of dumping shoes in the European market. Most of the shoes produced in China and Vietnam are low quality and low cost, but keeping them off the market would stimulate demand for European-produced shoes of higher quality and cost. In 2005, the EU trade commissioner announced tariffs of 19.4 percent on shoes imported from China 16.8 percent on shoes from Vietnam.

At the same time, the trade commissioner accused European retailers of failing to lower retail prices on low-cost goods manufactured in Asia. He indicated that the tariff would lead to higher costs for retailers, but he expected retailers to absorb the costs rather than pass them forward to consumers.

Sources: James Kanter, "Europe to phase in shoe tariffs", *New York Times*, Feb 24, 2006, p. C4; Alan Beattie, "India and EU buck dumping duties trend", *Financial Times*, Nov 23, 2006, p. 10.

Bra wars

In January 2005, a quota on textiles imported into the EU expired. Over the next few months, the volume of textiles imported from Asia increased 500 percent compared to the previous year. EU countries that produced large volumes of textiles, such as Italy, Spain, and Portugal, complained about the flood of cheap imports from China. In response, the European trade commissioner halted further imports from China, which froze three million bras and tons of other clothing in the warehouses and on ships at European ports.

Many European retailers complained that they could not obtain products for sale. They were joined with complaints by countries such as Sweden, Denmark, and Germany that were finished textile importers. The resulting dispute between the two sides – retailers and textile importers versus manufacturers and textile producers – became known as "bra wars."

The dispute was settled after several weeks when China and the EU reached a new quota agreement that allowed more imports of Chinese textiles than the previous quota allowed.

Sources: "Bra wars: The background", *Promotions and Incentives*, Oct 2005, p. 27; Charlotte Edwardes, Peter Goff, "EU import ban leaves High Street clothing stores facing 'biggest crisis since the war'", *Telegraph.co.uk*, Aug 21, 2005; George Parker, John Thornhill, "Europe and China reach deal to end 'bra wars' dispute", *Financial Times*, Sep 8, 2005, p. 10.

---

country's exports. Of course, a depreciated currency has the opposite effect on imports: goods and services from other countries become more expensive, so the volume of imports declines. The question of whether the policy makers want to please importers or exporters usually is a political issue, resolved the way most political issues are resolved.

In the days before markets determined currency values, governments set them. Officials frequently tried to promote domestic manufactures on world markets by devaluing the country's currency. Of course, when one country devalued, its trading partners would lose their competitive positions, so would devalue their own currencies in response. The result was a round of competitive devaluations that adversely impacted world trade and exacerbated the Great Depression of the 1930s.

Confidence, Again

In the chapter on monetary policy, we discussed what happens when people lose confidence in a nation's central bank; they begin to bail out of the financial system. A similar result happens when global investors lose confidence in a country: they bail out.

Box 7.6   The US dollar as a reserve currency

Treasuries and central banks frequently purchase foreign currencies or securities issued in foreign currencies to hold as assets. The major foreign currency held for this purpose early in the twenty-first century is the US dollar, which accounts for approximately 65 percent of all the world's currency reserves. The questions are: 1) How much longer will foreigners be willing to hold US dollars as a reserve, and 2) Which currencies will replace the US dollar as a reserve currency?

In a historical context, the dollar's term as the world's premier currency can be viewed as part of a cycle. Going back to the 1400s, Portugal's currency was the world's major currency for about 80 years, followed by Spain's for about 110 years, Holland's for 80 years, France's for 95 years, and England's for 115 years. The US dollar became the leading currency in about 1920, so by 2010 it has been in that position for 90 years and likely is approaching the end of its cycle.

The real determinants of a reserve currency are the country's underlying economic and political situations, confidence in the country, and the ability of the currency to hold value. Because of its continuing Current Account deficit and its position as an international debtor, the United States faces questions about its economic prowess. The recent United States financial crisis created further doubt about the United States economy. However, the major shift has been in the dollar's ability to retain value; since the 1960s, the dollar has fallen by about two-thirds compared to the German deutschemark/euro and the Japanese yen. Investors don't like to hold assets that depreciate in value.

Many authorities believe that the US dollar will continue to be a reserve currency for many years, but it will share the role with the euro and the Chinese yuan. In 2007, the United States accounted for about 20 percent of world GDP; the eurozone accounted for almost 15 percent, and China accounted for slightly more than 15 percent. The United States is no longer in a dominant position in the world economy.

Sources: Philip Thornton, Allister Heath, "Passing the Buck", *The Business*, Nov 17, 2007, p. 1; "The passing of the buck?", *The Economist*, Dec 4, 2004, p. 71; "Losing faith in the greenback", *The Economist*, Dec 1, 2007, p. 85; Benjamin J. Cohen, "The future of reserve currencies", *Finance and Development*, Sep 2009, p. 26.

Investors do this by liquidating investments in the country, from the stock market to plant and equipment. They also do this by dumping a country's currency: they sell it on the currency market and purchase currency of a country in which they have more confidence.

Earlier in this chapter we mentioned that central banks keep reserves consisting of gold, foreign currencies, and positions in the IMF. At the turn of the twenty-first century, the foreign currency that was the most widely held as a reserve was the US dollar. But foreign governments and central banks are beginning to reduce their holdings of dollars in favor of other currencies, particularly the euro and the Chinese yuan. This is a natural technique for them to diversify their portfolio of currencies, but it also is an indication that foreign governments and central banks are losing confidence in the dollar. Box 7.6 discusses the dollar's future as a reserve currency.

Conclusion

Countries don't operate by themselves; they are part of a global environment, so it is necessary to measure economic interactions between countries. The Balance of Payments consists of two primary accounts – the Current Account and the Financial Account – that measure trade and investment transactions between countries. Countries either gain or lose reserves through trade and investment activities, and a country can experience a financial crisis when it runs out of reserves.

Further Reading

Dornbusch, R. and S. Fischer (1984) *Macroeconomics*, New York: McGraw-Hill.

Farrell, D. and S. Lund (2007) What businesses need to know about the US current-account deficit, *The McKinsey Quarterly*.

Federal Reserve Bank of St. Louis (2000) Accounting and the economics of the trade deficit, *International Economic Trends*, Feb., p. 1.

Federal Reserve Bank of St. Louis (2004) Considering the capital account, *International Economic Trends*, Nov., p. 1.

International Monetary Fund (1993) *Balance of Payments Manual*, http://www.imf.org/external/np/sta/bop/BOPman.pdf, accessed 6/3/08.

Kearney, A.T. (2007) New concerns in an uncertain world: The A.T. Kearney Foreign Direct Investment Confidence Index, http://www.atkearney.com/shared_res/FDICI_2007.pdf, accessed 6/3/08.

US Department of Commerce (1990) *The Balance of Payments of the United States*, Washington DC: US Government Printing Office.

8 *Currencies*

Exchange rates frequently are a difficult topic for US executives. The US economy is so large that most Americans don't have to worry directly about the value of the dollar on the international currency market. We produce and consume many of our goods domestically, so foreign exchange is not a concern. When we purchase goods produced in other countries, someone else has already exchanged currency, so all we see is the US dollar cost of the products. When we sell goods to other countries, someone else worries about the value of the goods in foreign markets; we're content to receive our wages or salaries in US dollars.

It's not until we pack our bags for a trip to Europe, Asia, or Latin America that we suddenly face the question of how much our dollar is worth on a foreign market. And then we encounter professionals who deal with currencies on a daily basis. They either meet us at the airport with hands full of currency, shouting that they will buy our dollars, or they're waiting for us at exchange booths or banks. Either place, we're in unfamiliar territory.

Learning Objectives

After studying this chapter, you should be able to:

1. interpret exchange rates quoted in two ways;
2. explain and apply the concepts of currency appreciation and depreciation;
3. calculate the value in one currency of an asset or liability priced in a different currency;
4. discriminate between the spot rate and the forward rate;
5. explain the factors that influence the value of a currency;
6. explain the difference between fixed and floating exchange rate regimes;
7. explain the risk in a currency transaction caused by appreciation or depreciation of either currency.

What is an Exchange Rate?

An *exchange rate* is simply a price that tells you how much a currency is worth in terms of another currency. Because this book is intended for a US audience, most of the discussion will be in terms of how much a US dollar is worth, but the same reasoning applies to any other currency: how much a UK pound is worth in terms of euros, or how much a euro is worth in terms of Japanese yen. Any currency can be stated relative to another currency, and the price is its exchange rate.

The exchange rate can be established in two ways: by the government of a country, or by the international currency market. In the old days, before the Second World War, governments set exchange rates that initially were based on the gold content of each country's coins. When that system ran into complications, rates were set by agreements between governments in what was known as the Bretton Woods system. When the Bretton Woods system failed in the 1970s, most governments left it to markets to determine exchange rates. With a few notable exceptions, today most exchange rates are determined on the currency market.

When a government sets an exchange rate and attempts to maintain that value, it is called a *fixed exchange rate* regime. When governments give up the effort and allow markets to determine exchange rates, it is called a *floating exchange rate* regime. Between the two extremes are several variations, but those are the choices facing any government: the government can attempt to dictate the exchange rate, or it can leave the decision up to the market. Recall that the Washington Consensus advocates letting the market determine a currency's value.

The international currency market, known as *forex* or *FX*, operates around the clock and around the globe, so currency transactions are always occurring somewhere. The market consists of multinational firms, the world's largest commercial banks, the central banks of many countries, and a few firms large enough to trade independently of the commercial banks. Traders deal in millions of dollars in each transaction, not the penny-ante trades that you and I conduct at the exchange booth. Traders have only one objective – to make money. They worry about all the topics we've discussed in this book, and they do it on a daily basis. They also worry about the psychology of markets, which we haven't covered. Traders think short term and long term: they speculate on how much a currency is worth now relative to its value in 30 seconds, and they speculate on how much a currency is worth now relative to its value in six months or a year. Currency trading is a great way to develop indigestion.

Every currency has a three-letter abbreviation that specifies the country and currency. A "$" sign is almost never used without additional information because it is the symbol for dozens of currencies, from dollars to pesos. Instead, currency markets use USD for US dollar or AUD for Australian dollar, GBP for Great Britain pound, and JPY for Japanese yen. You can find the three-letter abbreviation on the Internet at www.oanda.com or any other foreign exchange home page. From now on, we will use the three-letter abbreviations when discussing currencies.

One complication is that there are really two ways to express the exchange rate for each currency relative to another currency, as you see in Table 8.1. For example, here are two ways to express the exchange rate for the US dollar, USD, relative to the euro, EUR:

$$1 \text{ EUR} = 1.3890 \text{ USD} \tag{1}$$

or

$$1 \text{ USD} = .7199 \text{ EUR} \tag{2}$$

They are inverses of each other, which means that 1/1.3890 equals .7199 and 1/.7199 equals 1.3890 (check the math to be sure). The rates are not one rate when you're buying and a different rate when you're selling; they are simply the same price quoted from two

Table 8.1   Exchange rates for the US dollar against selected currencies

Exchange Rates: New York Closing Snapshot

Thursday, June 18, 2009 (Reuters)

US-dollar foreign-exchange rates in late New York trading

Country/currency	In US$		Per US$	
	Thurs	**Wed**	**Thurs**	**Wed**
Europe				
Czech Rep. koruna	0.05260	0.05223	19.011	19.146
Denmark krone	0.1866	0.1874	5.3591	5.3362
Euro area euro	1.3890	1.3953	0.7199	0.7167
Hungary forint	0.004944	0.004943	202.27	202.31

Source: Wall Street Journal, http://online.wsj.com/mdc/public/page/2_3021-forex-20090618.html?mod
=mdc_pastcalendar, accessed 6/19/09.

perspectives: how many dollars it takes to purchase one euro and how many euros it takes to purchase one dollar. The exchange rate between currencies at any time is the *spot rate,* so these are spot rates of the USD against the EUR. (At least these were the spot rates in New York at 4:00 pm on 6/18/09, when I made up this example.)

The spot rate in (1), dollars per euro (USD/EUR), can be interpreted in two ways: a) if I have one euro, I can sell it for 1.3890 USD; or b) if I want to buy one euro, I must pay 1.3890 USD. Either way, 1 EUR is "worth" 1.3890 USD. In equation (2), euros per dollar (EUR/USD): a) if I have one US dollar, I can sell it for .7199 EUR; or b) if I want to buy one US dollar, I must pay .7199 EUR. Either way, 1 USD is "worth" .7199 EUR. Both equations convey the same point: how much is the dollar worth relative to the euro; only the perspective changes.

Equations (1) and (2) have another more sophisticated interpretation. From the US investor's perspective, equation (1) is called the direct quote for the EUR because it is like going to the deli and asking how much prosciutto costs ("Hey, Luigi! How much is that prosciutto?" "It's a dollar and thirty nine cents a slice.") How much is that euro? "It's 1.3890 dollars per euro." Equation (2) is called the indirect quote for the EUR because we don't usually ask "Hey, Luigi! How much prosciutto can I get for a dollar?" "You can get about three-fourths of a slice." How many euros can I get for a dollar? "You can get .7199 euros for a dollar."

Let's examine the quote in Table 8.1 in more detail, but we'll focus only on the 1.3890 USD/EUR.

- First, 1.3890 is the exchange rate for transactions of at least one million dollars. If you or I tried to buy euros, we would have to pay much more than USD 1.39 per euro. If we tried to sell euros, we would get nowhere near USD 1.39 for each euro. That's the difference between the big players in the currency market and the little tykes like us.
- Second, 1.3890 is an average of several banks, and it is a midpoint between the price traders buy euros and the price they sell euros. A trader will always buy euros at one

price but sell euros at a higher price; that's how they make profits. So if a trader buys euros from you, the price may be 1.36 USD/EUR. If the trader sells euros to you, the price may be 1.41 USD/EUR. The rates at which the trader buys and sells usually are referred to as the *bid rate* (buy) and *ask rate* (sell). The difference of USD 0.05 is the trader's profit.

- Third, 1.3890 is the price of a euro on Thursday. On Wednesday, the euro traded at 1.3953 USD/EUR. Prices in the currency market change every minute or so. In this case, the price of the euro fell from 1.3953 USD/EUR on Wednesday to 1.3890 USD/ EUR on Thursday. Something must have happened in the market between Wednesday and Thursday to cause the price of the euro to change. This chapter explores the forces that lead to changes in currency values.

Purchasing a French Government Security

Because we're global investors, let's examine how exchange rates influence our decision to invest in a foreign asset. Suppose we have an opportunity to purchase a security issued by the Treasury of France. The security is the French equivalent of a US Treasury bill. In France, they are called BTFs (*Bons du Trésor á taux fixe et á intérêts précomptés*). The security is denominated in euros because the euro is the currency of France. The security costs EUR 998,277.97 to purchase today, June 19, 2009. In three months (September 2009) we will receive the face value of the security, which is EUR 1,000,000. At this market price and face value, the security will give us the equivalent of an annual return of 0.69 percent. That's not a particularly high return, but it is typical of the investment environment of 2009 when central banks around the globe were lowering interest rates in an effort to stimulate economies.

The problem is that we're US investors, so we deal in dollars, while the security is an obligation of the Government of France, which deals in euros. There are two currency transactions in this situation. The first transaction occurs today when we purchase euros so that we can purchase the security. Three months from now, we will receive euros, so the second transaction occurs when we sell the euros for dollars. Let's look at the transaction that occurs right now: we purchase euros.

We know from equation (1) that each euro will cost 1.3890 dollars, so to purchase 998,277.97 euros, we must pay 1,386,608.10 dollars (998,277.97 EUR * 1.3890 USD/ EUR = 1,386,608.10 USD). We get the same answer if we use the alternate quotation of the exchange rate. To purchase 998,277.97 euros, we must pay 1,386,689.78 dollars (998,277.97 EUR/.7199 EUR/USD = 1,386,689.78 USD). The difference of 81.68 USD occurs because the exchange rates were quoted to four decimals, but the number we calculated contains eight digits; it is a rounding error.

It's not because we're buying euros that we know to multiply or divide by the exchange rate, it is the way the exchange rate is quoted. There is no universal rule that you always multiply or always divide by the currency quote, and it doesn't make any difference whether you're buying or selling. It all depends on how the exchange rate is quoted. All you have to do is make up a few examples using various prices, try exchange rates quoted in both directions, and practice them a few hundred times. Pretty soon it will become second nature. That's the advantage that many foreigners have over us Americans – they exchange currencies constantly, most of us do it only occasionally.

Appreciation and Depreciation

Now let's examine the other currency exchange: when we receive 1,000,000 euros from the Treasury of France in three months, we must sell those euros for dollars (another way of saying the same thing is that we must use the euros we receive to buy dollars). The difficulty is that we don't know now what will be the value of the euro in three months. Currencies constantly change value as factors in the currency markets fluctuate. Political situations, economic indicators, balance of payments, and market psychology are never constant, and exchange rates reflect the fluctuation. We are exposed to *currency risk* or *exchange risk*: the risk that one currency will exchange for a different amount of another currency.

When a currency increases in value, the currency is said to appreciate. *Appreciation* means the currency is worth more of another currency. If you own it, you can sell it for more of another currency. If you don't own it and need to buy it, you'll have to pay more for it than before it appreciated. It's just the opposite with *depreciation*, which means that the currency is worth less of another currency. If you own it, you can't sell it for as much of another currency. If you don't own it, you can buy it at a lower price than previously. Appreciation and depreciation occur within seconds on the currency market, although you and I don't notice it until we look at quotes on television or in the newspaper, or until we go abroad and see them in action. Box 8.1 shows appreciation of the dollar against the euro until 2002, followed by depreciation of the dollar against the euro afterward.

Box 8.1   Value of the dollar against the euro

The euro was introduced as the currency of the European Monetary Union in 1999. The table shows the value of the dollar against the euro on a monthly basis each year from 1999 through 2008. The rates are quoted as euros per dollar, so when the dollar appreciates it is worth more euros and the line slopes upward. As you see, the dollar appreciated against the euro until 2001, fluctuated for a year, and then began to depreciate after 2002.

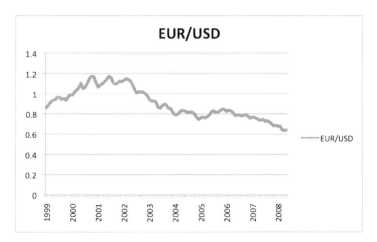

Source: FRED, St. Louis Federal Reserve Bank, http://research.stlouisfed.org/fred2/series/EXUSEU?cid=95.

In the old days when governments set exchange rates, the terms were *devaluation* (in place of depreciation) and *revaluation* (in place of appreciation). Operationally, the terms are synonyms. The difference is who makes the decision – the government or the market.

Let's return to the original values of the dollar and euro, and we will focus only on equation (1) because it tells us how many dollars each euro is worth.

$$1 \text{ EUR} = 1.3890 \text{ USD} \tag{1}$$

If the spot rate in three months is the same as today's spot rate in equation (1), we will sell the 1,000,000 euros for 1,389,000.00 dollars (1,000,000 EUR * 1.3890 USD/EUR = 1,389,000.00 USD). Unfortunately, we can't be certain that the spot rate in three months will be unchanged from its value today. In reality, three things might happen in three months: 1) the euro could appreciate, meaning it will be worth more dollars, 2) the euro could depreciate, meaning it will be worth fewer dollars, or 3) the euro could remain at the same value as it is today.

What will happen if the euro appreciates? Before putting down any numbers, just think about it. An appreciating euro means that each euro is worth more dollars: When we sell 1,000,000 euros, we will receive more dollars than we anticipated. If the euro appreciates ten US cents, the new exchange rate will be:

$$1 \text{ EUR} = 1.4890 \text{ USD} \tag{3}$$

Do you see how each euro is worth more dollars (1 EUR buys 1.49 USD after compared to 1.39 USD before) as a result of the euro's appreciation? Notice that we haven't used phrases such as "the exchange rate increased" or "the exchange rate decreased". Those terms aren't good guides because the number might increase when the exchange rate is a direct quote but decrease when it is an indirect quote, and both are equally valid. It's best to be as precise as possible. If the euro appreciates, we can sell it for more dollars, so plug a number into equation (1) representing more dollars for each euro.

If the euro appreciates during the three months to the value in equation (3), we will receive 1,489,000.00 dollars (1,000,000 EUR * 1.4890 USD/EUR = 1,489,000 USD), which is more dollars than we anticipated. We benefit from the euro's appreciation because we earn an additional 100,000 USD, not because the security is worth more (it is worth the same 1,000,000 EUR) but because the euro is worth more.

Of course, the euro might depreciate during the coming three months. Plug in a number representing fewer dollars per euro than at today's spot rate. If the euro depreciates by ten US cents from its spot rate now, the new exchange rate will be:

$$1 \text{ EUR} = 1.2890 \text{ USD} \tag{4}$$

Now, when we try to sell the euros in three months, we will receive only 1,289,000 dollars, which means we will lose 100,000 USD compared to what we anticipated. The risk facing us as a global investor is that once we invest abroad, the foreign currency might depreciate, making the investment less valuable in terms of our domestic currency.

The returns earned under the three possible outcomes are shown in Table 8.2. The base scenario is that the spot rate in three months is the same as the spot rate now. In that outcome, we will earn a return of 0.69 percent, which is what we anticipated. If the euro appreciates to 1.4890 USD/EUR, our return jumps to 29.537 percent. If the euro depreciates to 1.2890 USD/EUR, our return falls to -28.157 percent; we lose money on the investment. Remember that the gain or loss is because of currency value, not because of a change in the underlying investment. We face currency risk.

Of course, there is no guarantee that the euro will appreciate or depreciate to the values in this example. The movement could be much greater, so our potential gain or loss also will be much greater. Look again at Box 8.1 to see how much the dollar depreciated against the euro from 2003 to 2004. In 2003, one USD was worth approximately one EUR. In 2004, one USD was worth about 0.8 EUR, so the USD depreciated about 20 percent over that year. European investors who had put money in US dollar-denominated assets experienced a 20 percent decline in the euro value of their investment.

On the other hand, when the dollar is depreciating against the euro, it means the euro is appreciating against the dollar. So US investors who had invested in euro-denominated assets experienced a 20 percent rise in the dollar value of their investments during the same time frame.

Now you get a feel for why some countries try to set the value of their currency rather than leaving it to the market to determine the value: Pegging the currency frees global investors from the risk of a depreciating currency. Under a fixed rate regime, there is no currency risk, which could lead to more investing globally. Lest you think that currency appreciation or depreciation is a strictly academic exercise, read Box 8.2, which describes the risk facing homeowners who have borrowed in a different currency.

At this point, you may be asking yourself: "If there is a chance I might lose because of currency fluctuations, isn't there a way that I can protect myself against the risk that the foreign currency could depreciate?" It's a very good question, and we will address it in the next chapter. First, let's examine in more detail the issue of why currency values fluctuate in the first place.

Table 8.2   Return to US investor on a three-month French BTF

Market price now	998,277.97	EUR
	1,386,608.10	USD
Spot rate now	1.3890	USD/EUR
Face value 3 months	1,000,000.00	EUR

If the EUR:	To this value USD/EUR	US investor receives USD	Annual return to US investor
Appreciates	1.4890	1,489,000.00	29.537%
Unchanged	1.3890	1,389,000.00	0.690%
Depreciates	1.2890	1,289,000.00	-28.157%

Box 8.2 The carry trade and home mortgages

During the mortgage crisis in the United States, borrowers didn't have to worry about the value of the US dollar. Borrowers in Hungary were not as fortunate. Over the past decade, it has become popular in Eastern European countries such as Hungary and Poland to borrow in a currency other than their domestic currency. Many Hungarians borrow Swiss francs because interest rates are lower than interest rates in Hungary.

"Carry trade" is the finance term for borrowing in a currency where interest rates are low, exchanging currencies, then investing in a different currency where interest rates are higher. The process works fine as long as the currency you're borrowing doesn't appreciate. If it does, you must spend more of the domestic currency to repay the more expensive foreign currency.

That's what happened in Hungary. Mortgage rates to borrow in Swiss francs were between 1 and 2 percent, compared to 5 to 6 percent to borrow in Hungarian forints, so financially it was attractive to borrow Swiss francs. So many people and businesses borrowed that foreign currency loans accounted for 85 percent of all the loans outstanding in Hungary. In fact, the amount of foreign currency debt exceeded the foreign reserves of the central bank, making Hungary vulnerable to withdrawals by foreign investors.

In 2007, the Swiss franc began to appreciate against the forint. Over the next two years, borrowers found that the cost of paying their mortgages increased. Hungary faced a financial crisis because it tried to raise the value of the forint by increasing interest rates and using foreign currency reserves to purchase forints on the currency market. When the central bank ran low of reserves, the IMF had to help rescue the country.

Sources: Craig Karmin, Joellen Perry, "Homeowners abroad take currency gamble in loans", *Wall Street Journal*, May 29, 2007, p. A1; "Swiss franc wins foreign favour in funding asset purchases", *Financial Times*, Mar 22, 2007, p. 54; Thomas Escritt, Roman Olearchyk, "Hungary lifts rates to defend currency", *Financial Times*, Oct 23, 2008, p. 8.

Why do Exchange Rates Change?

If you've read the previous chapters, you're familiar with many of the forces that affect currency values: the political situation, economic policies such as government budget and inflation, and the balance of payments. Any factor or event that causes investors to lose confidence in a country will create pressure for its currency to depreciate: an unstable political situation or unpopular policies, high government budget deficits, a high rate of inflation, and an increasing Current Account deficit. Factors that create confidence in a country will create pressure for the currency to appreciate: stable politics, a budget surplus, low inflation, and a Current Account surplus.

Because we've discussed these forces already, we won't spend much time on them here. However, two forces have particular influence on exchange rates over time: the relative rates of inflation between two countries and relative interest rates between two countries.

PURCHASING POWER

An economic principle known as the law of one price argues that the exchange rate ought to reflect the relative purchasing power between two countries. If the exchange rate doesn't reflect underlying prices, it will be possible to earn profits by purchasing a product in one country and selling it in the other. Here is the reasoning.

Suppose a tube of toothpaste sells in Europe for 1 EUR. Using the spot rate in equation (1), the identical toothpaste ought to sell in the US for 1.3890 USD per tube. If it didn't, people would purchase toothpaste in one location and sell it in the other. For example, if the tube sold for 1 EUR in Europe but only 1.10 USD in the US, Europeans would purchase the toothpaste in the US for the equivalent of .7919 EUR (1.10 USD/1.3890 USD/EUR = .7919 EUR), ship it to Europe, and sell it for a profit of .2081 EUR per tube (1.00 EUR sales price − .7919 EUR cost = .2081 EUR profit). Americans would take their toothpaste to Europe and sell it for 1 EUR, exchange the 1 EUR for 1.3890 USD (1 EUR * 1.3890 USD/EUR = 1.3890 USD), and realize a profit of .2890 USD (1.3890 USD sales price − 1.1000 USD cost = 0.2890 USD profit).

The profit potential won't persist because so many people will buy dollars so they can buy toothpaste in the US that the dollar will appreciate against the euro. The situation will stabilize only when the exchange rate reflects the purchasing power of the currencies of each country. This is an example of a concept known as *arbitrage* – buying in one market and selling in another. Traders search for and exploit opportunities to profit through arbitrage.

Of course, countries don't produce only one product, but the principle applies to the price level in general: exchange rates ought to reflect relative price levels in each country.

There are several assumptions in the previous argument. One is that the product is virtually identical in both countries – the same size, same ingredients, similar presentation, and so on. In the past that was rare, although in the modern world there are many virtually identical products sold around the world. (I'm writing this chapter in Pula, Croatia, where I purchase a cereal of small wheat biscuits with icing on top. Here they are called Toppas. In the US, the same cereal is called Frosted Mini Wheats Bite Size. Both are manufactured by Kellogg's.) Another assumption is that transportation costs are zero. In fact, they would have to be incorporated into the prices. This would make the presentation more tedious without changing the point about purchasing power parity, so we ignored transportation costs.

This concept of currencies reflecting relative prices is so appealing that the popular press has begun using an index for a product that is sold almost everywhere in standard form – a McDonald's Big Mac hamburger. The Big Mac Index shows prices in a variety of currencies for a Big Mac, then how much the price would be in US dollars at current exchange rates. If the actual exchange rate does not match the implied Big Mac Index, the currency is either overvalued or undervalued against the dollar. Box 8.3 shows the Big Mac Index in April, 2002. I've put column headings on the table and inserted explanatory calculations to help you understand how the index is calculated. Your calculations may not match the numbers in the table precisely because the exchange rates in column D are rounded.

As my informal test of the Big Mac theory, I purchased a Big Mac in Ljubljana, Slovenia, then purchased other Big Macs in Zagreb and Pula, Croatia. Sure enough, they were identical to the Big Mac in the US. McDonald's has standardized a product worldwide. I didn't compare prices. There are other examples of products that are sold around the world, if you think about them for a moment.

If you're really astute and wish to link what you've learned, read the last sentence and date of the article in Box 8.3. Compare that information to what happened to the dollar after 2002 in Box 8.1. The Big Mac Index, which illustrates the law of one price, predicted that the dollar was overvalued against other major currencies. What happened to the dollar after 2002?

Box 8.3 "In the history of the Big Mac Index, the dollar has never been more overvalued"

	A	B	C	D	E
	Big Mac prices		Implied PPP* of the dollar	Actual dollar exchange rate Apr 23, 2002	Under (-)/over (+) valuation against the dollar, %
	In local currency	In dollars			
United States	$2.49	2.49	–	–	–
Canada	C$3.33	2.12	1.34	1.57	-15
China	Yuan 10.50	1.27	4.22	8.28	-49
Japan	¥262	2.01	105	130	-19
Switzerland	SFr6.30	3.81	2.53	1.66	+53
Britain ($ per £)	£1.99	2.88	1.25	1.45	+16
Euro area ($ per €)	€2.67	2.37	0.93	0.89	-5

* Purchasing power parity: local price divided by price in United States.

The Big Mac Index is based on the principle of purchasing power parity (PPP), which says that exchange rates should adjust so that the prices of identical goods and services would be equivalent in each country. McDonald's sold Big Macs in 120 countries in 2002, and the Big Mac is almost the same everywhere, so the Big Mac is used as a proxy for goods and services.

Here is how you interpret the Big Mac Index for currencies whose prices are quoted as foreign currency per dollar. Column A shows the price of a Big Mac in the local currency. Column B converts the local price into equivalent dollars using the actual exchange rate in Column D. [B = A/D]. Column C is the exchange rate implied by the selling price of a Big Mac in the local country compared to the price in the United States; this is the implied price according to PPP. [C = A for the US/A for each country].

Compare Column D, which shows the market exchange rate, to Column C, which shows the exchange rate implied by PPP. PPP predicts that it should require only 105 yen to buy one dollar, but you must pay 130 yen on the market. The yen is undervalued on the market. It should require 2.53 Swiss francs to purchase one dollar according to PPP, but you can buy a dollar for only 1.66 Swiss francs on the market. The Swiss franc is overvalued on the market. Column E shows in percentage terms how much the foreign currency is undervalued or overvalued against the dollar.

The British pound and the Euro area euro are quoted as dollars per foreign currency, so the process is the opposite of what we did above. In those cases, [B = A * D] and [C = A for that country/A for the US]. It should require $1.25 to purchase £1, but on the market it requires $1.45 to purchase £1. The pound is overvalued. It should require $.93 to purchase €1, but it only requires $.89 on the market. The euro is undervalued.

The Economist's conclusion in 2002 was that "the dollar now looks more overvalued against the average of the other big currencies than at any time in the life of the Big Mac Index," which was created 16 years earlier.

Source: The Economist, Apr 25, 2002.

When extended over time, the law of one price leads to a concept called *purchasing power parity (PPP)*, which argues that the exchange rate will adjust to reflect the relative rates of inflation between two countries. This means that if inflation in Europe is 0.6 percent over the coming year while inflation in the US is -0.7 percent (the latest data available in June 2009), the spot rate in one year ought to be:

$$\frac{USD}{EUR} \; next \; year = \frac{USD}{EUR} \; now \; x \; \frac{(1+US\;inflation\,)}{(1+EUR\;inflation\,)} = 1.3890 \; x \frac{(1-.007)}{(1+.006)} = 1.3711 \qquad (5)$$

In other words, the euro ought to depreciate against the US dollar because each euro will be worth fewer dollars. Right now 1 EUR sells for 1.3890 USD; next year 1 EUR will sell for only 1.3711 USD. Because the euro doesn't sell for as many dollars, the euro depreciates. If the concept of PPP holds, the currency of a country experiencing higher inflation should depreciate against the currency of a country with lower inflation.

PPP works better when there is a significant difference in inflation rates between countries. When the difference is small, PPP isn't as reliable. The PPP principle is tested whenever governments try to impose one value on their currency but economic fundamentals indicate another, as illustrated by Mexico in the late 1970s. In early 1977 the central bank of Mexico, the Banco de Mexico, decided to control the value of the peso around 23.0 MXN/USD, meaning it required 23 Mexican pesos to purchase 1 USD.

However, over the next five years the rate of inflation in Mexico was about 30 percent per year, compared to US inflation of about 8 percent per year. According to PPP, the peso should have depreciated against the dollar, but this was contrary to the Government's objective of a pegged exchange rate. Traders in the forex market sold pesos because they thought it was going to decrease in value. To prevent depreciation of the peso, the Mexican Government and central bank had to take steps to offset the pressure toward depreciation.

Ultimately, Mexico was unable to maintain the currency peg. In early 1982 the Banco de Mexico began to let the peso adjust incrementally, and its value began to decline. The peso fell to 30 MXN/USD in mid-February, then 40 MXN/USD two weeks later. The peso depreciated to 78 MXN/USD in August and 145 MXN/USD in September. The rapid decline of the currency created a currency crisis in Mexico as domestics bought dollars in an effort to preserve the value of their money and foreign investors tried to liquidate peso-denominated assets. The Government eventually defaulted on its foreign debt. The lesson is that if a country attempts to manage its exchange rate at a value different from its PPP value, it faces a difficult task.

This discussion leads to the concept of a *real exchange rate*, which is the market exchange rate adjusted for the effect of inflation between two countries. The real exchange rate, shown in equation (5), reflects the purchasing power between two countries. The real exchange rate sometimes differs from the spot rate on the forex market. When the difference becomes too great, the adjustment can be cataclysmic. In the resulting sell-off, panic frequently occurs and the market price can over-adjust.

Panic is precisely what led to the currency crisis in Mexico, and the discrepancy between the real and nominal exchange rates helps explain the panic. In 1972, the exchange rate was 23 MXN/USD. Over the next five years, Mexico's inflation averaged 30 percent compared to US inflation of 8 percent. We can use equation (5) with the inflation rates of Mexico and the US to determine the real exchange rate in 1982:

$$\frac{MXN}{USD}1982 = \frac{MXN}{USD}1977x\frac{(1+MX\ inflation)}{(1+US\ inflation)} = 23x\frac{(1+.30)^5}{(1+.08)^5} = 58$$

By 1982, the real exchange rate – the rate at which the currencies should trade according to PPP – was 58 MXN/USD. Instead, the Government tried to maintain the nominal exchange rate at 23 MXN/USD, less than half the dollar's real value against the peso. When the discrepancy became apparent to locals and foreign investors, they lost confidence that Mexico's Government and central bank could maintain the peg, so they sold pesos.

INTEREST RATES

Another major influence on exchange rates is relative interest rates between countries. To understand why, let's consider an investor who can invest now and receive the amount invested plus interest in a year. The investor will receive interest at whatever is the bank's deposit rate for that currency. The amount the investor accrues in one year is shown by the formula:

$$FV = PV + PV*i = PV * (1 + i) \tag{6}$$

where *FV* is the future value (the ending amount), *PV* is the present value (the amount invested), and *i* is the interest rate.[1] In other words, the investor will redeem the original amount plus the interest earned on the deposit.

If the investor is in the US, whose currency is the dollar, the investor deposits and redeems dollars at the USD interest rate:

$$FV_{USD} = PV_{USD} * (1 + i_{USD}) \tag{7}$$

The same situation faces an investor in France, whose currency is the euro. The investor deposits and redeems euros at the EUR interest rate:

---

1   This is the simplified form of a general formula: $FV = PV * (1+i/n)^{t*n}$, where FV is future value, PV is present value, i is the annual interest rate, t is the number of years, and n is the number of compounding periods per year. This formula is used constantly in finance. I used it to calculate the annual return on the French BTF that you see in Table 8.2.

$$FV_{EUR} = PV_{EUR} * (1 + i_{EUR}) \tag{8}$$

When you divide equation (7) by equation (8), here's what you get:

$$\frac{FV_{USD}}{FV_{EUR}} = \frac{PV_{USD}}{PV_{EUR}} \ x \ \frac{(1+i_{US})}{(1+i_{EUR})} \tag{9}$$

We know what $\frac{PV_{USD}}{PV_{EUR}}$ is: it's a dollar now per euro now, which is today's spot rate of USD per EUR: 1.3890.

$\frac{FV_{USD}}{FV_{EUR}}$ is a dollar per euro in one year. It is a new concept, the *forward rate* – the rate that banks are willing to contract now to exchange currencies in one year. The forward rate is an expectation of what the dollar will trade for against the euro in one year, based on the current level of interest rates in the countries. To put the formula into words, the forward rate equals the spot rate multiplied by the ratio of one plus the interest rates in the two countries.

We can add numbers to calculate the forward rate in three months. We know that today's spot rate is 1.3890 USD/EUR. According to the *Wall Street Journal's* Money Rates data on Thursday, June 18, 2009 shown in Table 8.3, the US prime rate is 3.25 percent. The prime rate is the rate that large banks charge their best customers, and frequently is used as an index on which other rates are based. On the same day, the prime rate for the eurozone is 1.00 percent. According to formula (9), the forward rate should be:

$$\frac{FV_{USD}}{FV_{EUR}} = \frac{PV_{USD}}{PV_{EUR}} \ x \ \frac{(1+i_{US})}{(1+i_{EUR})} = 1.3890 \ x \ \frac{(1+3.25\%/4)}{(1+1.00\%/4)} = 1.3968 \tag{10}$$

Notice that we adjusted the interest rates, which are quoted on an annual basis, for the fact that we are investing for only three months, or one-quarter of a year. We divided the interest rate by four.

Focus on the two numbers 1.3890, which is today's spot rate, and 1.3968, which is the forward rate in three months. Right now it takes 1.3890 USD to purchase one EUR, but you can agree with the bank now to buy one EUR to be delivered to you in three months for 1.3968 USD. The forex market thinks that the euro will appreciate over the coming three months, which is equivalent to saying that the forex market thinks that the dollar will depreciate.

Let's see how close we came to predicting the forward rate using the prime rates in the US and the eurozone. Table 8.4 shows forward rates for the dollar against various currencies on June 18, 2009. Find the row for the euro, then go to the column showing the rate for three months. You'll see the number 1.3953, which is pretty close to the 1.3968 we predicted.

Unfortunately, we're not always this lucky. If we followed the same process using different interest rates or a different currency set, we might not have been so accurate. For example, I tried the calculation using Libor and euro Libor interest rates and got a forward rate that predicted the USD would appreciate rather than depreciate. Not only was the forward prediction not accurate, it wasn't even in the right direction!

Table 8.3   Prime rates in selected countries

Money Rates:

Thursday, June 18, 2009

INTERNATIONAL RATES:

Prime rates [US Effective Date: 12/16/2008]

	Latest	Week ago
US	3.25	3.25
Canada	2.25	2.25
Euro zone	1.00	1.00
Japan	1.475	1.475
Switzerland	0.52	0.53
Britain	0.50	0.50
Australia	3.00	3.00
Hong Kong	5.00	5.25

Source: Wall Street Journal, http://online.wsj.com/mdc/public/page/2_3020-moneyrate-20090618.html?mod=mdc_pastcalendar, accessed 6/19/09.

Table 8.4   Spot and forward rates of US dollar against other currencies

Country	Currency	(June 18) Spot	Forward One month	Three month	One year
UK	pound	1.6345	1.6344	1.6342	1.6342
Europe	euro	1.3962	1.3959	1.3953	1.3964

Source: Financial Times, http://markets.ft.com/ft/markets/researchArchive.asp?report=DSP&cat=CU, accessed 6/19/09.

One thing that should be noted is that there is interplay between the banking market (called the money market) and the currency market. Any gain from investing in the US because of higher interest rates (3.25 percent is higher than 1.00 percent) will be offset by the depreciating dollar when the dollars are converted back to euros (1 USD buys 1/1.3890 = .7199 EUR now, but it will buy only 1/1.3968 = .7159 EUR in three months). The forward rate is a function of relative interest rates between the two countries. This is the principle of *interest rate parity*. The relationship usually is shown as:

$$\frac{\dfrac{FV_{USD}}{FV_{EUR}}}{\dfrac{PV_{USD}}{PV_{EUR}}} = \frac{(1+i_{USD})}{(1+i_{EUR})} \tag{11}$$

which in words says that the forward rate divided by today's spot rate (where both are quoted as USD per EUR) equals the ratio of one plus the USD interest rate divided by one plus the EUR interest rate.

In today's world, you don't really need to go to banks in different countries to deposit or borrow the currency of another country. Major banks typically accept deposits or lend in all the major currencies, although they price the deposits or loans at rates related to rates in the country of the currency they're borrowing or lending. For example, you can borrow or deposit dollars at banks in Paris, Tokyo, or Buenos Aires. These dollars that are outside the US are known as *eurodollars*, a name that derives from the growth of dollar deposits in Europe during the 1950s and 1960s. Even though you borrow dollars in Tokyo, the interest rate relates to rates in the US, not in Japan, and the dollars are still called eurodollars.

PPP and interest rate parity are the major influences on currency value in the long run, meaning over a period of years. In the short run, other forces can influence currency values. PPP and interest rate parity are founded on economic and financial theory, and they do a pretty good job relating to reality.

CENTRAL BANK INTERVENTION

Sometimes a government doesn't like the result of what the forex market thinks of its currency, or it may have policy reasons for reversing a trend in the currency's price. Sellers in the forex market may be creating pressure for a currency to depreciate for example, but for policy reasons the government may not favor depreciation. In this situation, the government may work with the central bank to purchase the country's currency on the forex market to offset the selling pressure.

How does a central bank purchase its own currency? It buys its own currency using the foreign currencies that make up part of its international reserves. (You'll recall that international reserves consist of foreign currency, gold, and borrowing rights at the IMF.) For example, if the US central bank, the Fed, wishes to create pressure for the dollar to appreciate against the euro, the Fed would purchase dollars using euros that it already owns. Central banks frequently own currencies of other countries, particularly major trading partners, for just such purposes. A central bank also could purchase its own currency by selling gold from its reserves. In fact, a trend around the world is for central banks to sell gold reserves.

The process works just as well in reverse. If the government wants to offset market pressure toward appreciation, it may direct the central bank to sell its domestic currency and purchase the foreign currency. Either way, the process is called central bank intervention. The central bank intervenes in the currency market by purchasing or selling its domestic currency. As a result, the central bank creates pressure for the currency to appreciate or depreciate.

Sometimes a country says that it has a policy of letting its currency float, which means that it lets the currency market determine the value of the currency. However, if the market value deviates from what the treasury or central bank think is the appropriate value, the central bank intervenes so that the currency returns to the target value. If the practice continues, it is referred to as a *dirty float* – a practice of intervening in the currency market, usually without announcing the act, to prevent a currency's value from deviating from some specified value. The US frequently accuses the Bank of Japan of practicing a dirty float in an effort to keep the yen from appreciating against the US dollar.

A frequent reason for central bank intervention is attempting to maintain a currency peg. A currency peg means the government has a policy of maintaining the price of its currency within a narrow range. If the currency begins to move outside of the range, the central bank must intervene by purchasing or selling the currency to offset the market pressure. When the central bank must use its international reserves to purchase its currency, there is a danger that the central bank will run out of reserves. Box 8.4 describes several examples of central bank intervention.

Another reason for central bank intervention is to send a signal to the forex market. For example, if traders are bidding down the dollar against the euro, the US and European central banks may intervene by purchasing a large quantity of dollars in a few hours.

Box 8.4   Central bank intervention

Central banks intervene in the currency market when they wish to influence the direction the currency is moving. The central bank buys its currency when it desires appreciation or sells its currency when it desires depreciation. Here are three examples of central banks intervening when their countries faced a currency crisis.

For years, Vietnam pegged its currency, the dong, to the US dollar (see Box 3.3 to refresh your memory). In late 2007, the central bank began to stop purchasing dollars as part of an effort to let the dong appreciate. Within a few months, economic conditions in Vietnam deteriorated: inflation increased, the trade deficit worsened, and the stock market plunged. Speculators began betting that the dong would depreciate, so they sold it. The central bank was forced to defend the dong's value by purchasing dong on the currency market using dollar currency reserves.

In August 2008, Russia engaged in a military conflict with Georgia over territory in South Ossetia. Within two weeks, global investors withdrew $28 billion of reserves from Russia, causing foreign currency reserves to fall at the fastest rate since Russia's 1998 currency crisis. The rouble depreciated as investors liquidated rouble-denominated assets. Russia's central bank used its currency reserves to purchase roubles on the currency market, helping to stem the currency crisis. Fortunately, Russia had the third-highest foreign reserves in the world: $582 billion. There was no danger that it would run out of reserves.

Of the three Baltic countries, Latvia's economy was in the worst shape in 2009. Its GDP shrank by almost 20 percent during the year, unemployment increased, and wages fell. The private sector had borrowed so much in foreign currency that it amounted to 130 percent of GDP, exposing the country to the risk of withdrawals by foreign investors. In spite of these forces, Latvia pegged its currency to the euro. The central bank had to purchase lats, causing the bank to "bleed forex reserves at an alarming rate" according to one observer. The IMF, the EU, and Government of Sweden had to provide assistance to Latvia.

Sources: "Vietnam currency crisis may loom" *Wall Street Journal*, May 29, 2008, p. C6; Amy Kazmin, "Vietnam's currency crisis causes headache", *Financial Times*, Feb 26, 2008, p. 1; Charles Clover, Peter Gamham, "Moscow forced to shore up the rouble", *Financial Times*, Sep 5, 2008, p. 1; "Baltic brinksmanship", *The Economist*, Oct 17, 2009, p. 64; Nouriel Roubini, "Latvia's currency crisis is a rerun of Argentina's", *Financial Times*, Jun 11, 2009, p. 11.

The intervention costs speculators a few million dollars and may change their expectations by sending a signal that the central banks are willing to support the dollar to some extent. Frequently, this is enough to stabilize the market or halt a trend.

SPECULATORS

Some organizations trade foreign currencies because they need to purchase or sell goods and services. However, transactions for these purposes make up only about 5 percent of the forex market. The other 95 percent consists of speculators trying to profit from buying and selling currencies. The Bank for International Settlements (sort of the central banker's clearing house) surveys central banks periodically in an effort to determine the size of the forex market. In 2004, the equivalent of approximately $1.9 trillion was traded on a daily basis. The USD was one side of 89 percent of the transactions, meaning most transactions were either to purchase or sell US dollars. The most active trading center was London, followed by New York.

There are many ways to speculate in the currency market. One of the most basic is to use one currency now to purchase another currency because you think the other currency will appreciate against the original currency. When it does, you sell it for more of the original currency and realize a profit. You use this strategy when you think the other currency is undervalued. It is the same process as purchasing a share of stock, waiting for the stock to increase in price, then selling the stock. You profit from the increase in price.

You can pursue a different strategy when you think the other currency is overvalued and you expect it to depreciate. You borrow that currency and sell it for the original currency. When the other currency depreciates, you buy it back; but because it has depreciated, it doesn't cost as much of the original currency. You end up with a profit equal to the amount of original currency you have left. You can also use this strategy by borrowing shares of stock, selling them at today's price, waiting for the price to decline, then buying them back at a lower price. You profit from the decrease in price.

Box 8.5 discusses a famous episode of a currency speculator, George Soros, betting against a central bank, the Bank of England, about the "correct" value of the pound. In this instance, the speculator won the bet.

Box 8.5   George Soros versus the Bank of England

Before the euro became the common currency of the eurozone, the Exchange Rate Mechanism (ERM) set exchange rates through agreements between governments. Although the United Kingdom was not initially a member of the ERM, it attempted to set the value of the pound so that it mirrored the value of the German deutschemark. When the UK ultimately entered the ERM in 1988, it insisted on a high value of the pound even though economic conditions in the UK did not justify a high value. Inflation was too high and interest rates were too low for the pound to maintain its value, particularly against the deutschemark.

By early 1992, George Soros, among other investors, thought that the UK could not maintain the high value of the pound, so began selling pounds on the currency market. He borrowed pounds and sold them for deutschemarks so that when the pound devalued, he would be able to repay the loan with fewer deutschemarks, realizing a profit on the transaction.

So many speculators sold pounds that the Bank of England was forced to defend the value of the pound by raising interest rates and purchasing pounds on the currency market using its reserves of deutschemarks. However, the Bank soon ran low of reserves.

In September 1992, the Bank of England finally acknowledged that the value of the pound was too high and devalued; the date became known as "Black Wednesday". Soros repaid the pounds he had borrowed using the appreciated deutschemarks, and in the process made a profit equivalent to 1 billion dollars in a few hours. Soros became famous as the man who broke the Bank of England.

The episode turned out especially bad for the Conservative party's parliamentary majority. When voters felt the adverse effect of high interest rates and learned of the Government's inept handling of the currency situation, they voted the Government out of office.

Sources: Daniel Dombey, "The billion-dollar memory lapse", *Financial Times*, Aug 5, 2006, p. 14; Steve H. Hanke, Alan Walters, "Easy money", *Forbes*, Jan 31, 1994, p. 141.

Exporters and Importers

Investors in other countries are not the only parties that need to worry about exchange rates. Trillions of dollars worth of international transactions occur each year because of the trade in goods and services. Whenever a US consumer purchases a Sony Playstation, a French manufacturer sells perfume in Japan, or a Peruvian copper miner exports to China, exchange rates play a role in the process.

IMPORTER

Consider a US distributor importing products from France. The French company requires payment in euros, but gives the purchaser 30 days from the day the shipment is received to pay the full contract amount, EUR 100,000. The US importer receives the shipment on June 19, 2009. Let's examine the situation facing the US importer.

The exchange rate quoted in Table 8.1 is 1.3890 USD/EUR, so the US importer owes EUR 100,000, which is worth USD 138,900 at today's exchange rate. Because it is a US business, the importer records an account payable of USD 138,900, although the exact amount of dollars paid may not be known for 30 days. When time comes for payment, the US importer must purchase EUR 100,000 to deliver to the French producer.

Now let's shift forward one month when the importer must purchase EUR 100,000 to pay the account. Table 8.5 shows the three scenarios that could occur over the month. Under the base scenario that the EUR/USD exchange rate doesn't change, the US firm pays USD 138,900, the same amount as the account payable. If the dollar appreciates over the month, each euro will not cost as much, so the importer will save money compared to the dollar-denominated account payable. For example, if the dollar appreciates ten cents to 1.2890 USD/EUR, the importer saves USD 10,000 on the transaction.

Conversely, if the dollar depreciates, each euro will cost more, so the importer will pay more than the dollar-denominated account payable. If the dollar depreciates ten cents to 1.4890 USD/EUR, the importer pays an additional USD 10,000. Of course, there is nothing certain about the exchange rates in Table 8.5. Actual appreciation or depreciation likely will be different from the amounts in the table.

We conclude that a US importer prefers an appreciating dollar because contracts denominated in foreign currencies cost fewer dollars when settlement occurs.

Table 8.5   Currency risk facing a US importer

Contract amount	100,000 EUR
Today's spot rate	1.3890 USD/EUR
USD account payable	138,900 USD

If the USD:	USD/EUR will be:	USD paid	USD gain (loss) on contract
Appreciates	1.2890	128,900	10,000
Is unchanged	1.3890	138,900	0
Depreciates	1.4890	148,900	-10,000

EXPORTER

We can look at a different situation: a US exporter selling to a French customer. The French customer wishes to pay in euros, and the exporter gives the customer 30 days after receipt of the goods to pay the EUR 400,000 contract amount. The French customer receives the goods on June 19, 2009. The US exporter records an account receivable of EUR 400,000, which is worth USD 555,600 at today's exchange rate of 1.3890 USD/EUR.

What happens in one month, when the US exporter receives EUR 400,000 from the customer in France? The results are shown in Table 8.6. The base scenario is that the dollar is unchanged over the month. If that scenario occurs, the exporter receives the same amount that is in the account receivable, USD 555,600. If the dollar appreciates over the month, each euro will not buy as many dollars. For example, if the dollar appreciates ten cents to 1.2890 USD/EUR, the exporter receives only USD 515,600, which is USD 40,000 less than anticipated.

The third scenario is that the dollar could depreciate, meaning that each euro will purchase more dollars. If the dollar depreciates ten cents to 1.4890 USD/EUR over the month, the exporter receives USD 595,600, which is USD 40,000 more than the original dollar equivalent of the contract.

We see that a US exporter prefers a depreciating dollar because a contract denominated in a foreign currency exchanges for more dollars. This is the opposite of what importers prefer. Importers prefer an appreciating dollar because they don't have to pay as many dollars to settle an account payable. Exporters prefer a depreciating dollar because they can sell the foreign currency received for more dollars.

Table 8.6   Currency risk facing a US exporter

Contract amount   400,000 EUR

Today's spot rate   1.3890   USD/EUR

USD account receivable   555,600 USD

If the USD:	USD/EUR will be:	USD received	USD gain (loss) on contract
Appreciates	1.2890	515,600	-40,000
Is unchanged	1.3890	555,600	0
Depreciates	1.4890	595,600	40,000

WHAT IS THE "CORRECT" EXCHANGE RATE?

Policy makers thus have a tough choice: should they strive for a weak (depreciating) dollar to make life easier for exporters, or should they strive for a strong (appreciating) dollar to make life easier for importers? Unfortunately, there is no correct answer to the question.

In part, the answer depends on power: Which of the two groups has the most power in swaying opinions of public officials? In many countries, exporters sway more public opinion than importers do. For example, exporters argue for international competitiveness, which can be achieved through a cheap currency. Importers don't compete with importers from other countries. Exporters frequently talk about job losses due to foreign competition, but you don't hear much about job losses at importers. Importers are able to pass higher prices to consumers, but exporters hurt by lower prices lay off workers or go out of business.

The answer also depends on the relative importance of exports or imports to the nation's economy. Japan, for example, is famous for being an export-oriented economy, so policy makers in Japan tend to adopt a "cheap yen" policy that makes Japanese exports less expensive on the global market. Because the US is a major competitor and purchaser of Japanese exports, US policy makers encourage the Japanese to let the yen appreciate.

Policy makers have to worry about other effects, too. Decreasing the value of the dollar on the currency market means that imports become more expensive. This in turn increases inflation because the price index measures the prices of all goods and services, whether domestic or imported. Thus, addressing one issue – making US exports more competitive globally – raises another issue: higher inflation.

So should policy makers leave the decision about a currency's value up to the currency market, or should they attempt to influence the value to achieve some policy objective? Many countries leave the decision to the market, although they sometimes intervene if the market generates an undesirable outcome. Box 8.6 describes US intervention in the currency market during several presidential administrations.

Box 8.6   Talking up the dollar

The tradition in the United States for at least the past two decades is for policy makers to let the currency market determine the value of the dollar. Only once or twice during the Clinton and George W. Bush administrations did officials make public statements attempting to influence the direction of the currency.

One reason is that a strong currency sounds more politically attractive, but a weak currency makes a country's exports more attractive, stimulates GDP, and leads to higher employment. There is an inherent conflict between the political and economy spheres. "Benign neglect" is the name for the practice of saying and doing nothing while market forces determine a currency's value.

In 2008, Treasury Secretary Henry Paulson and Fed Chairman Ben Bernanke both made public statements within a few days that the dollar had depreciated sufficiently and the Bush administration was in favor of a strong dollar. The statements temporarily reversed the downward trend of the dollar, which during the Bush administration had depreciated 25 percent against a basket of currencies of its major trading partners.

A danger of public officials attempting to influence a currency's value is that they may lose credibility if their talk is ineffective. In 2009, Treasury Secretary Tim Geithner made several statements that the Obama administration favors a "strong dollar," but the dollar continued to depreciate because the talk was not accompanied with policy changes. The *Financial Times* quipped that, "If one thing has been devalued, it is not so much the currency itself but the impact of the phrase." Another observer calls the practice of talking up a currency's value "open mouth operations," a pun on open market operations.

Sources: Deborah Solomon, Michael M. Phillips, "New vigor brought to defense of the dollar", *Wall Street Journal*, Jun 5, 2008, p. A3; Sudeep Reddy, Joanna Slater, Deborah Solomon, "Bernanke bolsters weak dollar", *Wall Street Journal*, Jun 4, 2008, p. A1; Tom Barkley, Don Curren, "Geithner and Bernanke rally around the dollar", *Wall Street Journal*, Oct 2, 2009, p. C2; Tom Braithwaite, Sarah O'Connor, "US mantra of strong dollar loses its value", *FT.com*, Oct 9, 2009.

STRATEGIC ISSUES

To this point we have looked only at the effects on importers and exporters of one transaction, as if it occurred in isolation. The firms in the importer and exporter examples face *transaction exposure* because a foreign-currency denominated cash flow that will occur in the future may be worth a different amount of domestic currency when settlement occurs.

A different risk is translation exposure, which arises when firms have international subsidiaries that have plant and equipment, equity investments from the parent company, and borrowings that are denominated in a foreign currency. *Translation exposure* addresses the issue of how much assets, liabilities, and equities are worth in terms of the domestic currency when the firm's financial statements are consolidated. Accountants have debated this question for years. In the US, the Financial Accounting Standards Board (FASB) provides guidelines about valuing international subsidiaries.

Strategic issues also arise in international operations. Let's return to the exporter example to see why. The exporter originally signed a contract to sell EUR 400,000 of merchandise to a French customer. At today's exchange rate, the contract is worth USD 555,600, meaning that the exporter expects that amount of revenue to cover the costs of the merchandise and provide a profit to the exporter. But if the euro appreciates to 1.4890 USD/EUR, the exporter can receive the same USD 555,600 on future contracts by selling the merchandise in France at a price of EUR 373,136 (USD 555,600/1.4890 USD/EUR = EUR 373,136). Because the dollar has depreciated, the US exporter has a price advantage relative to other firms selling in France. This is another reason that exporters prefer a weaker domestic currency: their goods become cheaper relative to the competition.

How should the firm react? It can maintain prices in France at EUR 400,000 and earn more USD revenue, so its profits will increase. Or it can lower prices in France to EUR 373,236 and maintain profits, but capture market share. These are strategic issues that arise whenever exchange rates change. Sometimes a currency moves in your favor, other times it moves against you, but you must consider the effect of the movement on the firm's operations.

Establishing a production facility in another country is a frequent strategic response to trends in exchange rates. Japanese auto manufacturers open facilities in the US so they can compensate for continual appreciation of the yen. If the manufacturer produces the cars in Japan for export to the US, all of its revenues are exposed to currency risk, but all of its expenses are in yen. If the yen appreciates, each dollar of revenue exchanges for fewer yen, so the manufacturer faces a strategic problem. If the manufacturer produces cars in the US for sale in the US, its revenues are in dollars and its expenses are in dollars, so only the profits are exposed to currency risk. Box 8.7 discusses strategic reactions by firms in other countries in the face of a weakening dollar.

Predicting Exchange Rates

Given the uncertainty of exchange rates and their effect on businesses and the country's economy, wouldn't it be nice to be able to predict the exchange rate in six months or a year? Yes, it would be nice, but sadly, it is not possible. If we could predict exchange rates, we'd all be rich by profiting from the movements in price. But such is not the case.

In a famous study two decades ago, Meese and Rogoff (1983) found that trying to predict exchange rates using the factors mentioned in this chapter weren't any better than flipping a coin. Exchange rates don't consistently follow trends, so tomorrow's dollar is as likely to appreciate or depreciate, regardless of yesterday's value or underlying trends. In finance theory, this is known as a "random walk" because there is no discernable pattern to exchange rate movements. Other studies through the years have supported the conclusions of Meese and Rogoff: models aren't any more effective than flipping a coin, and a model that is better in one period may not be better in the next period.

One explanation for failure of the models incorporating macroeconomic fundamentals is that models incorporate data that is based on history: What was the most recent growth of GDP? What was the most recent Current Account deficit? What was the most recent political crisis in the country? However, exchange rates are based on expectations about the future, not on what happened in the past. Because expectations are extremely difficult to measure, it is difficult to create a model of behavior based on them.

Box 8.7   Coping with a depreciating dollar

As the dollar depreciated 25 percent from 2002 to 2008, it meant that selling to the United States market was less profitable for foreign firms. Each dollar of revenue sold for fewer units of foreign currency, so revenues denominated in the foreign currency declined.

For example, Toyota Motor Corp., one of the world's largest automobile manufacturers, reported a decline in profits in the second quarter of 2004. Toyota attributed the decline to a strong Japanese yen. When repatriated to Japan, the value in yen of Toyota's overseas earnings declined because of the yen's appreciation. Toyota's Chairman said that the company would double overseas production.

A similar problem occurred at Airbus, the European aircraft manufacturer. The company was forced to lay off workers and close production facilities in 2007 because the company's profits declined. The underlying problem is that Airbus's expenses are in euros, but its revenues are in dollars because aircraft are sold in dollars. The dollar had depreciated 30 percent against the euro over five years, meaning euro-denominated revenues declined relative to expenses. One consultant recommended that Airbus send basic production to low-wage overseas countries with currencies pegged to the dollar and retain high value added assembly in Europe.

Craftsman Tools, Ltd manufactures machine-tool equipment in England, but 30 percent of its sales are to the United States. Appreciation of the British pound against the US dollar caused it to lose pound-denominated revenue during 2006. The company raised US prices 5 percent twice in two years and protected itself with forward contracts, but the moves were not sufficient to offset the revenue decline. Now the company is looking for a factory in the US.

Sources: Jathon Sapsford, "Toyota aims to rival GM production", *Wall Street Journal*, Nov 2, 2005, p. A3; "In place of Streiff", *The Economist*, Oct 14, 2006, p. 82; Alistair MacDonald, "European firms tackle dollar problem", *Wall Street Journal*, Dec 11, 2007, p. A12.

Another explanation for the failure of macroeconomic models concerns causality. It isn't obvious that macroeconomic fundamentals cause changes in exchange rates. It is possible that fluctuations in exchange rates cause changes in macroeconomic fundamentals. For example, in formula (9) showing the principle of interest rate parity, economists traditionally have posited that changes in interest rates affect the forward rate for a currency pair. But it is possible that causality goes the other way: changes in the forward rate cause changes in interest rates.

One thing economists have found out is that models based on macroeconomic fundamentals are better at predicting exchange rates in the long run than in the short run, where the long run is 12 quarters (three years) or more. Unfortunately, many business decisions incorporating exchange rates are made in the short run (one or two quarters), where macroeconomic fundamentals aren't as effective at predicting exchange rates.

In summary, it's not possible to predict exchange rates, although many late-night infomercials try to get your money based on their ability to predict. It's also a great field for academic research, particularly if you're into mathematics.

Conclusion

An exchange rate is the price of one currency in terms of another currency. When the government sets an exchange rate, it is called a pegged currency regime. When the market determines an exchange rate, it is called a floating currency regime. Exchange rates fluctuate constantly, depending on market participants' views about economic and political conditions, as well as market psychology. When a currency appreciates, it increases in value on the currency market; when a currency depreciates, it decreases in value. Fluctuations in the exchange rate can increase or decrease the return earned on an investment in another country.

Further Reading

Bank for International Settlements (2005) Central bank survey of foreign exchange and derivatives market activity in 2004, http://www.bis.org/press/p050316.htm, accessed February 28, 2006.

Duttagupta, R., G. Fernandez and C. Karacadag (2005) *Moving to a Flexible Exchange Rate*, International Monetary Fund.

Eichengreen, B. (1996) *Globalizing Capital*, Princeton University Press.

Malkiel, B.G. (1981) *A Random Walk down Wall Street*, New York: Norton.

Meese, R. and K. Rogoff (1983) Empirical exchange rate models of the seventies, *Journal of International Economics*, 14(1) p. 3.

Mitchell, K. and D.K. Pearce (2006) Can business economists predict interest-rate or exchange-rate movements? *Corporate Finance Review*, 10(6) p. 15.

Wang, J. (2008) Why are exchange rates so difficult to predict?, *Economic Letter*, Federal Reserve Bank of Dallas, 3(6).

9 *Managing Currency Risk*

Now that we realize that currency values can be influenced by a whirlwind of forces beyond the control of the average investor, let's return to the issue of whether we can avoid some of the currency risk associated with our French TBill. Fortunately, global financial institutions have developed numerous ways for us to avoid risk in foreign transactions, so let's discuss a few of them.

Just think of going to Las Vegas and walking into a casino. You see every sort of way for the casinos to take your money: blackjack, craps, roulette, keno, poker, and row upon row of slot machines. Modern finance is similar to gambling, although it goes by a different name: derivatives. You can use derivatives to protect yourself against certain risks, but you also can use derivatives to speculate. The trick is to know how derivatives work and what risks are associated with them. Even finance professionals sometimes don't know those two issues, as the financial collapse of 2008 made apparent.

This chapter covers some of the methods of protecting against the currency risk that arises in international investing. We'll use that discussion as the basis for understanding the reasons for the financial collapse that began in 2008.

Learning Objectives

After studying this chapter, you should be able to:

1. explain the advantages and disadvantages of various risk reduction strategies;
2. execute a forward contract, futures contract, or options contract;
3. explain the purpose of derivatives;
4. discuss reasons for the financial collapse of 2008.

The French Security Investment

Let's review the investment in the French Treasury security. Today is June 19 and we're investing in a Treasury Bill, called a BTF, issued by the Government of France. We purchase the BTF for EUR 998,277.97. When it matures in three months, we will receive EUR 1,000,000. We know today's dollar/euro spot rate from Table 9.1, but we don't know what the spot rate will be in three months. The potential returns on the investment under three scenarios are shown in Table 9.2.

If the exchange rate is the same in three months as it is today, we will receive an annual return of 0.69 percent. If the euro appreciates over the three months, we exchange the euros for more dollars and our return from investing in the security increases. If the euro depreciates over the period, we exchange them for fewer dollars and our return decreases. In fact, it is possible that we will lose money on the investment.

Some people may be willing to assume the risk of losing money on the investment. They may do it because they are risk lovers attracted by the high potential return. They may do it because they are confident the euro will appreciate over the three months. Perhaps they pay an investment advisory service that recommends euro-denominated assets over the next three months. For whatever reason, they are willing to speculate. These investors are attracted by the high return despite the risk inherent in the investment.

Other people may be more hesitant to take risks, particularly when there is a chance they could actually lose money on the investment, not simply earn a lower return. These people might be willing to give up a chance at higher profits in exchange for protection against the possibility of loss. In the language of risk and return, they are willing to accept a lower return if it is accompanied by lower risk.

The risk we're facing is similar to the risk faced by many firms conducting international transactions. Box 9.1 discusses how Japanese firms were exposed to currency risk due to their operations in the US.

Table 9.1   Spot rates for US dollar

Exchange Rates: New York Closing Snapshot

Thursday, June 18, 2009 (Reuters)

US-dollar foreign-exchange rates in late New York trading

	In US$		Per US$	
Country/currency	**Thurs**	**Wed**	**Thurs**	**Wed**
Europe				
Czech Rep. koruna	0.05260	0.05223	19.011	19.146
Denmark krone	0.1866	0.1874	5.3591	5.3362
Euro area euro	1.3890	1.3953	0.7199	0.7167
Hungary forint	0.004944	0.004943	202.27	202.31

Source: Wall Street Journal, http://online.wsj.com/mdc/public/page/2_3021-forex-20090618.html?mod=mdc_pastcalendar, accessed 6/19/09.

Hedging Currency Risk

There are numerous ways for investors to avoid currency risk if they choose to do so. We will not discuss all of them, but we will discuss the most popular. With the exception of forward contracts, all of these methods have been developed over the past three decades. Before the 1970s, there was little reason to protect against currency risk simply because governments, rather than the currency market, established exchange rates, so there was not so much volatility in currency prices.

Table 9.2   Return to US investor on a three-month French BTF

Market price now	998,277.97	EUR
	1,386,608.10	USD
Spot rate now	1.3890	USD/EUR
Face value 3 months	1,000,000.00	EUR

If the EUR:	To this value USD/EUR	US investor receives USD	Annual return to US investor
Appreciates	1.4890	1,489,000.00	29.537%
Unchanged	1.3890	1,389,000.00	0.690%
Depreciates	1.2890	1,289,000.00	-28.157%

Box 9.1   Japanese firms suffer from falling dollar

A depreciating dollar (an equivalent statement is "an appreciating yen") means that sales in the US market of Japanese products translate into fewer yen when the currency is repatriated. Japanese automobile and consumer goods manufacturers have been adversely affected as the dollar depreciated steadily against the yen from 2002 to 2008.

When profits at Toyota fell in 2004, the company attributed the decline to lower prices in the US due to discounting and to the depreciating US dollar. Lower prices meant Toyota earned fewer US dollars for each car sold, while a depreciating dollar meant that each dollar exchanged for fewer Japanese yen. Toyota generates two-thirds of its profits from sales in North America, so a change in the US or Canada has a major impact on the company. Toyota said that for every yen that the Japanese currency appreciates, the company loses about 20 billion yen of operating profit. (For example, if the yen appreciates to 117 per dollar from 118 per dollar, Toyota loses 20 billion yen of operating profits.) In 2003, the dollar sold for 118 yen, but in 2004 the dollar sold for only 110 yen, meaning a decline of 160 billion yen in Toyota's operating profit.

Nintendo manufactures Wii consoles, a popular videogame. Nintendo said that it would not reach its profit target for the year 2008 because of the appreciating yen. Unit sales in the US and Europe increased 26 percent in the second quarter of 2008, yet Nintendo did not receive as many yen because the yen appreciated against both the dollar and the euro. Although it sold more units, Nintendo did not receive as many yen per unit due to the yen's appreciation.

Sources: Todd Zaun, "Weaker dollar causes Toyota's profit to slip", *nytimes.com*, Nov 2, 2004; Kenneth Maxwell, "Nintendo's net rises on robust Wii sales", *Wall Street Journal*, Oct 31, 2008, p. B5.

The methods for avoiding risk are known collectively as *hedges* or *covers* – financial arrangements that reduce the risk of adverse movements in the value of an asset. Hedges can be relatively simple or unbelievably complex, but they all share the characteristic of shifting some or all of the risk away from the hedger and onto another party. Almost all of us hedge on a regular basis: insurance is a form of hedging. You pay the insurance company a premium to insure your car. If you get into an accident, the insurance company reimburses you for the cost of the accident, according to the terms of the policy. You have shifted the risk of the accident from yourself to the insurer.

Hedging always costs something. The cost may be direct, as in the premium you pay for auto insurance. Other times, the cost may be more subtle, such as giving up the potential for profits in exchange for accepting protection against losses. Either way, you pay something for protection.

As with any business decision, you compare the cost of an alternative to its reward. Hedging may not be an appropriate strategy if the cost of the hedge exceeds the benefit from the hedge. Also, market forces may be pushing in a direction that encourages you to believe that hedging is unnecessary. Perhaps you'll take a chance without the hedge.

But for those who wish to sleep soundly, hedging can be as beneficial as a sedative. You rest easy, knowing that you no longer have the possibility of losing thousands or millions of dollars.

FORWARD

The most straightforward of the hedges is the forward hedge, an agreement between the hedger and another party, usually a financial institution such as a bank. In a *forward hedge* (sometimes called a *currency forward*), the two parties agree now on a price that they will exchange two currencies in specified amounts at some date in the future. No money changes hands until the agreed-upon date. When the money changes hands, the value is the price agreed upon when the contract was written.

The forward market arises because banks trade currencies for delivery now, called the spot market, as well as for delivery in the future. Business firms typically extend credit for 30, 60, or 120 days, so banks receive requests from clients for quotes to exchange currencies that match the timing of those cash flows. One way to think of the forward market is that it reflects the currency needs of businesses 30, 60, or 120 days from now. If more businesses need to acquire dollars 30 days from now, the forward rate of the dollar will be higher than today's spot rate – the dollar appreciates in the forward market.

Forward contracts are available on major currencies, but not always on minor currencies because a bank may not be willing to assume the risk of currency fluctuation. If you want to arrange a forward contract on the Nigerian naira, for example, you may have to deal directly with a bank in Nigeria; your bank in New York may not be willing to quote a forward rate on the naira. Forward contracts are arrangements directly with a bank; there is no centralized exchange where forward contracts are bought and sold.

In the situation facing us when we purchased the EUR 1,000,000 French BTF, we have the information required to decide about a forward hedge. We know that we will receive EUR 1,000,000 in three months, so we know the amount and the time period. All we need is to find the counterparty – the financial institution that will quote us a price and agree to purchase the EUR 1,000,000 in three months and give us USD at the price we agree on.

When we go to the bank, the bank will quote us a forward rate of 1.3953 USD/EUR, as shown in Table 9.3. We sign the contract, wait three months for the French BTF to mature, receive EUR 1,000,000 from the Treasury of France, and take the euros to the bank. The bank gives us USD 1,395,300.00 (EUR 1,000,000 * 1.3953 USD/EUR = 1,395,300 USD) according to the contract. The return on the investment in the BTF is 2.51 percent, whether the euro appreciates or depreciates over the coming three months. We have fixed our return.

What actually happens to the value of the euro during the time period and whatever is its value on the date the French BTF matures now no longer matter to us. We have a contract that we will deliver EUR 1,000,000 and receive USD 1,395,300. Notice that we have avoided currency risk because if the euro depreciates, which was our risk exposure with the BTF investment, we still receive USD 1,395,300. On the other hand, we have given up the opportunity to profit from appreciation of the euro because even if the euro appreciates, we still receive USD 1,395,300. The price we pay for peace of mind is the opportunity to profit if the euro appreciates.

Unfortunately, a forward contract is not completely without risk. What happens if the Treasury of France fails to pay us EUR 1,000,000? We still are obligated to deliver to the bank EUR 1,000,000 on the date specified in the contract. If we don't receive them from the Treasury, we'll have to purchase them on the market, and the euro may have appreciated beyond the value specified in the contract. In that case, we'll lose money. The risk of nonpayment by a debtor is called *default risk* or *credit risk*. We incur default risk whenever we lend money to someone else, because the possibility exists that we may not get our money back. Governments of most major developed countries such as the US, France, the UK, and Japan, are pretty safe places to invest, so have low default risk. We can't make that general statement about all countries, however, because governments occasionally default on debts, as Argentina did in 2002.

Another disadvantage of a forward contract is that you can't get out of it easily. You can't sell the contract to someone else, and you must fulfill the obligations of the contract unless you are able to negotiate with the financial institution to change the terms. Box 9.2 shows what can happen to firms begin to speculate rather than simply hedge positions in currencies.

Table 9.3   Forward rates for the dollar

| | (June 18) | | | Forward | |
Country	Currency	Spot	One month	Three month	One year
UK	pound	1.6345	1.6344	1.6342	1.6342
Europe	euro	1.3962	1.3959	1.3953	1.3964

Source: Financial Times, http://markets.ft.com/ft/markets/researchArchive.asp?report=DSP&cat=CU, accessed 6/19/09.

Table 9.4   Return to US investor using forward hedge

Market price now	998,277.97	EUR
	1,386,608.10	USD
Spot rate now	1.3890	USD/EUR
Forward rate, 3 months	1.3953	USD/EUR
Face value 3 months	1,000,000.00	EUR

If the EUR:	To this value USD/EUR	US investor receives USD	Annual return to US investor
Appreciates	1.4890	1,395,300	2.51%
Unchanged	1.3890	1,395,300	2.51%
Depreciates	1.2890	1,395,300	2.51%

FUTURES

A currency *futures contract* is different from a forward contract. A futures contract is standardized in that each contract is for a stated amount of currency. For the euro, each futures contract is for EUR 125,000. A futures contract also is standardized for date of payment. Futures contracts mature on the third Friday of March, June, September, and December, although if there is sufficient demand, contracts may be offered for other months. Because the contracts are standardized, they can be bought and sold on an exchange, which in the US is the Chicago Mercantile Exchange (CME).[1]

When you buy a futures contract, you are obligating yourself to receive EUR 125,000 on the day the contract matures. When you sell a futures contract, you are obligating yourself to deliver EUR 125,000 on the third Friday of the maturity month. So remember that buy = receive and sell = deliver in the futures market.

Let's see how we would protect ourselves against possible depreciation on our EUR 1,000,000 French BTF. Because we will receive euros from the Treasury of France, we need to guarantee a price in dollars that we can sell the euros. Following our rubric from the previous paragraph, we sell enough futures contracts to hedge our exposure.

If we wish to hedge the entire EUR 1,000,000, and each contract is for EUR 125,000, we sell eight futures contracts. According to Table 9.5, the futures price is 1.3892 USD/EUR. At that price, we will receive USD 1,389,200 on September 18 when the contract matures and we deliver EUR 1,000,000 to the clearinghouse. That's it! We have avoided currency risk by selling in the futures market the euros we receive from the Treasury of France.

There is a little more to futures trading, however. For each contract, we must put on deposit a percentage of the value of the contract, called a margin. The margin helps guarantee our performance of the contract, and it also serves as a bank account in which we record gains or losses. The gains or losses occur because we have taken a position in the futures market and our position may be worth more money or less money according to what happens to futures prices over the next three months.

---

1   You can find out more about what currencies have futures contracts and learn more about trading contracts by going to the CME's home page at http://www.cmegroup.com/trading/fx/.

Box 9.2   Derivatives plague in Latin America

Derivatives can be a path to financial ruin if they are not used properly or are used for speculation but the market turns against your position. Companies in Latin America suffered a plague of losses on derivatives contracts when executives went beyond protecting an exposed position and began speculating using derivatives. The crisis was worst in Mexico and Brazil.

For several years in the mid-2000s, the US dollar depreciated steadily against the Mexican peso and the Brazilian real. Mexican and Brazilian firms exposed to dollar depreciation hedged their positions through currency derivatives. Some of the hedges were through exchanges, such as the peso futures contract at the Chicago Mercantile Exchange, while others were negotiated privately with banks.

Because of the dollar's continued depreciation, many of the firms placed bets against the dollar by taking positions that would profit when the dollar depreciated. At first, they won the bets. But when the global recession hit in 2008, the dollar appreciated quickly and unexpectedly against many currencies from developing countries, including Mexico and Brazil. Suddenly, the positions that generated profits instead generated losses.

Here are some of the firms experiencing losses due to speculation in derivatives:

- Comercial Méxicana, Mexico's third-largest supermarket chain, lost $1 billion in derivatives trading and declared bankruptcy.
- Cemex, North America's largest cement maker, lost $647 million and was forced to lay off 10 percent of its work force and close plants.
- Gruma, a producer of corn flour and tortillas, lost $847 million and was downgraded by Fitch Ratings.
- Aracruz, a large paper and pulp producer in Brazil, lost $1.8 billion.
- Sadia, a large Brazilian producer of processed meats, lost almost $800 million.
- Grupo Votorantim, a Brazilian conglomerate, lost $960 million.

Sources: Antonio Regalado, John Lyons, "Big currency bets backfire", *Wall Street Journal*, Oct 22, 2008, p. B1; "Mexican Cement cracks up", *LatinFinance*, Feb 2009; "No easy way out for Mexican firms", *Euromoney*, Aug 2009; Jonathan Wheatley, "Currency bets go wrong for Brazil's Aracruz", *Financial Times*, Mar 28, 2009, p. 11; Jonathan Wheatley, "Years of conservative lending could leave Brazil unscathed", *Financial Times*, Oct 15, 2008, p. 14.

Our position is that we have sold euros at 1.3892 USD/EUR. A good way to visualize whether our position makes or loses money is to compare that sale price to a different price on the futures market. For example, if the euro depreciates to 1.2890 USD/EUR on the futures market, our position is worth more. We have a contract to sell euros for 1.3892 USD/EUR. We could fulfill that contract by purchasing the euros for 1.2890 USD/ EUR, selling them for 1.3892 USD/EUR, and pocketing the difference of 0.1002 USD/EUR. We're ten US cents better off because the euro has depreciated below our futures price. The clearinghouse would deposit enough money so that our margin account had USD 100,200 in it. We make money in the futures market.

Unfortunately, the opposite happens if the euro appreciates to say, 1.4890 USD/EUR. Our futures contract says we sell euros for only 1.3892 USD/EUR. If we had to purchase the euros for 1.4890 USD/EUR, we would lose 0.0998 USD/EUR. We would have to deposit enough so that our margin account had USD 99,800 in it.

Futures contracts are *marked-to-market* at the end of each trading day, meaning the contract is always valued at current market prices, not the price at which we executed the contract. If the value of our position increases, the gain is added to our margin account. If the value of our position decreases, the loss is deducted from our margin account. Therefore, there may be cash flows between now and the date the contract expires. If our position loses money, we may be asked to put more into the margin account to cover the position, so we'd better have cash available. We also must pay a commission for each contract we purchase, although the amount is small relative to the value of the contract.

Notice that the outcomes described above are just the opposite of the outcomes associated with the French BTF. For the BTF, when the euro depreciates, we lose because we will receive fewer dollars when we sell the euros for dollars. But on the futures contract we benefit if the euro depreciates because our position is more valuable. We have constructed a situation in which the loss from one contract (the BTF) is offset by the gain from a different contract (the futures). In other words, we have hedged our exposure on the BTF.

One nice thing about a futures contract is that we can exit the market whenever we wish. We can't sell our contract, but we can take an offsetting position that would cancel our responsibility to deliver EUR 1,000,000. If we want to offset our short position (we sold eight contracts), we buy eight contracts, which means we expect to receive EUR 1,000,000. Our position in the market is zero because we have bought and sold EUR 1,000,000 worth of futures contracts. The only thing that changed is the price at which we bought or sold. We may make or lose money on the price difference, but at least we no longer have to deliver or receive EUR 1,000,000.

If we wish, we can close the futures position when we're ahead, which is what happens when the euro depreciates. If we do this before receiving the EUR 1,000,000 from the Treasury of France, we're back to speculating on that contract because we no longer have an offsetting position in the futures market. But maybe we're willing to take that chance.

Futures markets are a great way to speculate on currencies. If you think that the euro will appreciate to 1.4890 USD/EUR or beyond by September 18, you can purchase a euro futures contract now at 1.3892 USD/EUR. On September 18, you receive EUR 125,000 for which you pay USD 173,650. You sell them on the currency market at the spot rate of 1.4890 USD/EUR and receive USD 186,125 and pocket a tidy profit of USD 12,475. Shucks, that was so easy, we'll do it for ten futures contracts; or a hundred. But what happens if the euro depreciates rather than appreciates? That's the risk of speculating.

In fact, the futures market reflects the way investors and speculators are betting about the direction of the euro. If a lot of people anticipate that the euro will appreciate, they will purchase euro futures and the price will increase. If they anticipate that the euro will depreciate, they will sell euro futures and the price will decrease. Look at Table 9.5 and go to the column on the right. The abbreviation "Open Int" stands for open interest, and that is the number of contracts outstanding that do not yet have an offsetting position. Open interest consists of hedgers, like us selling eight euro contracts to protect our BTF position. It also consists of speculators taking a position in the futures market.

Table 9.5   Currency futures

Currency Futures

Thursday, June 18, 2009

Key to Exchanges: CME: Chicago Mercantile Exchange

Euro (CME) – 125,000 – $ per €

	Open	High	Low	Settle	Chg	Open Int
September 2009	1.3932	1.3994	1.3863	1.3892	-0.0063	108,507
December 2009	1.3966	1.3989	1.3864	1.3891	-0.0059	405

Source: *Wall Street Journal*, http://online.wsj.com/mdc/public/page/2_3023-fut_currency-futures-20090 619.html?mod=mdc_pastcalendar, accessed 6/19/09.

Table 9.6   Return to US investor using futures hedge

Market price now	998,277.97	EUR
	1,386,608.10	USD
Spot rate now	1.3890	USD/EUR
Futures price, 3 months	1.3892	USD/EUR
Face value 3 months	1,000,000.00	EUR

If the EUR:	To this value USD/EUR	US investor receives USD	Annual return to US investor
Appreciates	1.4890	1,389,200	0.75%
Unchanged	1.3890	1,389,200	0.75%
Depreciates	1.2890	1,389,200	0.75%

Another interesting thing about the futures market is what happens on the day the contract matures and we have to settle all the accounts. During the three months from June, when we sell eight futures contracts, until September, when the contracts mature, the futures price can go anywhere. Sometimes the euro might appreciate, other times it may depreciate. But as the day the contracts mature approaches, the futures price gets closer and closer to the daily spot rate until BINGO! On the maturity day, the futures price equals the spot rate for that day. Stop and think about it. What is the price of something in the future when the future is today? It must be today's price.

The implication of this is that on the day the contract matures in September, we can do either of two things: 1) we can deliver the euros to fulfill our futures contract, or 2) we can buy eight futures contracts to offset our exposure in the futures market and sell the euros on the currency market at the spot rate on that day. Either way, we net USD 1,389,200 because whatever we gained on the BTF contract was offset by losses in the futures market, or vice-versa. The futures hedge was constructed so that losses on one contract are offset by gains on the other contract.

The takeaway concerning using the futures market to hedge rather than the forward market is that the futures market is more liquid because we can sell or buy contracts, but there is the possibility of additional cash flows during the period we take a position in the market. We might have to put up more money to maintain our margin account.

OPTIONS

Are you getting tired of reading about ways to avoid currency risk? I hope not, because there are other methods that we should discuss. An *option* gives you the right, but not the obligation, to do something. Having an option – the ability to decide – is worth something, so options have a cost; you must pay for the option.

Table 9.7 shows a portion of the quotes for euro options from the *Wall Street Journal*. Let's discuss a few of the particulars and see how they influence our decision to avoid currency risk. One thing you notice is that each option contract is denominated at EUR 125,000, just like the futures contract. These are called options on futures because what you're really getting is an option on an underlying futures contract.

Another thing you'll see is the series of numbers in the first column, the strike price. The *strike price* is the exchange rate at which you would exercise the option if you decide to do so. If you place a decimal after the first 1 in each of the strike prices, it will make more sense: 1.3550, 1.3900, 1.4150. Now the figures look comparable to the market price of 1.3890 USD/EUR that we've been using all along. Table 9.7 shows only 13 of 100 strike prices that were listed at the *Wall Street Journal's* site that day, so it isn't possible to list them all.

Suppose we say to ourselves that we are willing to bear the risk of modest depreciation of the euro. We know that we will receive USD 1,389,000 if the spot rate in September is the same as today's spot rate. But we might be satisfied with receiving USD 1,355,000 as a lower limit, as long as we can capture the gain if the euro appreciates. This is the situation for an option contract. (I arbitrarily chose the strike price 13550; you may have a different risk preference.)

At a strike price of 13550, which in our language is 1.3550 USD/EUR, we have a choice. If the euro falls below that level, we will exercise our option to sell the euros at the strike price. If the euro appreciates, or depreciates but stays above 1.3550 USD/EUR, we will not exercise our option; we will simply let the option expire and sell the euros at the market price. We have limited our downside risk to selling the euros for no less than 1.3550 USD/EUR, so the least we will earn is USD 1,355,000.

Having the ability to exercise the option is a luxury, and we have to pay for it. That is the cost of the option, called the *premium*. You'll see in Table 9.7 that there are two sets of columns to the right of the column of strike prices. One set is labeled calls, the other is labeled puts. An option to purchase is a *call option*; an option to sell is a *put option*. We want an option that will allow us to sell the euros we receive from the Treasury of France at either the strike price or the market price, whichever is greater, so we will purchase a put option. We'll also try to match the period of the option to the period of the BTF, so we purchase a put option maturing in September.

If you look in Table 9.7 across from the strike price 13550, under the September puts heading, you'll see the number 2.140. That is the option premium, expressed as cents per euro. Because we're purchasing EUR 1,000,000 worth of protection, we must pay USD 21,400 for eight options contracts (125,000 EUR per contract * 8 contracts * 0.0214 USD/

Table 9.7   Currency futures options

Thursday, June 18, 2009

EURO (CME)

125,000 euros, cents per euro

Strike Price	Calls			Puts		
	Jul	Sep	Dec	Jul	Sep	Dec
13550	3.790	5.550	7.200	0.370	2.140	3.800
13600	3.380	5.230	6.910	0.460	2.320	4.010
13650	2.990	4.930	6.620	0.570	2.510	4.220
13700	2.630	4.640	6.350	0.710	2.720	4.450
13750	2.290	4.350	6.080	0.870	2.930	4.680
13800	1.980	4.080	5.830	1.060	3.160	4.920
13850	1.690	3.820	5.580	1.270	3.400	5.170
13900	1.430	3.580	5.340	1.510	3.660	5.430
13950	1.200	3.340	5.100	1.780	3.920	5.690
14000	1.000	3.120	–	2.080	4.200	–
14050	0.830	2.910	4.660	2.410	4.490	6.240
14100	0.680	2.710	4.450	2.760	4.790	6.530
14150	0.550	2.520	4.250	3.130	5.090	6.830

Note: All prices are settlement prices. Volume and open interest are from the previous trading day.

Source: Wall Street Journal, http://online.wsj.com/mdc/public/page/2_3024-futopt_currency.html? mod=topnav_2_3000, accessed 6/19/09.

EUR = 21,400 USD). We have to pay that amount just to purchase the option, and we pay it whether we exercise the option or do not exercise the option. So whatever the amount of dollars we receive, we must deduct 21,400 USD as the cost of the option.

Now let's see what decision we make. If the euro appreciates, that's good for us. We won't exercise our option and instead will sell the euros at the spot rate, which is 1.4890 USD/EUR in Table 9.8. Because we have to pay for the option, we net USD 1,467,600 after deducting the cost of the option. If the euro stays the same in June, we won't exercise the option, but we still must pay the cost of the option. The neat part of an option contract is what happens if the euro depreciates to, say, 1.2890 USD/EUR. If that happens, we exercise the option to sell euros at the strike price of 1.3550 USD/EUR. After deducting the cost of the option, we receive USD 1,353,600. In fact, that is the least amount we can receive, because any time the euro depreciates below the strike price, we will exercise the option to sell at the strike price.

Table 9.8   Return to US investor using futures options hedge

Market price now	998,277.97	EUR
	1,386,608.10	USD
Spot rate now	1.3550	USD/EUR
Strike price	1.3750	
Option cost per euro	0.0214	USD/EUR
Number of options	8	
Contract size	125,000	EUR
Face value 3 months	1,000,000.00	EUR

If the EUR:	To this value USD/EUR	Total cost of option (USD)	Exercise option?	US investor receives USD	Annual return to US investor
Appreciates	1.4890	21,400	No	1,467,600	23.36%
Unchanged	1.3890	21,400	No	1,367,600	-5.48%
Depreciates	1.2890	21,400	Yes	1,353,600	-9.52%

Unfortunately, we experience a negative return even if the spot rate in September is the same as it was in June. We attribute this to the cost of the option, which we have to pay even if we don't exercise the option.[2]

SWAP

A *swap* is an arrangement in which you trade a series of cash flows for a series of cash flows of another party. Swaps may be an exchange of interest payments, such as fixed interest for floating interest, or an exchange of currency payments. Swaps usually involve cash flows that occur over a longer period of time, such as several years, although swaps for shorter terms may be negotiated.

In our situation, we have to buy euros in June, then sell euros in September. We would love to find someone who needs to sell euros now, then buy euros in three months, the opposite of each of our transactions. In fact, it would really be nice if the counterparty needed to sell EUR 998,277.97 for dollars now and in September needed to buy EUR 1,000,000 with dollars. In that situation, we could swap our euro cash flows for their dollar cash flows and we would be happy.

The chances of us finding someone out there in the finance universe who needs those specific cash flows at that specific time are pretty slim. Fortunately, this is one of the services that a bank offers to its clients. The bank will serve as the counterparty for our transactions, so we go to the bank to negotiate a swap just as we would negotiate a forward contract. In fact, the bank will quote us a swap rate for the September cash

---

2   If you'd like to learn more about futures and options, the CME provides a thorough tutorial at: http://www.cmegroup.com/cmegroup/education/interactive/intro_to_futures/player.html.

flow that turns out to be pretty close to the forward rate because swap rates are based on relative interest rates between countries, just as forwards are.

In a swap arrangement, we're trying to locate someone with the opposite risk exposure. We are exposed to depreciation of the euro over the next three months because a depreciating euro causes a lower return on our investment in the BTF. There always is someone else exposed to appreciation of the euro over the next three months. All we have to do is find that someone else. That's where the bank comes in. The bank serves as the intermediary in the transaction as each of the parties tries to protect against risk.

Unfortunately, like a forward contract, a swap is not without risk. What happens if the counterparty fails? If we arranged the swap privately, without going through the bank, we need to worry about default risk. If we go through the bank, we don't worry about the person on the other side of the transaction, but we worry about the bank. This risk became painfully apparent during the financial crisis of 2008, when numerous financial institutions failed and clients faced threat of default by counterparties. For example, AIG, a large US insurance company, had issued billions of dollars of "credit default swaps" (CDS) – guarantees of protection against defaults on mortgages. When the housing crisis occurred and more people defaulted on mortgages than AIG had anticipated, AIG had to pay out more money than it had, so the US Government provided financial support to the institution. We'll discuss this episode in more detail later in the chapter.

WHICH TO CHOOSE?

So that's it. We have a panoply (a particularly appropriate word; look it up in the dictionary) of methods for avoiding currency risk, and we haven't even covered all the possibilities. Which one should we choose? There's no single answer to that question.

The most obvious answer is that we should choose the method that gives us the most dollars in September. That's fine, but perhaps that choice also involves cash flows between now and September, and we're short on cash. Choosing the method with no intermediate cash flows might be appropriate, but then we may give up the opportunity to magnify our return if the euro appreciates significantly. And what about the ability to get out of a contract? Forwards and swaps aren't traded, while futures and options can be bought and sold on a centralized exchange. An option is attractive because it sets a limit on the amount we can lose but doesn't limit the amount we can gain, but we have to pay for the option even if we decide not to use it.

So there is no easy answer to the question of which method is appropriate. Each has attractive features, but each also has drawbacks. We have to fit our risk reduction strategy to the situation of our organization.

Remember back at the beginning of the chapter where I described financial markets as similar to the gaming floor of a casino? You probably wondered about the comparison then, but I hope now you see the similarities. Modern financial markets offer at least the four risk-reduction methods described in this chapter. All are sold as ways to reduce risk, which is how we're using them. But to use them, we give up some of our ways to profit. We pay for the reduction in risk. When you deal with financial institutions, they will always get some of your money, just like a casino does.

Is Hedging Always Necessary?

One issue we haven't discussed is how much of our exposure we want to hedge. It isn't always necessary to hedge 100 percent of our exposure or speculate 100 percent. We may want to protect a portion and speculate with a portion.

In our BTF example, we may want to protect 60 percent of the EUR 1,000,000 we receive in September, but are willing to speculate with the remaining 40 percent. The percentages you wish to protect or speculate depend on your attitude toward risk. If you are risk averse, you will try to protect 100 percent of the investment. If you are a risk lover, you will speculate 100 percent. Chances are, you're somewhere between the extremes.

Hedging vs. speculating also depends on the type of cash flow. Our example is an investment in a security. But what if we are selling goods to a client in a foreign currency? The contract will include a portion that covers our cost of producing the goods and a portion that represents our profit on the sale. We may wish to hedge the portion associated with our cost of producing the goods, but we may be willing to gamble with our profits. If the foreign currency depreciates, we'll lose some profit, but if it appreciates we'll make even more profits. We might be willing to make that tradeoff.

The decision about protecting the exposure of one cash flow also depends on the other cash flows the firm is facing. For example, if we know that in September we'll have to pay EUR 1,000,000, perhaps for something we purchased in the eurozone, then there is no reason to hedge the BTF investment. Why? Because we'll use the EUR 1,000,000 we receive on the BTF to pay the EUR 1,000,000 account payable, so there is no currency risk on either transaction. If we looked at them in isolation, we might wish to hedge one or both cash flows. But when we consider all potential cash flows, we may find that hedging isn't necessary.

What Happens to Risk?

You may have asked yourself throughout this chapter, "What does the bank do about its risk?" If you asked yourself this question, you've noticed a principle about risk reduction strategies: Risk doesn't go away, it just moves from one party to another. When we selected one of the methods for reducing risk, we paid another party to assume the risk instead of us. Now the risk is on their shoulders.

The other party in turn may have methods for reducing its risk exposure, but writing about them would consume another book. Refer to a book about management of financial institutions to get a feel for how commercial banks, investment banks, and insurance companies handle risk. If they adopt a risk-reduction strategy, they simply shift their risk to someone else down the line.

That risk doesn't go away is an important point that was unappreciated until the financial crisis of 2008. Financial institutions passed risk to other parties until ultimately, only one party assumed much of the risk. When that party was unable to fulfill its obligations, institutions that had tried to pass the risk to it found that they were exposed. The risk had not gone away, it had merely been passed around.

Derivatives

The financial arrangements covered in this chapter go by a general name: derivatives. A derivative gets its name because it has no inherent value. Instead, its value is derived from the behavior of an underlying asset, such as currency in this chapter. The value of the futures contract increases or decreases according to movement in the USD/EUR exchange rate. Without the currencies, the derivative would have no value.[3]

Table 9.9 provides a different view of derivatives. The table is a summary of one of the financial statements from Citigroup, a large US bank. It shows the derivative position of the bank at the end of 2008. The two columns show the derivatives the bank uses to hedge its exposure (nontrading derivatives) and the derivatives the bank provides as a service to its customers or for speculation (trading derivatives). In the table you'll see the derivatives covered in this chapter: forwards, futures, options, and swaps.

A few points should impress you about the information in Table 9.9:

- The value of derivatives is enormous. If you look at the totals in the bottom row, you'll see that the notional amounts add up to more than $33 trillion. That's twice the GDP of the US, and this is only one bank. There are dozens of other banks dealing in derivatives throughout the world.
- Swaps are used more frequently to protect against interest rate risk, while forwards and futures are used more frequently to protect against currency risk.
- An entry near the bottom, "Total credit derivatives", contains credit default swaps, which were the source of great angst in the 2008 financial crisis.

Here are some cautions about interpreting the numbers in Table 9.9:

- You'll see the term "Notional amount" or "Notionals" throughout the table. Many derivatives are based on a principal amount that is used to calculate monetary values. For example, interest rate swaps trade fixed for floating interest rates that have to be multiplied by the notional principal amount in order to determine a monetary value for interest. Borrowing or lending of principal is not involved in an interest rate swap, so there is no risk of principal repayment. Instead, the notional amount is used to calculate interest cash flows. In this sense, notional amount is a fictitious number. Or at least that was the thinking until the financial crisis in 2008.
- The table doesn't reflect offsetting exposures. Citigroup may have positions in which the bank's risk in one derivative is offset by its risk in another derivative. The $32 trillion figure represents only the total value of all the derivative contracts, and doesn't include any adjustment for net exposure.
- In a written option, Citigroup collects the price of the option, but the option belongs to the client. A purchased option is an agreement where Citigroup has the option to exercise. Generally, written options have greater exposure to risk than do purchased options, where the loss is limited to the amount of the premium.
- So even though $32 trillion sounds like an enormous number, it isn't a reliable guide to Citigroup's exposure on derivative contracts. You'll have to do more investigating to evaluate the bank's real risk.

---

3   Other derivatives are based on stocks, interest rates, or bonds, among others. You can view the variety of derivatives offered on only one exchange, the CME, at: http://www.cmegroup.com/. You can even find derivatives based on the weather!

Table 9.9   Citigroup derivatives position, 12/31/2008

	Trading Derivatives	Non-trading Derivatives
Interest rate contracts		
Swaps	$15,096	$764
Futures and forwards	2,620	118
Written options	2,963	25
Purchased options	3,067	38
Total interest rate contract notionals	23,747	946
Foreign exchange contracts		
Swaps	882	62
Futures and forwards	2,165	41
Written options	483	3
Purchased options	539	1
Total foreign exchange contract notionals	4,070	107
Equity contracts		
Swaps	98	
Futures and forwards	17	
Written options	507	
Purchased options	472	
Total equity contract notionals	1,095	
Total commodity and other contract notionals	169	
Total credit derivatives	3,033	
Total derivative notionals	**$32,114**	**$1,053**

Note: Notional amount, billions of dollars.

Source: Citigroup Annual Report, 2008, p. 90 http://www.citigroup.com/citi/fin/data/ar08c_en.pdf, accessed 9/2/09.

One thing that is factual is that derivatives are unregulated. There is no regulatory oversight by the Fed, the Treasury, the Securities and Exchange Commission (which regulates stocks and bonds), or the Commodities Futures Trading Commission. Derivatives exist in a world all their own, free of oversight by financial authorities, not just in the US, but in other countries as well. However, this may be changing. The 2008 financial crisis exposed the risks of unregulated derivatives markets, so financial authorities are discussing the need for supervision and perhaps regulation of derivatives. It is still too soon after the crisis to know the extent of the regulation, but it is being discussed.

The 2008 Financial Crisis

BACKGROUND AND DESCRIPTION OF THE CRISIS

Now we're sufficiently familiar with terminology and concepts that we can discuss the 2008 financial crisis. The discussion will be brief, but we'll cover enough of the important points to understand what happened and why governments intervened to the extent that they did. We'll focus on the role played by financial innovations and derivatives while ignoring other causes. Entire books have been and will be written about the crisis, so we can't cover all the aspects in the next few pages.

Financial crises occur periodically, so there is nothing unusual about them. The last major financial crisis in the US occurred in the 1980s and early 1990s when the savings and loan industry collapsed. However, that crisis was largely limited to the US; the 2008 crisis was worldwide. The US experienced another crisis as a result of the collapse of Enron Corporation, but that was a bankruptcy of a large firm; the 2008 crisis threatened the entire US and global financial systems. The most recent world financial crisis was the collapse of many Asian economies in 1997 and 1998. The US and world economies recovered from each of these crises, just as they will recover from the 2008 crisis.

Let's begin by placing the crisis in its historical context. For decades, the US Government has promoted home ownership. Several government-owned agencies, including the Federal Housing Administration (FHA) and the Federal National Mortgage Association (FNMA), were created to help achieve the goal. The FHA insured lending institutions against default by qualifying borrowers and set standards for mortgages. FNMA purchased qualifying mortgages from financial institutions, especially savings and loans, which originated the mortgages. This led to creation of a secondary market in which mortgages could be bought and sold independently of either the borrower or the financial institution originating the loan.

Originally, mortgage terms were conservative, requiring the borrower to put up a large portion of the purchase price of the house in the form of a down payment. In the 1990s, policymakers encouraged the FHA and FNMA to enable more people to purchase houses. The effect was that house buyers were not required to put as much equity in the purchase and instead could borrow a larger percentage of the price through a mortgage. This increased leverage, which doesn't create a problem as long as housing prices and incomes are increasing. It also enabled people who previously could not qualify for a mortgage to borrow, and people who could qualify moving into larger houses or speculating in the housing market.

Prior to the 1980s, many interest rates in the US were determined by the Treasury, the Fed, or government agencies such as the FHA. Because of the inflation of the 1970s, Congress passed two laws that had the effect of deregulating almost all interest rates in the US. Now rates were determined by markets, which increased the chance of interest rate volatility.

Many financial innovations emerged during the following years, including a process called asset securitization, in which a series of future cash flows is grouped with other cash flows to form a security. Portions of the security then are sold to investors. David Bowie, for example, securitized the royalties from his future earnings so he could borrow against them. When this principle is applied to mortgages, the asset is called a "mortgage backed security" (MBS). A MBS is a collection of mortgages that are packaged together, then portions of the package are sold to investors. At the time, the securities were considered to have low risk because they were backed by mortgages, which seldom defaulted in large numbers.

Other financial innovations in the 1980s and 1990s included the CDS and the interest-only mortgage. A CDS is comparable to an insurance policy, where one party pays another party a series of cash flows in exchange for the promise that the other party will reimburse the payer if the underlying asset defaults. This sounds like an insurance policy, but because the swaps are traded as contracts in the derivatives market, they are free from insurance regulations.

CDSs were sold on a variety of assets, such as corporate bonds, but a large portion of market was for mortgage-backed securities. A major seller of CDSs was American International Group (AIG), a large insurance company. Premiums on CDSs represented a significant source of revenue for AIG, while the risk was considered to be low because widespread mortgage defaults had never occurred. Investors worldwide purchased MBSs and other asset-backed securities, then insured them by purchasing CDSs.

CDSs also were easy to issue, and it was not necessary to own the underlying asset in order to purchase a CDS. In other words, it was easy to speculate in the CDS market. The CDS market grew to $62 trillion in 2007, more than the world's GDP and significantly more than the $6.2 trillion in US corporate debt. The earlier caveat about notional amounts and offsetting positions applies to this figure, but it still is an incredible growth of a financial derivative.

An interest-only mortgage is a mortgage on which the borrower has the ability to pay only the interest portion of the scheduled mortgage payment. A typical mortgage is self-amortizing, which means that the mortgage principal is retired through regular payments of principal and interest over the term of the mortgage. Payment on an interest-only mortgage covers only the interest but does not pay off the principal. After a few years, the interest-only mortgage is replaced by a traditional self-amortizing mortgage.

An interest-only mortgage enables low-income homeowners to enter the housing market because the mortgage payments are lower than they would be under a self-amortizing mortgage. By the time the interest-only mortgage is replaced by a self-amortizing mortgage, the homeowner's income should have increased to the point that the payments are affordable. An interest-only mortgage also encourages speculation in the housing market because the investor does not have to repay the principal on a regular basis. Instead, the investor sells the house when its value increases after a few years and uses the proceeds to repay the mortgage principal.

Mortgages issued to credit-worthy borrowers are known as prime mortgages; mortgages issued to borrowers with poor credit are known as subprime mortgages. Mortgage-backed securities based on subprime mortgages were particularly attractive to investors because they offered high returns but little risk because they received high ratings from credit rating agencies such as Moody's and Standard and Poor's, and widespread defaults on mortgages had not occurred previously.

Originators of mortgages and traders in mortgage-backed securities and CDS receive a fee for each transaction, so they have an incentive to originate more mortgages or trade more derivatives. The fee is not adjusted for the riskiness of the borrower or the underlying asset, so originators and traders do not have an incentive to consider risk. The result is a large volume of trading regardless of the riskiness of the asset being traded. Another result is large bonuses for traders: Merrill Lynch paid bonuses of more than $1 million each to almost 700 employees in 2008, at the same time the firm reported a loss in excess of $27 billion.

In 2007, the housing market in the US began to slow. Prices started to decline, sometimes to the point where the value of the house was less than the amount owed on it. Homeowners began to default on mortgages, particularly in areas where growth in the housing market had been greatest. Mortgage defaults became so widespread that MBSs declined in value. This meant that financial institutions that owned these assets also decreased in value and required more capital to make up for the loss.

One problem was the difficulty of determining the value of a MBS. It is not possible to link each portion of a MBS to specific properties, so the investor cannot evaluate the risk of default on a particular MBS. This creates uncertainty, which is like adding fuel to the fire during a financial panic.

Uncertainty about asset values and reduced equity created so much uncertainty in credit markets that financial institutions decreased lending, both to other financial institutions and to business and individual borrowers. Credit stopped flowing in the US. Financial institutions began to fail internationally, either because they did not have sufficient capital, or because they could not obtain financing for normal operations. They simply ran out of money.

AIG, the large issuer of CDSs, was in a precarious situation. It had issued CDSs on the assumption that widespread mortgage defaults would not occur. Now, investors around the world were presenting AIG with claims to make good on the insurance it had issued. Some of the insurance contracts required that AIG pledge securities as collateral to guarantee performance, so many of AIG's assets were obligated for that purpose. AIG was in the position of having to pay a large amount of claims without the cash to pay them. AIG was out of money and did not have sufficient capital.

We see that there was a confluence of factors that helped magnify the financial crisis:

- *Separation of borrowers from lenders*. In the old days, a financial institution lent money to people it knew, and kept the loans on the bank's books. Now loans can be made over the Internet, and loans are quickly sold through the asset-backed securities market.
- *Political objectives*. Political objectives play a role in economic and financial decisions. Encouraging home ownership was a political objective, as was extending ownership to a wider spectrum of society. Some of the blame for the crisis must go to Congress and the President, who explicitly or implicitly encouraged financial institutions to relax credit standards so more people could borrow. This led to greater speculation in the housing market and higher leverage throughout the economy.
- *Lack of understanding of derivatives*. Wall Street is very good at financial innovations such as derivatives. The financial crisis showed that Wall Street is not as good at understanding the risks associated with the innovations. Or if it does understand the risks, Wall Street's culture is such that it ignores them, perhaps because it has no incentive to pay attention to them.

RESPONSES AND OUTCOMES

The risk of widespread defaults of financial institutions throughout the world compelled policy makers to act. They had to restore confidence in financial institutions to forestall a financial collapse. The immediate reaction was to restore liquidity, because financial institutions themselves were running out of money. Central banks in the US and UK flooded money and capital markets with cash.

In the US, the Fed and Treasury provided financial support to FNMA and the Government National Mortgage Association (GNMA), another organization specializing in packaging mortgages for resale. They also paid particular attention to AIG, which was the center of a worldwide web of derivatives. Failure of AIG could lead to failure of financial institutions around the world. To forestall a global panic, the Fed provided cash in the form of a loan, and provided additional cash by purchasing a portion of the firm. The Fed and Treasury allowed some institutions to fail, while requiring other institutions to merge with healthier institutions.

At the time I'm writing this chapter, it is too soon to know the direction of several trends in the US:

- US households may have changed attitudes toward borrowing. For decades, borrowing had increased, but there are signs that consumers are instead saving a larger portion of their incomes. This trend would reduce leverage and make the US economy less susceptible to risk when there is a downturn in the economy.
- Attitudes may be shifting in favor of increased regulation, at least in the financial services industry. Since the Reagan revolution, Congress and the President had deregulated financial markets and institutions, either through lack of enforcement of existing laws, or passing new laws to liberate markets. The crisis may reverse this trend.
- The incentive system at large financial institutions may change. Rather than basing bonuses solely on the volume of trading activity, they would be based on long-run profitability of the institution. This would have the effect of incorporating risk into the decision about bonuses. The effort at incorporating risk is led by Christine Lagarde, Minister of Economic Affairs in France, but it will be a topic of discussion at the G20 and the Bank for International Settlements.

One takeaway from the financial crisis is that risk doesn't go away, it just moves from one party to the next. Ultimately, AIG and other issuers of CDSs ended up with much of the risk. They were the firms ultimately responsible for making good on defaults, but they did not have financial resources to do so.

Conclusion

Financial markets provide numerous ways to protect against currency risk. We discussed forwards, futures, options, and swaps. There is no "best" hedge because each of them has advantages and disadvantages, and hedging to protect against currency risk may create other risks. Failure to understand derivatives was one of the contributing factors to the financial crisis of 2008.

Further Reading

Bray, C. (2009) Crisis on Wall Street: Merrill gave $1 million each to 700 of its staff, *Wall Street Journal*, 2/12/09, p. C3.

Craig, S. (2009) Merrill's $10 million men – top 10 earners made $209 million in 2008 as firm foundered, *Wall Street Journal*, 3/4/09, p. A1.

Elliott, L. (2008) Credit crisis: How it all began, *The Guardian*, http://www.guardian.co.uk/business/2008/aug/05/northernrock.banking, accessed 9/5/09.

Markowitz, H.M. (2009) Proposals concerning the current financial crisis, *Financial Analysts Journal*, 65(1), p. 25.

Ng, S. (2008) The financial crisis: AIG at risk, *Wall Street Journal*, 9/17/08, p. A10.

Shore, B. and S. Manwani (2009) The financial crisis on Wall Street: Complexity, stability, and information technology, *Journal of Global Information Technology Management*, 12(1), p. 1.

Varchaver, N. and K. Benner (2008) The $55 trillion question, *Fortune*, 158(7), p. 134.

Summary of Risk Measures

Here is a thumbnail summary of the risk measures used throughout this book. For a more complete explanation, refer to the appropriate chapter.

Chapter 2: Economic Indicators

- Growth of GDP
- Inflation
- Per capita GDP
- Income distribution
- Unemployment
- Interest rates

Chapter 3: A Frame of Reference

- Fiscal discipline
- Public spending priorities
- Tax reform
- Interest rates
- Exchange rate
- Trade policy
- Foreign direct investment
- Privatization
- Deregulation
- Property rights

Chapter 4: Evaluating Governance and Culture

- Worldwide Governance Indicators (WGI): http://info.worldbank.org/governance/wgi/index.asp.
- Corruption Perceptions Index: http://www.transparency.org/policy_research/surveys_indices/cpi.
- Global Competitiveness Index: http://www.weforum.org/en/initiatives/gcp/Global%20Competitiveness%20Report/index.htm.
- Index of Economic Freedom: http://www.heritage.org/Index/.
- Freedom in the World: http://www.freedomhouse.org/template.cfm?page=475&year=2009.

- Ease of Doing Business: http://www.doingbusiness.org/economyrankings/.
- Hofstede's cultural dimensions: http://geerthofstede.nl.
- GLOBE Leadership Survey: http://www.thunderbird.edu/sites/globe/index.htm.

Chapter 5: Evaluating Fiscal Policy

- Government spending ratio:
$$Government\ spending\ ratio = \frac{Total\ government\ spending}{GDP}$$

- Budget deficit ratio:
$$budget\ deficit\ ratio = \frac{budget\ surplus\ (deficit)}{GDP}$$

- Debt ratio:
$$debt\ ratio = \frac{national\ debt}{GDP}$$

- External debt to exports ratio:
$$debt\ to\ exports\ ratio = \frac{external\ debt}{exports}$$

- External debt to GNI ratio:
$$debt\ to\ GNI\ ratio = \frac{external\ debt}{gross\ national\ income}$$

Chapter 6: Evaluating Monetary Policy

- Inflation
- Money supply growth relative to real GDP growth

Chapter 7: Evaluating International Transactions

- Current account ratio:
$$Current\ account\ ratio = \frac{Current\ account\ surplus\ (deficit)}{GDP}$$

- Debt service ratio:
$$Debt\ service\ ratio = \frac{debt\ service}{exports\ of\ goods\ and\ services}$$

Index